About Our Plans

Our goal is to provide our clients with a design that perpetuates a constant feeling of pride. Each home owner should step into their dream home each day knowing they made the best possible decision, not only with their home design, but with their surroundings. Our experienced staff offers creativity and efficiency, and can modify any of our plans to suit your needs, saving time and guaranteeing customer satisfaction.

Table of Contents

Tier A B C D E F G

Nelson Design Group Collection Directory

CHARTED Neighborhoods®

"Solutions for Master Planned Communities"
Planning - Home Design - Marketing

A "Charted Neighborhood" is Nelson Design Group's approach for design *"plus"* marketing

services making your job easier when developing "Master Planned Communities." As the name implies,

a *Charted Neighborhood*® *represents a distinctive new direction and concept in residential and commercial design with*

marketing – an approach that is unique to Nelson Design Group.

*T*oday, a public awakening now highly values its heritage of great neighborhoods. Updated interiors of the homes many of us grew up in are now incorporated into Neo-Traditional, or Traditional Neighborhood Design. Hence, the pursuit of the American Dream has taken an indirect path, away from suburban sprawl and back to a renewed appreciation of development patterns of our predecessors. Some of these planning and design principals date back to the late 1800's.

*I*n more recent years, New Urbanism has caused a revival among historic towns, cities and villages, where the home-buying public wants more than just a place to sleep after work. A new appreciation for a richer social and civic life is integral to today's Master Planned Communities, in which families can get to know their neighbors by relaxing on spacious front porches and walking along tree covered streets and sidewalks.

*T*o meet the rising demand of Traditional Neighborhood Designs, today's building professional is

NDG 314
pg. 38

looking for a design firm that can be much more than just a vendor of stock plans. Until now, residential and commercial builders and developers have indicated that a true "total resource" for planning, design, cost-analysis and value-added marketing services, is almost unheard of. Most builders need a home plan source that essentially functions as their very own "in-house, complete source" for new home design and associated services. Nelson Design Group is a firm that concentrates on true personal service, and one that will modify plans as necessary, always delivering much more one on one attention that you deserve.

No longer will you need several firms to provide plans or modifications, and still be on your own to market the project afterwards. Regardless of your Company's size and volume, whether builder or developer, residential or commercial, we want to be your "personal design and promotional partner." We are ready to consult with you on individual plans or small in-fill projects, and yet we are large enough to work with you on the design of new large-scale Charted Neighborhood Communities. Quite simply, we do it all - always with a personal touch and at a reasonable fee.

Because builders and developers across the country already rely on us to provide their plans and marketing resources, we cater daily to a diverse marketplace with a broad mix of consumers, real estate professionals and home builders. We know what buyers want, how builders 'build,' and how to design and market homes that sell quickly. Each Nelson Design Group plan offers stunning elevations and fresh interior floor plans with unique features such as kid's nooks, hearth rooms, home theater or media rooms and grilling porches to attract homeowner interests and promote a carefree lifestyle. Our designs are supported with our wide array of economically customized marketing

materials to promote your project during construction, and then facilitate a quick sale – often at premium appraisal values.

NDG 209
pg. 219

**Pictures provided by
Scott Bilby**

Village at Windstone

*I*n the following pages, you will find individual designs and numerous groups of plans – our collections – such as our new *Historical, Stone Village, Olde Towne and Jim Barna Log Systems Collections.* Our designs have complementary themes that work together to build a single home, a neighborhood, or a full-scale development. There is certainly something you can immediately incorporate into your building program.

*W*hen online, point your browser to our comprehensive website, nelsondesigngroup.com. Our site features a handy "search" option where you can select from hundreds of plans to simplify locating designs that accommodate your lot dimensions and preferred architectural style. Give us a call or send us an e-mail. Above all, please let us know if you have any questions or special requirements. We are always interested in hearing about your projects and how we might serve you now – and in the future.

*A*s we say, "Welcome to our Neighborhood..." On behalf of Michael E. Nelson and our entire staff of friendly designers, marketing specialists, cost-analysts and customer service team including our architect, we are pleased to introduce Nelson Design Group, LLC, America's fastest growing residential and commercial design, planning, and marketing firm.

The Florida Collection

HISTORICAL COLLECTION

The Historical Collection features six home plans that reflect warmth and familiarities while updated interiors cater to today's family needs. Porches are used on the front and rear of the home allowing areas for visiting, grilling and overall cover from the elements. Contemporary vaulted ceilings and large storage areas are modernized additions to these timeless dwellings. Spacious great rooms, open to both kitchen and dining areas, create wonderful open floor plans for comfortable family gatherings. These outstanding designs have laundry rooms and side loading garages for better street appeal.

Nelson Design Group LLC

RESIDENTIAL & COMMERCIAL PLANNERS - DESIGNERS

786

Madison Avenue

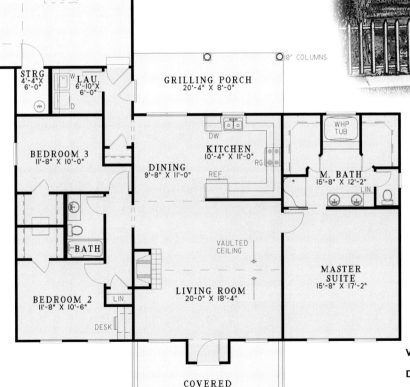

© 2002 NELSON DESIGN GROUP, LLC.

GARAGE
22'-0" X 22'-0"

STRG
4'-4" X 6'-0"

LAU.
6'-10" X 6'-0"

GRILLING PORCH
20'-4" X 8'-0"

10" COLUMNS

BEDROOM 3
11'-8" X 10'-0"

KITCHEN
10'-4" X 11'-0"

DINING
9'-8" X 11'-0"

DW

REF.

RG

WHP TUB

M. BATH
15'-8" X 12'-2"

LIN.

BATH

VAULTED CEILING

MASTER SUITE
15'-8" X 17'-2"

BEDROOM 2
11'-8" X 10'-6"

LIN.

LIVING ROOM
20'-0" X 18'-4"

DESK

COVERED PORCH
20'-8" X 10'-0"

10" COLUMNS

Welcome family and friends into this Historical Southern Traditional home by Nelson Design Group. Dormer windows enhance the front of the home while the front porch with columns and railing provides an elegant entry. The expansive great room with vaulted ceiling and cozy fireplace will provide a wonderful atmosphere for visiting with your guests. A U-shaped kitchen provides you ample counter space for preparing dinner while the nearby grilling porch awaits the family chef. This split bedroom design offers privacy for all household members and ample closet space in each bedroom. Enjoy the luxurious master suite and private bath with relaxing whirlpool tub.

WIDTH: 59' 0"

DEPTH: 69' 0"

TOTAL LIVING: 1,683 SQ. FT.

PRICE TIER: **B**

MAIN CEILING: 9 FT.

BEDROOMS: 3

BATHS: 2

FOUNDATION: CRAWL, SLAB, OPTIONAL BASEMENT, OPTIONAL DAYLIGHT BASEMENT

PLAN OPTIONS: PAGE 282

BUILDING SYSTEM
NGi
Next Generation Industries
COMPATABLE

790
Madison Avenue

Beautiful round columns accent the front porch of this Southern Historical Nelson Design Group creation. Enter this home and marvel at the openness of the great room with a warming fireplace for cozy gatherings. Charming round columns again accent the brightly lit dining room and kitchen-with a handy island workspace with seating. All bedrooms in this design have spacious walk-in closets that will aid in keeping them clutter free. The secluded master suite will provide a private retreat with a spacious walk-in closet and private bathroom packed with amenities.

WIDTH: 59' 8"

DEPTH: 69' 0"

TOTAL LIVING: 1,914 SQ. FT.

PRICE TIER: B

MAIN CEILING: 9 FT.

BEDROOMS: 3

BATHS: 2

FOUNDATION: CRAWL, SLAB, OPTIONAL BASEMENT, OPTIONAL DAYLIGHT BASEMENT

PLAN OPTIONS: PAGE 282

BUILDING SYSTEM
NGI
Next Generation Industries
COMPATABLE

© 2002 NELSON DESIGN GROUP, LLC.

GRILLING PORCH
9'-10" X 11'-10"

GARAGE
20'-8" X 21'-8"

MASTER SUITE
15'-4" X 15'-4"
10' BOXED CEILING

M.BATH
12'-6" X 15'-4"

WHP TUB

LAU.
5'-8" X 5'-6"

KITCHEN
9'-10" X 14'-2"

DINING
10'-2" X 14'-2"

BEDROOM 2
12'-6" X 14'-6"

ISLAND

LINEN

PAN

8" COLUMNS

BATH

GREAT ROOM
16'-0" X 21'-6"
10' BOXED CEILING

BEDROOM 3/ STUDY
12'-6" X 15'-4"

FRENCH DOORS

COVERED PORCH
26'-0" X 8'-0"

12" COLUMNS

To Order Call 1.800.590.2423   Similar plans can be viewed and ordered at www.nelsondesigngroup.com

787

Madison Avenue

MASTER SUITE
15'-4" X 13'-0"
10' BOXED CEILING

COVERED PORCH
34'-8" X 10'-0"

10" COLUMNS

MASTER BATH
15'-4" X 15'-0"

BREAKFAST ROOM
10'-4" X 11'-4"

LAU.
8'-0"X
8'-0"

STORAGE
7'-6" X
8'-0"

WHP TUB

GLASS SHWR

SEAT

GREAT ROOM
18'-10" X 19'-0"
10' BOXED CEILING
IN LIEU OF BONUS ABOVE

REF.

BATH

LIN

LIN

OPT. BASEMENT STAIRS

UP

MW
RG
KITCHEN
10'-4" X 12'-0"

DW

PAN.

GARAGE
20'-0" X 23'-0"

BEDROOM 2
11'-6" X 11'-10"

FOYER
7'-0" X 9'-0"

OPT. FRENCH DOORS

DINING ROOM
12'-2" X 12'-0"

BEDROOM 3 / STUDY
13'-2" X 12'-9"

8" COLUMNS

© 2002 NELSON DESIGN GROUP, LLC.

MAIN FLOOR

COVERED PORCH
34'-10" X 14'-0"

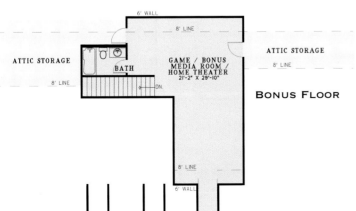

6' WALL

8' LINE

ATTIC STORAGE

8' LINE

ATTIC STORAGE

8' LINE

BATH

GAME / BONUS MEDIA ROOM / HOME THEATER
21'-2" X 29'-10"

8' LINE

DN.

8' LINE

BONUS FLOOR

6' WALL

Nelson Design Group has created a functional home while maintaining the charm of a Historical Southern Traditional plan. Entertaining family during the holidays will be easy with the spacious dining room and expansive great room–with even more room for guests to relax on the rear covered porch. The accommodating kitchen offers a snack bar for serving delicious meals buffet-style for a more casual lifestyle. Optional French doors are available for the front bedroom-making the perfect study for both quiet time and office work. Family will feel like royalty in the upstairs home theater and game room with a convenient bathroom and plenty of attic storage.

WIDTH: 66' 0"	**MAIN CEILING:** 9 FT.
DEPTH: 63' 0"	**BONUS CEILING:** 9 FT.
TOTAL LIVING: 1,989 SQ. FT.*	**BEDROOMS:** 3
*OPTIONAL BONUS 471 SQ. FT.	**BATHS:** 2
PRICE TIER: B	**FOUNDATION:** CRAWL, SLAB, OPTIONAL BASEMENT, OPTIONAL DAYLIGHT BASEMENT

BUILDING SYSTEM NGI Next Generation Industries **COMPATABLE**

PLAN OPTIONS: PAGE 282

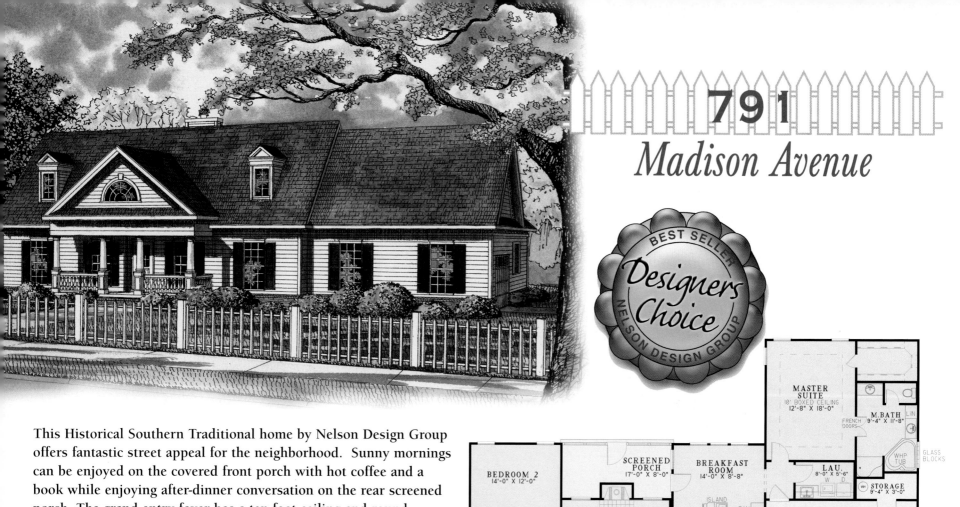

791
Madison Avenue

BEST SELLER — Designers Choice — NELSON DESIGN GROUP

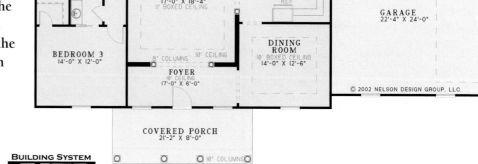

This Historical Southern Traditional home by Nelson Design Group offers fantastic street appeal for the neighborhood. Sunny mornings can be enjoyed on the covered front porch with hot coffee and a book while enjoying after-dinner conversation on the rear screened porch. The grand entry foyer has a ten-foot ceiling and round columns making a lavish entry into the great room with fireplace and an eleven-foot ceiling. Many dining options are available in both formal dining room and breakfast room, which are separated by the open kitchen complete with center work-island with seating. This split bedroom design offers privacy to the master suite placed at the rear of the home featuring French doors into the private bathroom and corner whirlpool tub.

WIDTH: 70' 0"	MAIN CEILING: 9 FT.
DEPTH: 57' 10"	BEDROOMS: 3
TOTAL LIVING: 1,999 SQ. FT.	BATHS: 2
PRICE TIER: B	FOUNDATION: CRAWL, SLAB
	PLAN OPTIONS: PAGE 282

BUILDING SYSTEM — NGI — Next Generation Industries — COMPATABLE

789
Madison Avenue

GRILLING PORCH
25'-10" X 8'-0"

BREAKFAST ROOM
12'-10" X 9'-8"

HEARTH ROOM
11'-10" X 16'-5"

M. BATH
12'-8" X 15'-4"

WHP TUP

LIN

MASTER SUITE
13'-6" X 15'-4"
10' BOXED CEILING

GREAT ROOM
13'-10" X 19'-2"

REF   DW

ATTIC STORAGE

KITCHEN
11'-8" X 12'-3"

BATH

PANTRY

RG

LAU.
8'-6" X 5'-10"

D W

8' COLUMNS

LIN

FOYER
7'-6" X 9'-0"

BENCH W/ HANGING

KID'S NOOK

BEDROOM 3
10'-8" X 11'-0"

BEDROOM 2 / STUDY
11'-2" X 11'-2"

DINING ROOM
12'-4" X 16'-4"

OPTIONAL BASEMENT STAIRS

GARAGE
22'-0" X 23'-6"

COVERED PORCH
32'-4" X 8'-0"

10" ROUND COLUMNS

© 2002 NELSON DESIGN GROUP, LLC.

Relatives may never want to leave this dynamic historically inspired Nelson Design Group home. Elegant round columns are carefully placed throughout to enhance room entries as well as porches. All family areas in this home wrap around the centralized kitchen allowing family the enjoyment of a cozy fireplace to gather around in the great room or cozy hearth room. An angled kitchen counter allows extra seating or is perfect for dining entertainment 'buffet-style" and has a handy kid's nook nearby. The master suite has a ten-foot boxed ceiling and magnificent private bathroom with French doors and large walk-in closet. Two additional bedrooms are located nearby keeping family within close distance.

WIDTH: 66' 4"

DEPTH: 58' 7"

TOTAL LIVING: 2,163 SQ. FT.

PRICE TIER: C

MAIN CEILING: 9 FT.

BEDROOMS: 3

BATHS: 2

FOUNDATION: CRAWL, SLAB, OPTIONAL BASEMENT, OPTIONAL DAYLIGHT BASEMENT

PLAN OPTIONS: PAGE 282

BUILDING SYSTEM
NGI
Next Generation Industries
COMPATABLE

Exterior details on this Historical Nelson Design Group home add character to this stately, symmetrical design. Upon entering the foyer, French doors lead to an optional study where privacy awaits and beautiful antique furniture can be showcased. While the formal dining room enhanced with elegant columns, leads to the well-equipped kitchen. The great room separates the master suite quarters from the additional bedrooms with an optional basement stairway next to the garage entry. Retire to your master suite full of amenities, treat yourself to a soak in the corner whirlpool tub, and afterwards enjoy private access to the rear-grilling porch for late night stargazing.

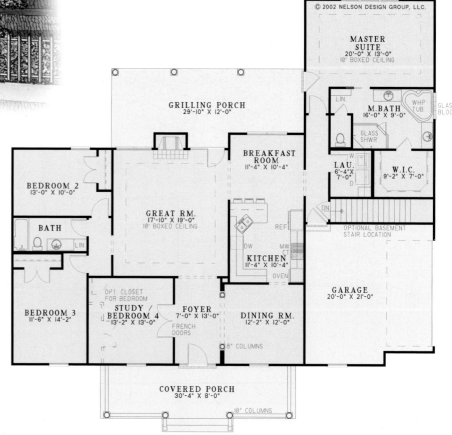

WIDTH: 66' 0"

DEPTH: 63' 8"

TOTAL LIVING: 2,246 SQ. FT.

PRICE TIER: C

MAIN CEILING: 9 FT.

BEDROOMS: 4

BATHS: 2

FOUNDATION: CRAWL, SLAB, OPTIONAL BASEMENT, OPTIONAL DAYLIGHT BASEMENT

PLAN OPTIONS: PAGE 282

BUILDING SYSTEM
NGI
Next Generation Industries
COMPATABLE

THE Burlington COLLECTION

The Burlington Collection is a collaboration of eight narrow lot line home designs that are economical to build as well as highly functional for today's family. These homes have a combination of brick and siding exteriors, shutters, front loading garages as well as optional basements. These traditional designs range between 1,250 to 1,800 square feet, include open floor plans, and feature spacious master suites with large walk-in closets. Simplicity, energy efficiency and well-designed floor plans make these homes highly desirable. Welcome to our neighborhood...with seventeen collections available.

Nelson Design Group LLC

RESIDENTIAL & COMMERCIAL PLANNERS · DESIGNERS

634 Burlington Cove

A starter home or empty nester home best describes this Nelson Design Group traditional style home. A quaint covered entry welcomes you into a foyer separating two bedrooms and a full bath from the master suite, creating a private split bedroom plan. Convenient to the living area, this spacious master suite has a private bath with a double vanity and extra large walk-in closet. The great room has a vaulted ceiling, plenty of wall space and a sliding glass door to the back yard. A quaint dining area has two large windows and opens to the kitchen. The garage accesses the home through the laundry room.

Width: 40' 0" · Depth: 43' 2"
Total Living: 1,250 sq. ft.
Main Ceiling: 8 ft.
Bedrooms: 3 · Baths: 2
Foundations: Crawl, Slab, Optional Basement, Optional Daylight Basement
Plan Options: page 282
Price Tier: A

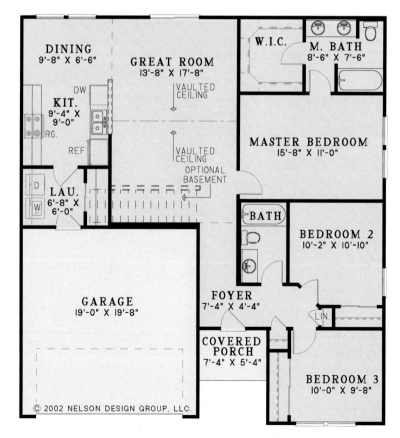

DINING
9'-8" X 6'-6"

GREAT ROOM
13'-8" X 17'-8"
VAULTED CEILING

W.I.C.

M. BATH
8'-6" X 7'-6"

DW

KIT.
9'-4" X 9'-0"

RG.

REF

VAULTED CEILING

OPTIONAL BASEMENT

MASTER BEDROOM
15'-8" X 11'-0"

D
W

LAU.
6'-8" X 6'-0"

BATH

GARAGE
19'-0" X 19'-8"

FOYER
7'-4" X 4'-4"

BEDROOM 2
10'-2" X 10'-10"

LIN.

COVERED PORCH
7'-4" X 5'-4"

BEDROOM 3
10'-0" X 9'-8"

© 2002 NELSON DESIGN GROUP, LLC.

To Order Call 1.800.590.2423   Similar plans can be viewed and ordered at www.nelsondesigngroup.com

640 Burlington Cove

Friends and family will enjoy gatherings in this quaint Nelson Design Group home. This open floor plan allows the great room to open into a spacious dining area with large windows for plenty of natural light. A sliding glass door at the rear of the great room allows family to comfortably access the rear patio while entertaining. The U-shaped kitchen has a convenient half bath near the basement and garage access. All bedrooms and the laundry room are located upstairs including the master suite with a large walk-in closet and private bathroom.

Width: 34' 0" · Depth: 36' 0"

Main Floor: 611 sq. ft. · Upper Floor: 675 sq. ft.

Total Living: 1,289 sq. ft.

Main Ceiling: 8 ft. · Upper Ceiling: 8 ft.

Bedrooms: 3 · Baths: 2 1/2

Foundations: Crawl, Slab, Optional Basement, Optional Daylight Basement

Plan Options: page 282

Price Tier: A

BUILDING SYSTEM
NGI
Next Generation Industries
COMPATABLE

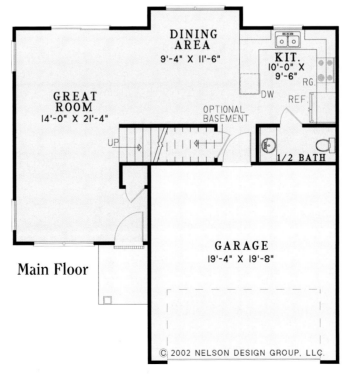

Main Floor

DINING AREA
9'-4" X 11'-6"

KIT.
10'-0" X 9'-6"

GREAT ROOM
14'-0" X 21'-4"

OPTIONAL BASEMENT

UP

1/2 BATH

GARAGE
19'-4" X 19'-8"

© 2002 NELSON DESIGN GROUP, LLC.

Upper Floor

BEDROOM 3
9'-2" X 9'-4"

BEDROOM 2
10'-0" X 9'-6"

W.I.C.

DN

BATH

LAU.
7'-8" X 5'-4"

M.BATH

MASTER SUITE
14'-0" X 14'-8"

W.I.C.

636 Burlington Cove

Imagine your family in this traditional Nelson Design Group home. The main level has a great room that opens to the dining room and kitchen with a handy work-island creating the ultimate family area. For convenience, a half bath and hall closet are located just off the foyer. Upstairs are all three bedrooms, each with walk-in closets, a full bathroom and the spacious laundry room. The master bedroom has a large walk-in closet, private bathroom and plenty of wall space. The double garage has an entry door into the main living area.

Width: 40' 0" • Depth: 34' 8"
Main Floor: 875 sq. ft. • Upper Floor: 723 sq. ft.
Total Living: 1,598 sq. ft.
Main Ceiling: 8 ft. • Upper Ceiling: 8 ft.
Bedrooms: 3 • Baths: 2 1/2
Foundations: Crawl, Slab, Optional Basement,
Optional Daylight Basement
Plan Options: page 282
Price Tier: **B**

Main Floor

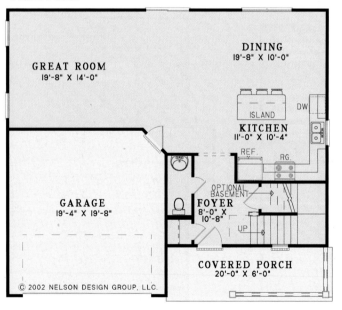

GREAT ROOM
19'-8" X 14'-0"

DINING
19'-8" X 10'-0"

ISLAND
DW

KITCHEN
11'-0" X 10'-4"

REF.
RG.

GARAGE
19'-4" X 19'-8"

OPTIONAL
BASEMENT

FOYER
8'-0" X
10'-8"

UP

COVERED PORCH
20'-0" X 6'-0"

© 2002 NELSON DESIGN GROUP, LLC.

Upper Floor

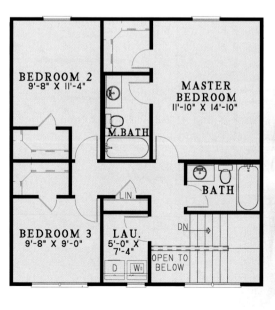

BEDROOM 2
9'-8" X 11'-4"

MASTER
BEDROOM
11'-10" X 14'-10"

M.BATH

BATH

LIN.

BEDROOM 3
9'-8" X 9'-0"

LAU.
5'-0" X
7'-4"

DN

D   W

OPEN TO
BELOW

To Order Call 1.800.590.2423   Similar plans can be viewed and ordered at www.nelsondesigngroup.com

635 Burlington Cove

This Nelson Design Group traditional home is the perfect starter home. Enter from a large covered porch and into a spacious great room perfect for family gatherings. This main floor contains a master suite with a private bath and an extra large walk-in closet. The kitchen has a work island with bar seating and opens to a large dining area. A half bath and laundry room are both centrally located for convenience. The upper floor contains two large bedrooms with creative ceiling heights, a large hall closet and a full bathroom.

Width: 39' 0" • Depth: 39' 10"

Main Floor: 1,048 sq. ft. • Upper Floor: 556 sq. ft.

Total Living: 1,604 sq. ft.

Bedrooms: 3 • Baths: 2 1/2

Foundations: Crawl, Slab, Optional Basement, Optional Daylight Basement

Main Ceiling: 8 ft. • Upper Ceiling: 8 ft.

Plan Options: page 282

Price Tier: B

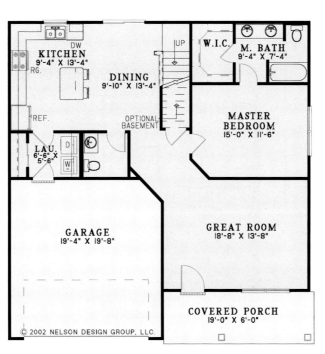

Main Floor

KITCHEN 9'-4" X 13'-4"
DINING 9'-10" X 13'-4"
W.I.C.
M. BATH 9'-4" X 7'-4"
MASTER BEDROOM 15'-0" X 11'-6"
LAU. 6'-6" X 5'-6"
OPTIONAL BASEMENT
GARAGE 19'-4" X 19'-8"
GREAT ROOM 18'-8" X 13'-8"
COVERED PORCH 19'-0" X 6'-0"

© 2002 NELSON DESIGN GROUP, LLC.

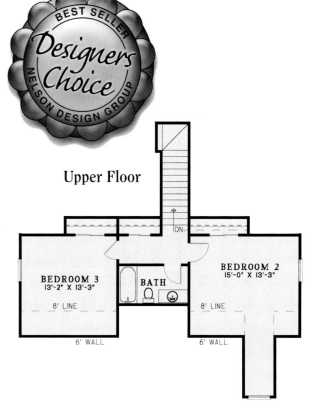

Upper Floor

BEDROOM 3 13'-2" X 13'-3"
8' LINE
6' WALL
BATH
BEDROOM 2 15'-0" X 13'-3"
8' LINE
6' WALL

BEST SELLER
Designers Choice
NELSON DESIGN GROUP

639 Burlington Cove

An entry porch with a grand ceiling height elegantly welcomes guests into this Nelson Design Group home. Immediately upon entry, this split level design will lead you up to the main living areas including a large great room adjoining the kitchen and dining area, a spacious master suite and two bedrooms and full bath. The lower level option has a fourth bedroom and full bath, perfect for weekend guests or a teenager's hideaway! The laundry room, a TV room or optional study and garage are also located on the lower level.

Width: 40' 0" • Depth: 30' 0"
Main Floor: 1,134 sq. ft. • Lower Floor: 480 sq. ft.
Total Living: 1,614 sq. ft.
Bedrooms: 4 • Baths: 3
Foundations: Crawl, Slab, Optional Basement, Optional Daylight Basement
Main Ceiling: 8 ft. • Lower Ceiling: 8 ft.
Plan Options: page 282
Price Tier: B

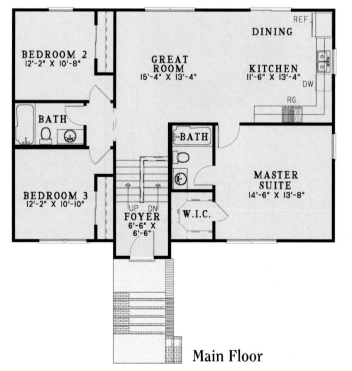

Main Floor

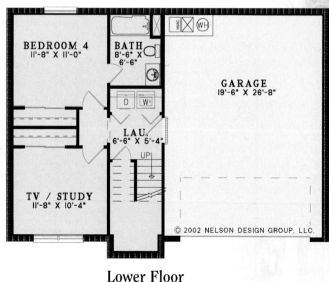

Lower Floor

© 2002 NELSON DESIGN GROUP, LLC.

To Order Call 1.800.590.2423   Similar plans can be viewed and ordered at www.nelsondesigngroup.com

638 Burlington Cove

This beautifully designed Nelson Design Group home has everything a growing family needs. A wide foyer provides a half bath while leading to an enormous great room with sliding glass doors to the deck, perfect for grilling. A step-saver kitchen has a bar for extra counter space and additional seating. The second story stairs are located in the entry foyer and lead to a massive master bedroom with private bath and large walk-in closet. Two additional bedrooms share a full bathroom and are located near the laundry room for added convenience.

Width: 45' 0" • Depth: 36' 0"

Main Floor: 789 sq. ft. • Upper Floor: 888 sq. ft.

Total Living: 1,677 sq. ft.

Bedrooms: 3 • Baths: 2 1/2

Foundations: Crawl, Slab, Optional Basement, Optional Daylight Basement

Main Ceiling: 8 ft. • Upper Ceiling: 8 ft.

Plan Options: page 282

Price Tier: B

BUILDING SYSTEM
NGi
Next Generation Industries
COMPATABLE

Main Floor

WALL LINE ABOVE

GREAT ROOM
24'-0" X 15'-0"

DECK
12'-4" X 12'-4"

DINING
10'-6" X 6'-6"

OPTIONAL BASEMENT

FOYER
6'-0" X 16'-4"

GARAGE
20'-0" X 20'-0"

KITCHEN
13'-10" X 9'-10"
RG.   REF.
DW   UP

COVERED PORCH
24'-4" X 4'-0"

© 2002 NELSON DESIGN GROUP, LLC.

Upper Floor

W.I.C.

MASTER BEDROOM
18'-2" X 12'-4"

M. BATH

BATH

LAU.
W   D

DN

BEDROOM 2
10'-0" X 12'-0"

BEDROOM 3
13'-8" X 12'-0"

633 Burlington Cove

A covered porch with a shed type roof and quaint captain's window add great street appeal to this Nelson Design Group home. Enjoy entertaining friends and family in your large great room with a sliding glass door for backyard grilling. A large bay window in the dining room adds plenty of light while viewing the backyard. For convenience, the garage access is located in the kitchen area as well as a half bath. The upper floor features a large laundry room, full bath and three spacious bedrooms. The master suite has plenty of wall space for large furniture, a private bathroom and an extra large walk-in closet.

Width: 38' 0" · Depth: 32' 0"
Main Floor: 688 sq. ft. · Upper Floor: 1,083 sq. ft.
Total Living: 1,771 sq. ft.
Bedrooms: 4 · Baths: 2 1/2
Foundations: Crawl, Slab, Optional Basement,
Optional Daylight Basement
Main Ceiling: 8 ft. · Upper Ceiling: 8 ft.
Plan Options: page 282
Price Tier: **B**

Main Floor

UPPER FLOOR WALL LINE

DINING
9'-6" X 11'-8"

DW.

KITCHEN
14'-0" X 10'-0"

RG.

REF.   PAN.

OPTIONAL
BASEMENT

GREAT
ROOM
13'-10" X 24'-4"

GARAGE
19'-0" X 19'-0"

UP

COVERED
PORCH
18'-0" X 5'-0"

© 2002 NELSON DESIGN GROUP, LLC.

Upper Floor

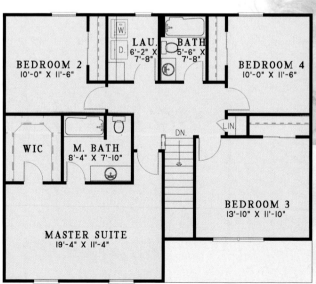

BEDROOM 2
10'-0" X 11'-6"

LAU.
6'-2" X
7'-8"

W
D.

BATH
5'-6" X
7'-8"

BEDROOM 4
10'-0" X 11'-6"

WIC

M. BATH
8'-4" X 7'-10"

DN.

LIN.

MASTER SUITE
19'-4" X 11'-4"

BEDROOM 3
13'-10" X 11'-10"

To Order Call 1.800.590.2423   Similar plans can be viewed and ordered at www.nelsondesigngroup.com

637 Burlington Cove

Sit back and relax in this very spacious two-story beautifully designed Nelson Design Group home. An open floor plan gives you many options for furniture placement as well as entertaining guests. The great room opens to the dining area and kitchen, which sensibly includes a half bath for convenience. The second level includes a large master bedroom suite with sizeable private bath and walk-in closet. Three additional bedrooms, a full bathroom and the laundry room complete this delightful plan.

Width: 37' 0" • Depth: 34' 0"
Main Floor: 733 sq. ft. • Upper Floor: 1,056 sq. ft.
Total Living: 1,789 sq. ft.
Bedrooms: 4 • Baths: 2 1/2
Foundations: Crawl, Slab, Optional Basement, Optional Daylight Basement
Main Ceiling: 8 ft. • Upper Ceiling: 8 ft.
Plan Options: page 282
Price Tier: B

BUILDING SYSTEM
NGi
Next Generation Industries
COMPATABLE

Main Floor

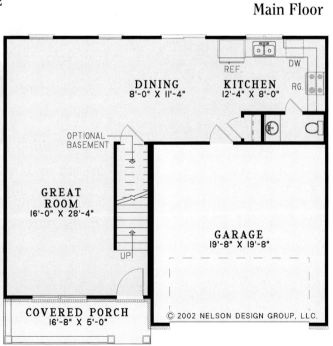

DINING
8'-0" X 11'-4"

KITCHEN
12'-4" X 8'-0"

REF.

DW

RG.

OPTIONAL BASEMENT

GREAT ROOM
16'-0" X 28'-4"

UP

GARAGE
19'-8" X 19'-8"

COVERED PORCH
16'-8" X 5'-0"

© 2002 NELSON DESIGN GROUP, LLC.

Upper Floor

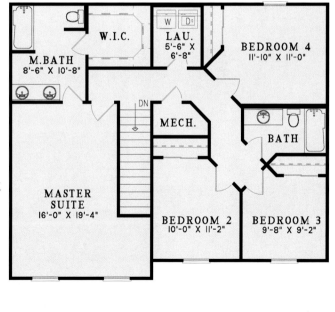

W.I.C.

LAU.
5'-6" X 6'-8"

W D

BEDROOM 4
11'-10" X 11'-0"

M.BATH
8'-6" X 10'-8"

DN

MECH.

BATH

MASTER SUITE
16'-0" X 19'-4"

BEDROOM 2
10'-0" X 11'-2"

BEDROOM 3
9'-8" X 9'-2"

THE
PROVIDIAN
COLLECTION

The Providian Collection includes five narrow lot designs featuring open floor plans for great family interaction. Spacious great rooms combined with dining rooms and kitchens create a much larger appearance. Half baths are great step savers as well as convenient for visitors. Upstairs you'll find the master suites complete with private bathrooms, walk-in closets and double vanities. Two additional bedrooms and full bathrooms, laundry rooms and linen closets are also located on the upper level completing these delightful plans. Stroll through our neighborhood of home plans at our website as well.

Nelson Design Group LLC

RESIDENTIAL & COMMERCIAL PLANNERS - DESIGNERS

Main Floor

OPTIONAL GRILLING PORCH
9'-0" X 8'-0"

DINING
11'-10" X 9'-4"

OPTIONAL FIREPLACE

GREAT RM.
13'-0" X 14'-8"

DW

RG.

KITCHEN
11'-4" X 11'-6"

REF.

PAN.

UP

FOYER
13'-2" X 13'-0"

STOR.

WH

PORCH
6'-4" X 5'-0"

GARAGE
19'-0" X 20'-0"

© 2002 NELSON DESIGN GROUP, LLC.

Upper Floor

BATH

BEDROOM 3
9'-10" X 8'-10"

BEDROOM 2
9'-4" X 11'-2"

LIN.

DN

MASTER SUITE
11'-4" X 13'-8"

W   D

M.BATH
13'-2" X 5'-0"

VAULTED CEILING

643 PROVIDIAN PLACE

Nelson Design Group has designed this two-story home with consideration for a growing family. The main level contains all family areas, which flow together to create a wonderful family environment. The kitchen opens the dining room and has a handy island for extra counter space as well as additional seating. The foyer has a convenient half bath near the stairs, that lead up to all three bedrooms including the master suite. A space-saver laundry area is located in the master suite bathroom.

Width: 25' 6" • Depth: 56' 8"
Main Floor: 697 sq. ft. • Upper Floor: 678 sq. ft. • Total Living: 1,375 sq. ft.
Main Ceiling: 9 ft. • Upper Ceiling: 8 ft.
Bedrooms: 3 • Baths: 2 1/2
Foundations: Crawl, Slab, Optional Basement, Optional Daylight Basement
Plan Options: page 282
Price Tier: **A**

To Order Call 1.800.590.2423   Similar plans can be viewed and ordered at www.nelsondesigngroup.com

Main Floor

GRILLING PORCH
13'-10" X 6'-2"

DINING
12'-6" X 9'-0"

GREAT ROOM
13'-6" X 17'-0"

REF.

OPTIONAL
FIRE PLACE

DW

KITCHEN
12'-10" X 10'-8"

RG.

FOYER
7'-0" X 7'-2"

UP

PORCH
7'-4" X 5'-0"

WH   STOR

GARAGE
19'-0" X 23'-0"

© 2002 NELSON DESIGN GROUP, LLC.

Upper Floor

W.I.C.

MASTER
SUITE
12'-6" X 13'-8"

WHP
TUB

M.BATH
13'-5" X 8'-0"

BATH
9'-2" X 5'-0"

DN

BEDROOM 2
9'-0" X 10'-6"

RAIL

LAU.
6'-2" X 5'-6"

D

W

BEDROOM 3
10'-0" X 10'-0"

642 PROVIDIAN PLACE

A quaint porch leads guests into this delightful Nelson Design Group home. A spacious great room with fireplace opens to the kitchen and dining room making for cozy entertaining. The large kitchen island is perfect for extra seating as well as counter space serving as a buffet for an afternoon barbecue. All three bedrooms are upstairs including a master suite with a large walk-in closet, a spacious laundry room with nearby linen closet and a full bathroom.

Width: 27' 0" • Depth: 50' 10"
Main Floor: 666 sq. ft. • Upper Floor: 812 sq. ft. • Total Living: 1,478 sq. ft.
Main Ceiling: 9 ft. • Upper Ceiling: 8 ft.
Bedrooms: 3 • Baths: 2 1/2
Foundations: Crawl, Slab, Optional Basement, Optional Daylight Basement
Plan Options: page 282
Price Tier: A

BUILDING SYSTEM
NGI
Next Generation Industries
COMPATABLE

To Order Call 1.800.590.2423   Similar plans can be viewed and ordered at www.nelsondesigngroup.com

Main Floor

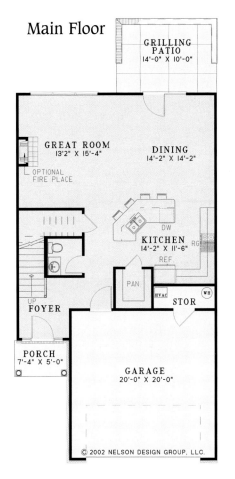

GRILLING PATIO
14'-0" X 10'-0"

GREAT ROOM
13'2" X 15'-4"

OPTIONAL FIRE PLACE

DINING
14'-2" X 14'-2"

DW

KITCHEN
14'-2" X 11'-6"

REF

PAN.

HVAC   STOR   WH

UP

FOYER

PORCH
7'-4" X 5'-0"

GARAGE
20'-0" X 20'-0"

© 2002 NELSON DESIGN GROUP, LLC.

Upper Floor

M. BATH
8'-2" X 9'-0"

W.I.C.

MASTER SUITE
12'-0" X 15'-4"

BEDROOM 2
15'-0" X 10'-2"

DN

W D

LAU.   LIN

LIN

BEDROOM 3
15'-0" X 10'-0"

BATH
12'-0" X 5'-8"

ATTIC STORAGE

644 PROVIDIAN PLACE

T his charming two-story home by Nelson Design Group is perfect for a growing family. A large island in the kitchen allows for extra counter space and additional seating during holiday gatherings. An open floor plan allows both the dining room and kitchen a cozy view of the great room fireplace. The upstairs includes a spacious master suite with an extra large walk-in closet, two additional bedrooms and a full bathroom.

Width: 28' 0" • Depth: 60' 0"
Main Floor: 824 sq. ft. • Upper Floor: 884 sq. ft. • Total Living: 1,708 sq. ft.
Main Ceiling: 9 ft. • Upper Ceiling: 8 ft.
Bedrooms: 3 • Baths: 2 1/2
Foundations: Crawl, Slab, Optional Basement, Optional Daylight Basement
Plan Options: page 282
Price Tier: B

BUILDING SYSTEM
NGI
Next Generation Industries
COMPATABLE

GRILLING PORCH
14'-8" X 10'-6"

DINING
13'-2" X 12'-0"

OPTIONAL
FIRE PLACE

KITCHEN
12'-2" X 11'-8"

DW

GREAT ROOM
15'-2" X 17'-6"

PAN REF RG

WH

STOR

VAULTED
CEILING

UP

FOYER
8'-0" X 15'-2"

GARAGE
19'-0" X 21'-6"

PORCH
8'-4" X 6'-0"

© 2002 NELSON DESIGN GROUP, LLC.

MASTER
SUITE
13'-2" X 16'-6"

BEDROOM 2
13'-10" X 12'-0"

WHP
TUB

BATH
13'-10" X 5'-0"

M.BATH
9'-4" X 15'-10"

LIN

DN

W.I.C.

LIN

LAU.
5'-6" X 6'-6"

OPEN TO
BELOW

W D

BEDROOM 3
13'-2" X 15'-3"

WINDOW
SEAT

VAULTED
CEILING

Upper Floor

645 PROVIDIAN PLACE

Nelson Design Group has created a lovely two story home
perfect for entertaining. A cozy entry hall leads to an open floor
plan containing a spacious great room, kitchen and large dining room. The
L-shaped kitchen has an angled island serving as extra counter space and
additional seating. Nearby is a corner grilling porch with columns for lazy
summer afternoons. The upper level has a spacious master suite, two
additional bedrooms, a full bathroom and nearby laundry room.

Width: 28' 0" • Depth: 53' 10"

Main Floor: 851 sq. ft. • Upper Floor: 990 sq. ft. • Total Living: 1,841 sq. ft.

Main Ceiling: 9 ft. • Upper Ceiling: 8 ft.

Bedrooms: 3 • Baths: 2 1/2

Foundations: Crawl, Slab, Optional Basement, Optional Daylight Basement

Plan Options: page 282 • **Price Tier: B**

BUILDING SYSTEM
NGI
Next Generation Industries
COMPATABLE

To Order Call 1.800.590.2423   **Similar plans can be viewed and ordered at www.nelsondesigngroup.com**

Main Floor

OPTIONAL
GRILLING PORCH
14'-8" X 8'-0"

OPTIONAL
FIREPLACE

MASTER
SUITE
13'-0" X 14'-0"

GREAT ROOM
14'-0" X 13'-0"

DINING
14'-0" X 8'-8"

M. BATH
13'-0" X 15'-10"

LIN

W.I.C.

WHP
TUB

RG

W D

DW   REF

KIT.
10'-2" X 11'-0"

LAU.
6'-0" X 5'-10"

WH   STOR

UP

GARAGE
19'-0" X 20'-0"

FOYER

PORCH
8'-4" X 4'-8"

© 2002 NELSON DESIGN GROUP, LLC.

BEST SELLER
Designers Choice
NELSON DESIGN GROUP

Upper Floor

BEDROOM 2
13'-6" X 14'-8"

BEDROOM 3
13'-6" X 14'-8"

DN

BATH
9'-8" X 8'-8"

OPT. GAME
ROOM
10'-8" X 20'-0"

OPEN TO
BELOW

8' LINE

5'6" WALL

641 PROVIDIAN PLACE

Many options are available in this well designed Nelson Design Group home. The long entry hall leads to a step saver kitchen flowing through to the dining area and great room. The master suite is privately located at the rear of the main level and includes a whirlpool tub, separate shower and large walk-in closet. For everyday convenience, a half bath and laundry room are also on the main level. Upstairs you'll find an optional game room, a full bath and two large bedrooms with double closets for extra storage.

Width: 28' 0" • Depth: 60' 0"

Main Floor: 1,190 sq. ft. • Upper Floor: 700 sq. ft.

Total Living: 1,890 sq. ft.* • *Optional Bonus: 224 sq. ft.

Bedrooms: 3 • Baths: 2 1/2

Foundations: Crawl, Slab, Optional Basement, Optional Daylight Basement

Main Ceiling: 9 ft. • Upper Ceiling: 8 ft.

Plan Options: page 282 • **Price Tier: B**

BUILDING SYSTEM
ngi
Next Generation Industries
COMPATABLE

Village at
WINDSTONE

When you choose a Nelson Design Group collection, you not only create beautiful homes, you achieve ideal master planned communities. The Village at Windstone Collection features living spaces of 1,800 to 2,800 square feet replicating historical Southern style designs. Each of these plans complement the other, resulting in an effective Traditional Neighborhood Design theme — making development easy for you. All plans are designed to fit lots of 50 feet to 80 feet. Nelson Design Group also offers complementary collections with the same traditional appeal and quality as our Village at Windstone Collection at our website.

Nelson Design Group
LLC

RESIDENTIAL & COMMERCIAL PLANNERS - DESIGNERS

Upper Floor

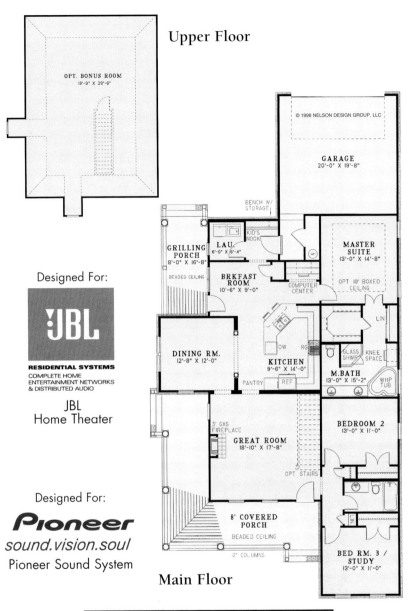

OPT. BONUS ROOM
19'-9" X 29'-6"

© 1998 NELSON DESIGN GROUP, LLC

GARAGE
20'-0" X 19'-8"

BENCH W/ STORAGE

GRILLING PORCH
8'-0" X 16'-8"
BEADED CEILING

LAU.
6'-0" X 6'-4"

KID'S NOOK

MASTER SUITE
13'-0" X 14'-8"

OPT 10' BOXED CEILING

BRKFAST ROOM
10'-6" X 9'-0"

COMPUTER CENTER

LIN

DINING RM.
12'-8" X 12'-0"

KITCHEN
9'-6" X 14'-0"

DW   RG

GLASS SHWR   KNEE SPACE

M.BATH
13'-0" X 15'-2"

WHP TUB

PANTRY   REF

3' GAS FIREPLACE

GREAT ROOM
18'-10" X 17'-8"

BEDROOM 2
13'-0" X 11'-0"

OPT. STAIRS

8' COVERED PORCH
BEADED CEILING

12" COLUMNS

BED RM. 3 / STUDY
13'-0" X 11'-0"

Main Floor

Designed For:

JBL
RESIDENTIAL SYSTEMS
COMPLETE HOME
ENTERTAINMENT NETWORKS
& DISTRIBUTED AUDIO

JBL
Home Theater

Designed For:

Pioneer
sound.vision.soul
Pioneer Sound System

321 Windstone Place

Windstone Collection I

An eight-foot corner wrap-around entry porch with classic southern columns allows you to enjoy an exquisite view from every direction of this Nelson Design Group home. Take advantage of hours of quality family time in a marvelous great room with an open stairway leading to the upper level. A double bedroom area with connecting full bath is ideal for kids of all ages. A bright breakfast area with access to a spacious kitchen and rear grilling porch conveniently provides entertaining and relaxing family dinners. Traveling to the upper level, find a huge bonus area for use as a game room or even another private suite.

Width: 41' 4"	Main Ceiling: 9 ft.
Depth: 83' 8"	Upper Ceiling: 8 ft.
Total Living: 1,845 sq. ft.*	Bedrooms: 3
*Optional Bonus: 1,191 sq. ft.	Baths: 2
Price Tier: B	Foundation: Crawl, Slab, Optional Basement, Optional Daylight Basement
	Plan Options: page 282

BUILDING SYSTEM
NGI
Next Generation Industries
COMPATABLE

317 Windstone Place

Windstone Collection I

This master-planned Nelson Design Group home is designed to capture the classic style and splendor of historical Southern architecture. Let summer days slip away on a traditional eight-foot covered front porch. An elegant foyer leads directly to a marvelous great room complete with a built-in media center, computer nook and efficient gas fireplace. Pass through remarkable wooden columns into a formal dining area — perfect for elegant dinner parties and conveniently located with fluid access to the kitchen. Invite friends over for a cookout using the side covered grilling porch. Intricate French doors lead to a grand master suite and adjoining full master bath with all the amenities you've come to expect.

Width: 39' 0"

Depth: 72' 0"

Total Living: 1,915 sq. ft.

Price Tier: **B**

Main Ceiling: 10 ft.

Bedrooms: 3

Baths: 2

Foundation: Crawl, Slab

Plan Options: page 282

BUILDING SYSTEM
NGI
Next Generation Industries
COMPATABLE

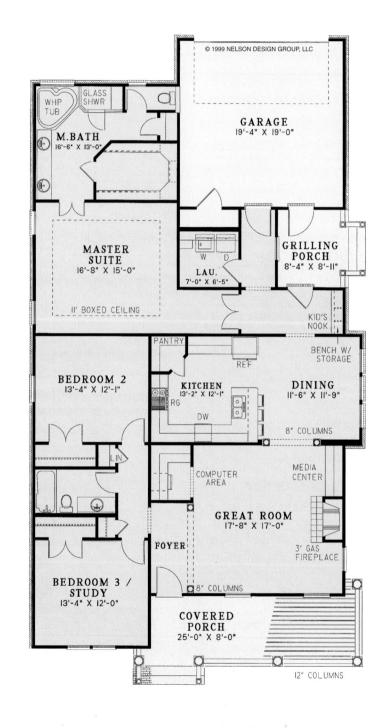

© 1999 NELSON DESIGN GROUP, LLC

GARAGE
19'-4" X 19'-0"

M.BATH
16'-6" X 13'-0"

WHP TUB

GLASS SHWR

MASTER SUITE
16'-8" X 15'-0"

11' BOXED CEILING

LAU.
7'-0" X 6'-5"

GRILLING PORCH
8'-4" X 8'-11"

KID'S NOOK

BENCH W/ STORAGE

PANTRY

REF

BEDROOM 2
13'-4" X 12'-1"

KITCHEN
13'-2" X 12'-1"

DINING
11'-6" X 11'-9"

RG

DW

8" COLUMNS

LIN

COMPUTER AREA

MEDIA CENTER

GREAT ROOM
17'-8" X 17'-0"

3' GAS FIREPLACE

FOYER

BEDROOM 3 / STUDY
13'-4" X 12'-0"

8" COLUMNS

COVERED PORCH
25'-0" X 8'-0"

12" COLUMNS

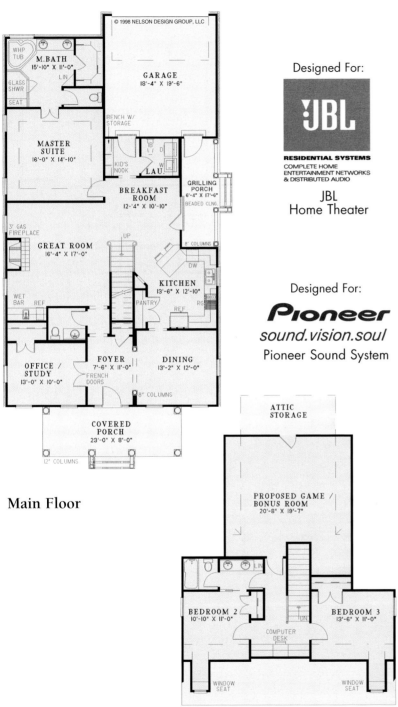

Main Floor

Upper Floor

318 Windstone Place

Windstone Collection I

Pamper yourself with Southern charm when you select this Nelson Design Group home. Become instantly immersed in tradition as you step into an elegant foyer designed with an open entrance to the formal dining room. Brilliant French doors open to a private study for late night work or quiet time with your favorite book. Enjoy romantic nights in front of a roaring fire while you sip drinks from the built-in wet bar in the great room. Plan a fun cookout and show off your famous barbeque skills while utilizing the side grilling porch. A spacious upper level with a bonus room – perfect for a game or study area – allows plenty of space for the kids to be kids.

Width: 35' 4"	Main Ceiling: 9 ft.
Depth: 71' 6"	Upper Ceiling: 8 ft.
Main Floor: 1,698 sq. ft.	Bedrooms: 3
Upper Floor: 533 sq. ft.	Baths: 2 1/2
Total Living: 2,231 sq. ft.*	Foundation: Crawl, Slab, Basement, Daylight Basement
*Optional Bonus: 394 sq. ft.	
Price Tier: C	Plan Options: page 282

BUILDING SYSTEM
NGi
Next Generation Industries
COMPATABLE

BEDROOM 3
13'-2" X 11'-0"

© 1999 NELSON DESIGN GROUP, LLC

GARAGE
20'-10" X 20'-0"

LIN.

GRILLING PORCH
BEADED CEILING

BEDROOM 2
12'-4" X 11'-1"

W.
D.
LAU.

KID'S NOOK

HANGING
BENCH W/ STORAGE

60X60 WHP TUB

SEAT

BUILT-INS

M.BATH
12'-4" X 15'-6"

GREAT ROOM
17'-4" X 15'-6"
10' BOXED CEILING

LIN.

BUILT-INS

KIT.
9'-8" X 11'-1"

RG.

NOOK
8'-0" X 11'-1"

REF
DW

MASTER SUITE
15'-0" X 17'-5"

PAN

8" COLUMNS

FOYER

SITTING AREA

DINING
11'-10" X 11'-0"
10' BOXED CEILING

8' PORCH
BEADED CEILING

12" FIBERGLASS COLUMNS

338 Windstone Place

Windstone Collection II

Step inside this traditional Nelson Design Group home and leave the world behind. Enjoy comfortable evenings relaxing in your spacious great room, complete with gas fireplace and built-in shelving. Dinner parties are a breeze in the comfort of your formal dining area enhanced by eight-inch wood columns. For more casual gatherings, invite friends over for a delicious cookout on your grilling porch, accessible from sitting nook and garage. Finally, relish in the privacy of your large master suite and relax in the corner whirlpool tub of the master bath.

Width: 38' 0"
Depth: 79' 6"
Total Living: 1,848 sq. ft.
Price Tier: B

Main Ceiling: 9 ft.
Bedrooms: 3
Baths: 2
Foundation: Crawl, Slab
Plan Options: page 282

BUILDING SYSTEM
NGI
Next Generation Industries
COMPATABLE

Main Floor

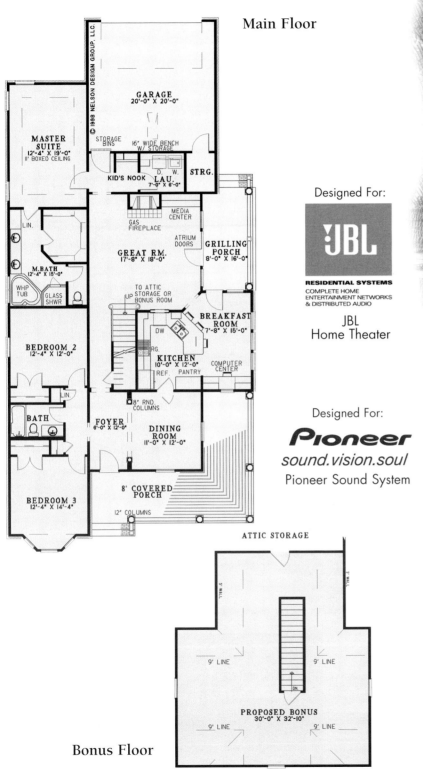

© 1998 NELSON DESIGN GROUP, LLC

GARAGE
20'-0" X 20'-0"

MASTER SUITE
12'-4" X 19'-0"
11' BOXED CEILING

STORAGE BINS

16" WIDE BENCH W/ STORAGE

KID'S NOOK

LAU.
7'-0" X 6'-0"

D. W.

STRG.

LIN.

M.BATH
12'-4" X 15'-0"

GAS FIREPLACE

MEDIA CENTER

WHP TUB

GLASS SHWR

ATRIUM DOORS

GREAT RM.
17'-8" X 18'-0"

GRILLING PORCH
8'-0" X 16'-0"

TO ATTIC STORAGE OR UP BONUS ROOM

DW

REG.

BREAKFAST ROOM
7'-8" X 15'-0"

BEDROOM 2
12'-4" X 12'-0"

KITCHEN
10'-0" X 12'-0"

REF. PANTRY

COMPUTER CENTER

LIN.

8' RND. COLUMNS

BATH

FOYER
6'-0" X 12'-0"

DINING ROOM
11'-0" X 12'-0"

BEDROOM 3
12'-4" X 14'-4"

8' COVERED PORCH

12" COLUMNS

Designed For:

JBL

RESIDENTIAL SYSTEMS
COMPLETE HOME
ENTERTAINMENT NETWORKS
& DISTRIBUTED AUDIO

JBL
Home Theater

Designed For:

Pioneer
sound.vision.soul
Pioneer Sound System

ATTIC STORAGE

5' WALL

5' WALL

9' LINE

9' LINE

PROPOSED BONUS
30'-0" X 32'-10"

DN.

9' LINE

9' LINE

Bonus Floor

355 Windstone Place
Windstone Collection II

Imagine yourself in this Nelson Design Group home. Each day is a dream come true as you enjoy quiet summer evenings over iced tea and conversation on your covered front porch. Become the perfect host or hostess of charming dinners in your dining room easily and conveniently accessible to the kitchen and breakfast room. A side grilling porch just off the breakfast room provides ample space for entertaining as well. After dining, adjourn to the great room for coffee in front of a gas fireplace. Then retreat to a wonderful master suite complete with master bath including a whirlpool tub and double vanity. But don't worry about the kids, they'll have plenty of space to play in the proposed upper level bonus area with nine-foot ceilings.

Width: 39' 0"	Main Ceiling: 10 ft.
Depth: 82' 4"	Bedrooms: 3
Total Living: 1,927 sq. ft.	Baths: 2
*Optional Bonus: 909 sq. ft.	Foundation: Crawl, Slab, Basement, Daylight Basement
Price Tier: B	Plan Options: page 282

BUILDING SYSTEM
NGI
Next Generation Industries
COMPATABLE

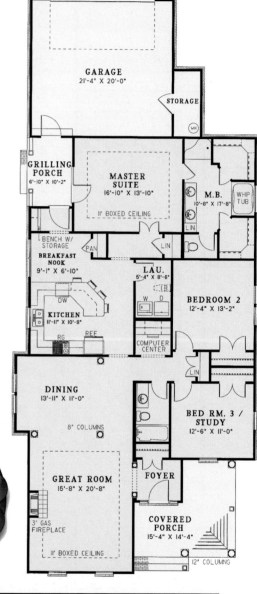

314 Windstone Place

Windstone Collection I

Step back in time as you journey onto the eight-foot covered porch of this Nelson Design Group home. Historical southern style accents the traditional foyer as you enter the large great room accented by an eleven-foot boxed ceiling and dining area divided by majestic eight inch wooden columns. Off the dining area, you'll find a bright kitchen area with breakfast nook — perfect for lazy Sunday mornings and an eat-in bar perfect for weekday meals on the run. A rear grilling porch with access to the master suite and kitchen makes entertaining a breeze.

BEST SELLER
Designers
Choice
NELSON DESIGN GROUP

Width: 36' 8"	Bedrooms: 3
Depth: 85' 0"	Baths: 2
Total Living: 1,934 sq. ft.	Foundation: Crawl, Slab
Main Ceiling: 10 ft.	Plan Options: page 282
Price Tier: B	

BUILDING SYSTEM
NGI
Next Generation Industries
COMPATABLE

To Order Call 1.800.590.2423   To view the rest of this collection visit www.nelsondesigngroup.com

Main Floor

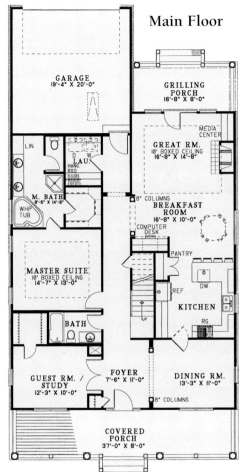

GARAGE
19'-4" X 20'-0"

GRILLING PORCH
16'-8" X 8'-0"

MEDIA CENTER

GREAT RM.
10' BOXED CEILING
16'-8" X 14'-8"

LIN.

D W
LAU
HANG ROD

M. BATH
8'-5" X 14'-8"

WHP TUB

8" COLUMNS

BREAKFAST ROOM
16'-8" X 10'-0"

COMPUTER DESK

PANTRY

MASTER SUITE
10' BOXED CEILING
14'-7" X 13'-0"

REF.

DW.

KITCHEN

UP

RG.

BATH

GUEST RM. / STUDY
12'-3" X 10'-0"

FOYER
7'-6" X 11'-0"

DINING RM.
13'-3" X 11'-0"

8" COLUMNS

COVERED PORCH
37'-0" X 8'-0"

Upper Floor

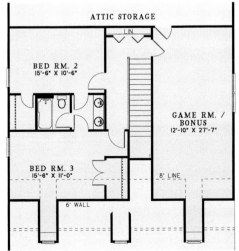

ATTIC STORAGE

LIN.

BED RM. 2
15'-6" X 10'-6"

GAME RM. / BONUS
12'-10" X 27'-7"

BED RM. 3
15'-6" X 11'-0"

8' LINE

6' WALL

307 Windstone Place
Windstone Collection I

This Nelson Design Group home is full of all the amenities of true southern style. Lazy summer afternoons slip by as you sit and visit with friends and family on the traditional eight-foot covered entry porch. A formal foyer with eight-inch wood columns leads you through to an elegant dining area. A master suite and bath will pamper you as you enjoy the luxury of a corner whirlpool tub with privacy glass block windows, large walk-in closet, corner glass shower and his and her vanities with linen cabinet. The rear grilling porch with atrium doors leads to the great room – perfect for entertaining any time of year. The upper floor creates a wonderful area for kids of all ages with two spacious bedrooms with walk-through bath and a large game room.

Width: 37' 0"	Main Ceiling: 9 ft.	
Depth: 73' 0"	Upper Ceiling: 8 ft.	
Main Floor: 1,713 sq. ft.	Bedrooms: 3	
Upper Floor: 610 sq. ft.	Baths: 3	
Total Living: 2,323 sq. ft.*	Foundation: Crawl, Slab, Optional Basement, Optional Daylight Basement	
*Optional Bonus: 384 sq. ft.		
Price Tier: C	Plan Options: page 282	

BUILDING SYSTEM
NGI
Next Generation Industries
COMPATABLE

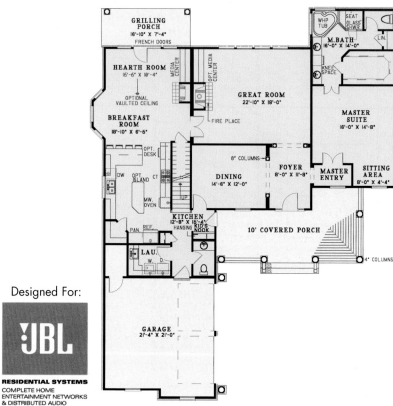

354 Windstone Place

Windstone Collection II

This grand one and a half story Nelson Design Group home combines historic southern charm with modern technology and design. A spacious two-car garage and engaging covered front porch with fourteen-inch columns allow optimum convenience. A marvelous foyer leads directly to an elegant dining room and comfortable great room — perfect for family fun. A separate entrance opens to a sitting area joined to the master suite, providing ample privacy and comfort. The family will love cookouts on your grilling porch — accessible to both a hearth room and breakfast nook by way of French doors. Traveling to the upper level you'll find ample bedrooms for the kids — complete with a computer area.

Designed For:

JBL
RESIDENTIAL SYSTEMS
COMPLETE HOME
ENTERTAINMENT NETWORKS
& DISTRIBUTED AUDIO

JBL
Home Theater

Upper Floor

Designed For:

Pioneer
sound.vision.soul
Pioneer Sound System

Width: 59' 4"
Depth: 74' 2"
Main Floor: 2,082 sq. ft.
Upper Floor: 695 sq. ft.
Total Living: 2,777 sq. ft.*
*Optional Bonus: 310 sq. ft.
Price Tier: D

Main Ceiling: 9 ft.
Upper Ceiling: 8 ft.
Bedrooms: 4
Baths: 2
Foundation: Crawl, Slab, Optional Basement, Optional Daylight Basement
Plan Options: page 282

BUILDING SYSTEM
NGI
Next Generation Industries
COMPATABLE

To Order Call 1.800.590.2423   To view the rest of this collection visit www.nelsondesigngroup.com

Main Floor

© 1999 NELSON DESIGN GROUP, LLC

SEA | GLASS SHWR | WHP TUB

M.BATH
16'-10" X 13'-0"

LIN.

FRENCH DOORS

GARAGE
21'-0" X 20'-0"

MASTER SUITE
10" BOXED CEILING
16'-10" X 12'-2"

LAU.
7'-0" X 6'-6"
W.
D.

LIN.

UP

OPT. GAS FIREPLACE

BREAKFAST ROOM
11'-4" X 12'-0"

COVERED PATIO
6'-0" X 20'-0"

COURT YARD PATIO

KITCHEN
12'-3" X 12'-0"

RG.

DW

REF.

PANTRY

© 1999 NELSON DESIGN GROUP, LLC

8" COLUMNS

MEDIA CENTER

FOYER
7'-6" X 11'-2"

DINING
11'-8" X 14'-0"

GREAT ROOM
17'-8" X 18'-0"

PORCH
21'-6" X 8'-0"

VAULTED CEILING

Upper Floor

8' LINE | FUTURE BONUS SPACE

4'-0" HALF ROUND WINDOW

DN.

BEDROOM 2
12'-0" X 12'-0"

BEDROOM 3
11'-3" X 12'-0"

DESK

391 Windstone Place

Windstone Collection III

Welcome your friends and family to this traditional Nelson Design Group home. Leading your guests into the foyer, they'll notice all the beautiful columns surrounding all entrances from the foyer to the adjoining rooms. Your spacious great room has a warm fireplace for those cold mornings. The gorgeous courtyard can be viewed by accessing the side covered patio from either the great room or master suite. The optional fireplace in the breakfast room will create a cozy environment for family breakfasts. Upstairs, you'll find two more bedrooms with walk-thru access to the bath.

Width: 38' 10"	Main Ceiling: 9 ft.
Depth: 70' 4"	Upper Ceiling: 8 ft.
Main Floor: 1,654 sq. ft.	Bedrooms: 3
Upper Floor: 492 sq. ft.	Baths: 2 1/2
Total Living: 2,146 sq. ft.	Foundation: Crawl, Slab, Optional Basement,
Price Tier: C	Optional Daylight Basement
	Plan Options: page 282

BUILDING SYSTEM
NGI
Next Generation Industries
COMPATABLE

Main Floor

Main Floor plan labels:
WHP TUB · M.BATH 11'-4" X 15'-0" · GLASS SHWR · GARAGE 19'-8" X 20'-0" · BENCH W/ STORAGE · LAU. 7'-10" X 6'-0" · HANGING · MASTER SUITE 18'-8" X 14'-0" · ATRIUM DOORS · GRILLING PORCH 8'-10" X 10'-0" · MEDIA CENTER · BUILT-INS · GAS FIRE PLACE · BREAKFAST ROOM 14'-4" X 9'-0" · GREAT ROOM 15'-7" X 17'-2" · REF. · KIT. 11'-7" X 12'-0" · DW · RG · PANTRY · BUTLER'S PANTRY · GUEST ROOM / STUDY 11'-7" X 12'-0" · FOYER 7'-6" X 12'-0" · DINING ROOM 11'-3" X 12'-0" · 8" RND COLUMNS · COVERED PORCH 32'-8" X 8'-0" · 12" COLUMNS

343 Windstone Place

Windstone Collection II

Upon entering this Nelson Design Group home notice the elegant dining room, adjoined to a butler's pantry, creating fluid entry to a marvelously spacious kitchen. The great room, complete with a romantic gas fireplace and built-in media center, is at the heart of the design with an open entry to a breakfast room. Enjoy countless possibilities entertaining on your convenient grilling porch. Stairs with left and right hand volutes take you to the spacious upper level. Two bedrooms with window seats, a full bath and bonus area with attic storage provide plenty of room for the kids.

Width: 32' 0"	Main Ceiling: 9 ft.
Depth: 83' 4"	Upper Ceiling: 8 ft.
Main Floor: 1,831 sq. ft.	Bedrooms: 4
Upper Floor: 455 sq. ft.	Baths: 3
Total Living: 2,286 sq. ft.	Foundation: Crawl, Slab, Basement, Daylight Basement
Price Tier: C	Plan Options: page 282

BUILDING SYSTEM
NGI
Next Generation Industries
COMPATABLE

Upper Floor plan labels:
REAR SPAN · BONUS AREA / ATTIC STRG. · LIN · BATH 12'-1" X 5'-0" · LIN · BEDROOM 3 12'-1" X 11'-0" · LIN · BEDROOM 4 11'-11" X 11'-0" · WDW SEAT · WDW SEAT

Upper Floor

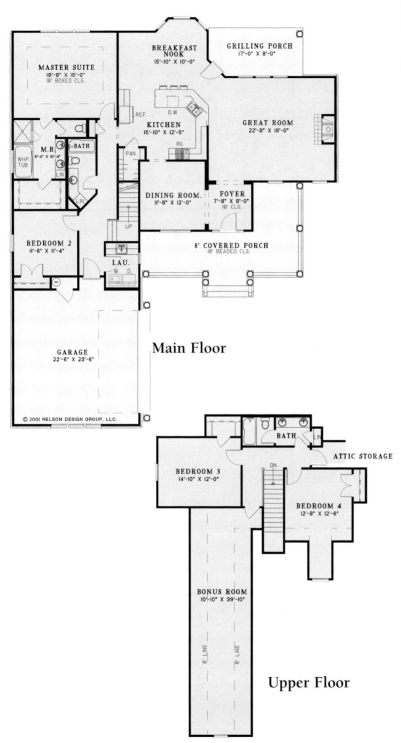

MASTER SUITE
18'-8" X 15'-0"
10' BOXED CLG.

BREAKFAST NOOK
15'-10" X 10'-0"

GRILLING PORCH
17'-0" X 8'-0"

M.B.
9'-4" X 10'-4"

BATH

WHP TUB

KITCHEN
15'-10" X 12'-5"

REF.

D.W.

PAN.

R.G.

GREAT ROOM
22'-8" X 18'-0"

DINING ROOM
11'-8" X 12'-0"

FOYER
7'-8" X 8'-0"
10' CLG.

UP

BEDROOM 2
11'-6" X 11'-4"

LAU.
W. D.

8' COVERED PORCH
10' BEADED CLG.

GARAGE
22'-6" X 23'-6"

© 2001 NELSON DESIGN GROUP, LLC.

Main Floor

BATH

ATTIC STORAGE

BEDROOM 3
14'-10" X 12'-0"

DN.

BEDROOM 4
12'-8" X 12'-6"

BONUS ROOM
10'-10" X 39'-10"

8' LINE

8' LINE

Upper Floor

538 Windstone Place

Windstone Collection III

A wrap around porch with a ten-foot beaded ceiling, round columns and gentle arches welcomes you into this Nelson Design Group home. The foyer also carries a ten-foot ceiling and leads into a great room with fireplace and a view overlooking the grilling porch. A wide walkway leads you into a breakfast bay adjoining the kitchen and through to the formal dining room. Entertaining will be enjoyable for both you and guests with this easy flowing floor plan. The master suite adorned with a boxed ceiling, as well as one bedroom and full bath are on the main floor. Upstairs has two additional bedrooms, a full bath and large bonus room located over the garage.

Width: 58' 6"	Main Ceiling: 9 ft.
Depth: 71' 10"	Upper Ceiling: 9 ft.
Main Floor: 1,992 sq. ft.	Bedrooms: 4
Upper Floor: 643 sq. ft.	Baths: 3
Total Living: 2,635 sq. ft.*	Foundation: Crawl, Slab, Optional Basement,
*Optional Bonus: 468 sq. ft.	Optional Daylight Basement
Price Tier: D	Plan Options: page 282

BUILDING SYSTEM
NGI
Next Generation Industries
COMPATABLE

To Order Call 1.800.590.2423   To view the rest of this collection visit www.nelsondesigngroup.com

43

Arts&Crafts™ collection

"A step back in time"

This collection of timeless narrow lot home designs celebrates the most functional use of space and building materials. With emphasis on simplicity, these designs feature lovely front porches, columns and built-ins and are suitable for narrow lots. These beautiful designs focus on family areas while allowing adequate storage to help create an uncluttered environment. Although these designs have been updated to suit today's busy lifestyle, the integrity of the Arts and Crafts era is maintained by using craftsman quality interior and exterior finishes.

Nelson Design Group LLC

RESIDENTIAL & COMMERCIAL PLANNERS · DESIGNERS

GARAGE
19'-0" X 19'-8"

LAU.
5'-8" X 6'-2"
D. W.

M.BATH

WH

MASTER SUITE
13'-4" X 11'-4"

DINING
10'-0" X 12'-0"

OPT. GAS FIREPLACE

GREAT ROOM
17'-4" X 13'-0"

PAN.
REF.

KITCHEN
10'-0" X 10'-2"
RG. DW

BATH

FOYER
7'-0" X 6'-6"

BEDROOM 2
10'-0" X 9'-6"

BEDROOM 3
10'-0" X 10'-8"

COVERED PORCH
11'-0" X 6'-0"

BUILDING SYSTEM
NGi
Next Generation Industries
COMPATABLE

626 Fir

Greet your family and friends on the lovely covered porch of this Nelson Design Group Arts and Crafts style home. The warmth of this split bedroom design will capture the attention of your guests as they enter the foyer. Two bedrooms are gently placed at the front of the home for privacy and possibly used as a study if desired. An attractive great room offers you the perfect place to relax and has an abundance of wall space for treasured antiques. The convenience of the kitchen to dining room will keep dinnertime less hectic and more enjoyable. As evening falls find seclusion in the master suite complete with spacious walk-in closet and private bathroom.

Width: 28' 4" • Depth: 69' 0" • Total Living: 1,259 sq. ft.
Main Ceiling: 9 ft. • Bedrooms: 3 • Baths: 2
Foundation: Crawl, Slab, Opt. Basement and Opt. Daylight Basement
Plan Options: page 282
Price Tier: A

628 Mulberry

Indulge yourself in this timeless Arts and Crafts style home by Nelson Design Group. Columns and a beaded ceiling gracefully adorn the front covered porch. Relax with family in the spacious great room with optional fireplace. A lovely step saver kitchen with angled bar and a large pantry adjoins the dining room for the ultimate dinner gathering. The laundry room is located just steps away from the kitchen for convenience and if two bedrooms are sufficient, use the third as an optional study or den. The master suite is quietly placed at the rear of the home and has plenty of wall space, a spacious walk-in closet, and a private bathroom.

Width: 32' 8" • Depth: 65' 2" • Total Living: 1,348 sq. ft.
Main Ceiling: 9 ft. • Bedrooms: 3 • Baths: 2
Foundation: Crawl, Slab, Opt. Basement and Opt. Daylight Basement
Plan Options: page 282
Price Tier: A

To Order Call 1.800.590.2423   Similar plans can be viewed and ordered at www.nelsondesigngroup.com

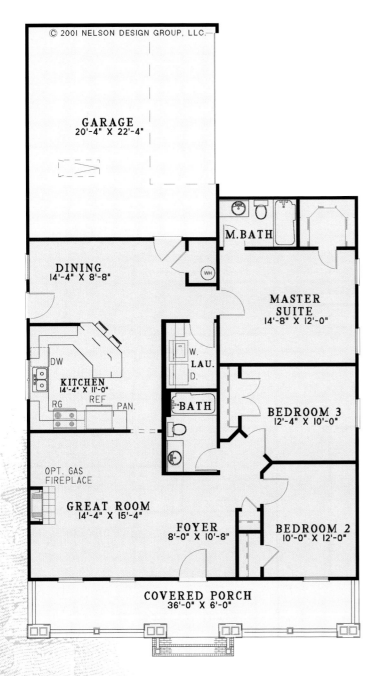

GARAGE
20'-4" X 22'-4"

© 2001 NELSON DESIGN GROUP, LLC.

M.BATH

DINING
14'-4" X 8'-8"

MASTER
SUITE
14'-8" X 12'-0"

W.
LAU.
D.

DW

KITCHEN
14'-4" X 11'-0"

RG   REF   PAN.

BATH

BEDROOM 3
12'-4" X 10'-0"

OPT. GAS
FIREPLACE

GREAT ROOM
14'-4" X 15'-4"

FOYER
8'-0" X 10'-8"

BEDROOM 2
10'-0" X 12'-0"

COVERED PORCH
36'-0" X 6'-0"

625 Sycamore

A covered porch with brick columns and railing add great street appeal to this Nelson Design Group Arts and Crafts style home. Enjoy conversation with friends and loved ones in the great room with cozy fireplace. Easy access from the kitchen to the dining room across an angled counter makes serving your meals a delight. This design offers a double bedroom area with full bath that is ideal for the kids or overnight guests while separate from the master suite entry. For privacy and convenience, the master suite is located at the rear of the house and has a private bathroom and large walk-in closet.

Width: 36' 0" • Depth: 65' 0" • Total Living: 1,374 sq. ft.
Main Ceiling: 9 ft. • Bedrooms: 3 • Baths: 2
Foundation: Crawl, Slab, Opt. Basement and Opt. Daylight Basement
Plan Options: page 282
Price Tier: A

© 2001 NELSON DESIGN GROUP, LLC.

STOR.

GARAGE
20'-4" X 20'-0"

WH

GRILLING
PORCH
10'-10" X 13'-0"

BATH

MASTER SUITE
15'-4" X 12'-4"

LIN.

BENCH
SEAT
STRG.
BINS

KID'S
NOOK

BATH

DW.

NOOK
10'-2" X 7'-8"

KITCHEN
9'-10" X 7'-8"

REF.   RG.

BEDROOM 2
12'-6" X 11'-0"

LIN.

LAU.
8'-8" X 5'-8"

W.   D.

GREAT ROOM
16'-0" X 16'-6"

OPT. GAS
FIREPLACE

BEDROOM 3
12'-6" X 10'-4"

COVERED PORCH
26'-0" X 8'-0"

629 Redwood

This Nelson Design Group home has detail and style reminiscent of the Arts and Crafts era. Enjoy a cup of coffee with neighbors on the expansive front porch detailed with double columns and railing. Upon entry notice a large closet perfect for seasonal storage and on to the large great room complete with a cozy fireplace for cherished family time. A breakfast nook is attached to the kitchen and just steps from the grilling porch entry. A nearby kid's nook keeps clutter at a minimum. The master suite has a private bath, a large walk-in closet and is located at the rear of the home. For convenience, the laundry room is centrally located next to the two additional bedrooms and bathroom.

Width: 39' 0" • Depth: 68' 6" • Total Living: 1,399 sq. ft.
Main Ceiling: 9 ft. • Bedrooms: 3 • Baths: 2
Foundation: Crawl, Slab, Opt. Basement and Opt. Daylight Basement
Plan Options: page 282
Price Tier: A

BUILDING SYSTEM
NGI
Next Generation Industries
COMPATABLE

To Order Call 1.800.590.2423   Similar plans can be viewed and ordered at www.nelsondesigngroup.com

© 2001 NELSON DESIGN GROUP, LLC.

GARAGE
19'-0" X 19'-8"

BATH

LAU.
5'-8" X 6'-2"

D. W.

WH

GRILLING PORCH
6'-6" X 10'-0"

PANTRY

MASTER SUITE
13'-4" X 11'-5"

DINING
14'-4" X 11'-0"

OPT. GAS FIREPLACE

PANTRY

GREAT ROOM
23'-8" X 13'-0"

REF.

KIT.
10'-0" X 11'-2"

RG.

DW

BATH

LIN.

FOYER
13'-4" X 4'-6"

BEDROOM 2
10'-0" X 9'-6"

BEDROOM 3
10'-0" X 10'-8"

COVERED PORCH
13'-4" X 8'-0"

BUILDING SYSTEM
NGI
Next Generation Industries
COMPATABLE

630 Maple

This Nelson Design Group home is styled in the Arts and Crafts era with an updated floor plan. Once inside the foyer, bedrooms on either side are away from the private master suite at the rear of the home. An expansive great room with fireplace is centrally located and opens to a large dining room. The U-shaped kitchen is a step saver and includes a bar counter for serving buffet style. Dining will be fun for the whole family with easy access to the grilling porch. After the kids are in bed, find solitude in your master suite with private bath and 'his and her' walk-in closets.

Width: 34' 8" • Depth: 69' 0" • Total Living: 1,442 sq. ft.
Main Ceiling: 9 ft. • Bedrooms: 3 • Baths: 2
Foundation: Crawl, Slab, Opt. Basement and Opt. Daylight Basement
Plan Options: page 282
Price Tier: A

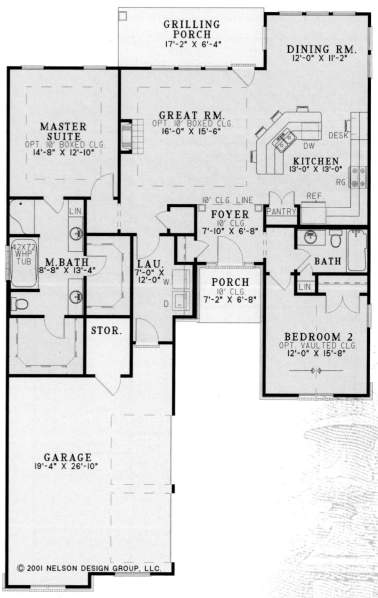

GRILLING PORCH
17'-2" X 6'-4"

DINING RM.
12'-0" X 11'-2"

GREAT RM.
OPT. 10' BOXED CLG.
16'-0" X 15'-6"

MASTER SUITE
OPT. 10' BOXED CLG.
14'-8" X 12'-10"

KITCHEN
13'-0" X 13'-0"

DESK

DW

RG.

REF.

10' CLG. LINE

FOYER
10' CLG.
7'-10" X 6'-8"

PANTRY

LIN

42X72 WHP TUB

M. BATH
8'-8" X 13'-4"

LAU.
7'-0" X 12'-0"

PORCH
10' CLG.
7'-2" X 6'-8"

BATH

LIN

W

D

STOR.

BEDROOM 2
OPT. VAULTED CLG.
12'-0" X 15'-8"

GARAGE
19'-4" X 26'-10"

© 2001 NELSON DESIGN GROUP, LLC.

589 Magnolia

Nelson Design Group has created an elegant design reflective of the Arts and Crafts era. Copper roofing and carriage style garage doors warmly welcome guests into this split bedroom plan. Ten-foot ceilings and an abundance of windows allow natural light to flow throughout. An elegant master suite is fully suited as a private hideaway while the opposite side of the home includes a large kitchen and dining room with large bar island for additional seating. A courtyard entry garage allows for the utmost in security and convenience.

Width: 43' 0" • Depth: 66' 6" • Total Living: 1,474 sq. ft.
Main Ceiling: 9 ft. • Bedrooms: 2 • Baths: 2
Foundation: Crawl, Slab, Opt. Basement and Opt. Daylight Basement
Plan Options: page 282
Price Tier: A

BUILDING SYSTEM
NGI
Next Generation Industries
COMPATABLE

To Order Call 1.800.590.2423   Similar plans can be viewed and ordered at www.nelsondesigngroup.com

Upper Floor

ATTIC STORAGE

BEDROOM 2
10'-0" X 13'-0"

LOFT

BATH

LIN.

DN.

OPEN TO BELOW

WDW. SEAT

BEDROOM 3
12'-0" X 10'-4"

Main Floor

© 2001 NELSON DESIGN GROUP, LLC.

GARAGE
18'-4" X 20'-0"

GRILLING PORCH
11'-0" X 8'-0"

BENCH W/ HANGING

LAU.
6'-2" X 5'-6"

D.

STOR.

W.

WH

BREAKFAST NOOK
13'-0" X 6'-8"

DW

RG

KITCHEN
13'-0" X 9'-8"

REF.

DINING
12'-0" X 10'-0"

UP

M.BATH
12'-0" X 8'-8"

OPT. GAS FIREPLACE

COMPUTER CENTER

LIN.

GREAT ROOM
16'-0" X 13'-0"

FOYER
4'-8" X 7'-4"

MASTER SUITE
12'-0" X 13'-4"

COVERED PORCH
20'-8" X 6'-0"

BEST SELLER
Designers Choice
NELSON DESIGN GROUP

627 Pin Oak

This Arts and Crafts style home by Nelson Design Group is simple yet elegant. A beaded ceiling and double columns set atop brick pillars enhance the covered front porch. As you enter the foyer, admire eight-inch columns inviting you into a spacious great room with fireplace and swinging door to the kitchen. Family can enjoy a sunny breakfast nook adjoining the kitchen and accessing a rear-grilling porch. Just across the hall is a formal dining room for large family gatherings. For privacy and convenience, this split bedroom plan places the spacious master suite on the main level. Two additional bedrooms, a full bath and a loft area with window seat are located upstairs.

Width: 34' 4" • Depth: 59' 6"
Main Floor: 1,063 sq. ft. • Upper Floor: 496 sq. ft.
Total Living: 1,559 sq. ft. • Main Ceiling: 9 ft. • Upper Ceiling: 8 ft.
Bedrooms: 3 • Baths: 2
Foundation: Crawl, Slab, Opt. Basement, Opt. Daylight Basement
Plan Options: page 282 • **Price Tier:**   B

BUILDING SYSTEM
NGi
Next Generation Industries
COMPATABLE

588 Cypress

This crafty design by Nelson Design Group combines a rustic exterior with an elegant interior. Ten-foot ceilings and an abundance of windows enhance the family areas for plenty of natural lighting. The breakfast room and kitchen are combined and enjoy a counter for additional seating. A large laundry room with pantry is located between the kitchen and garage access for convenience. On the opposite side of the home are two bedrooms, a full bath and a luxurious master suite with a ten-foot boxed ceiling, his and her walk-in closets and large bathroom with glass shower, whirlpool bath and double vanities.

Width: 41' 4" • Depth: 84' 2" • Total Living: 1,747 sq. ft.
Main Ceiling: 9 ft. • Bedrooms: 3 • Baths: 2
Foundation: Crawl and Slab • Plan Options: page 282

Price Tier: B

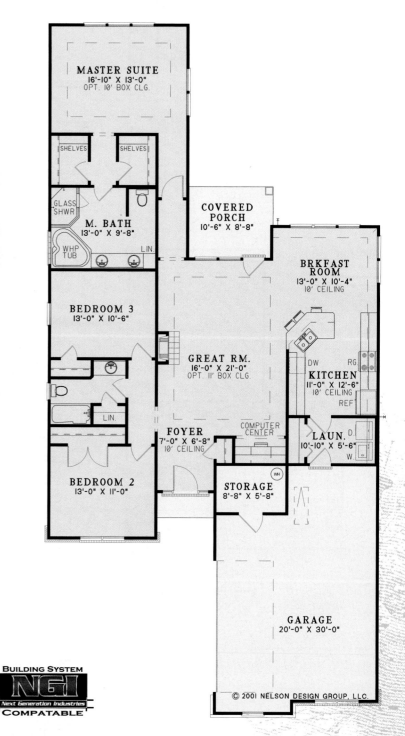

BUILDING SYSTEM
NGi
Next Generation Industries
COMPATABLE

© 2001 NELSON DESIGN GROUP, LLC.

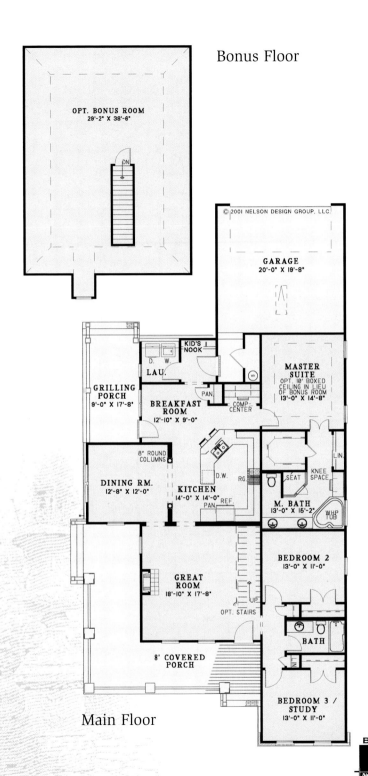

Bonus Floor

OPT. BONUS ROOM
29'-2" X 38'-6"

DN

Main Floor

© 2001 NELSON DESIGN GROUP, LLC.

GARAGE
20'-0" X 19'-8"

GRILLING
PORCH
9'-0" X 17'-8"

KID'S
NOOK

D. W.

LAU.

BREAKFAST
ROOM
12'-10" X 9'-0"

PAN.

COMP
CENTER

MASTER
SUITE
OPT. 10' BOXED
CEILING IN LIEU
OF BONUS ROOM
13'-0" X 14'-8"

8" ROUND
COLUMNS

DINING RM.
12'-8" X 12'-0"

KITCHEN
14'-0" X 14'-0"

D.W.

RG.

PAN.

REF.

SEAT

KNEE
SPACE

LIN.

M. BATH
13'-0" X 15'-2"

WHP
TUB

BEDROOM 2
13'-0" X 11'-0"

GREAT
ROOM
18'-10" X 17'-8"

OPT. STAIRS

UP

BATH

8' COVERED
PORCH

BEDROOM 3 /
STUDY
13'-0" X 11'-0"

595 Jasmine

Nelson Design Group has created a cozy historical home with a corner wrapped wooden porch and large brick columns with railing. This split floor plan has a great room immediately upon entry with access to the two bedrooms and full bath. An efficient kitchen with an angled bar counter allows for additional seating and adjoins a large breakfast room and access to a side grilling porch. Also nearby is a convenient kid's nook located near the rear load garage entry. The luxurious master suite is enhanced with an optional ten-foot boxed ceiling and has French door access to the master bathroom packed with amenities. An optional bonus room is available upstairs for future needs.

Width: 41' 10" • Depth: 83' 8"
Main Floor: 1,836 sq. ft.* • *Opt. Bonus Floor: 1,116 sq. ft.
Total Living: 1,836 sq. ft. • Main Ceiling: 9 ft. • Bonus Ceiling: 8 ft.
Bedrooms: 3 • Baths: 2
Foundation: Crawl and Slab • Plan Options: page 282
Price Tier: B

BUILDING SYSTEM
NGI
Next Generation Industries
COMPATABLE

Upper Floor

BEDROOM 2
11'-0" X 13'-4"

8' LINE

4' WALL

BATH

DN.

BEDROOM 3
12'-8" X 13'-10"

8' LINE

5' WALL

ATTIC STORAGE

WHP. TUB

M. BATH
14'-0" X 15'-0"

W.I.C.

W.I.C.

LIN

GRILLING PORCH
12'-4" X 6'-0"

MASTER SUITE
14'-0" X 13'-6"

BREAKFAST ROOM
12'-0" X 9'-6"

STORAGE

COMPUTER CENTER

LAU.
6'-10" X 6'-10"

W. D.

GARAGE
17'-8" X 19'-4"

D.W.

RG.

ISLAND

UP

REF.

KITCHEN
12'-0" X 14'-0"

BUILT-INS

© 2001 NELSON DESIGN GROUP, LLC.

DINING
11'-8" X 12'-0"

GREAT RM.
14'-0" X 13'-8"

COVERED PORCH
20'-4" X 7'-0"

Main Floor

586 Ivy

This Nelson Design Group home is reminiscent of days gone by. A lovely front covered porch is enhanced with railing and square tapered columns atop brick pillars. Upon entering a quaint foyer, the great room welcomes you with a large fireplace and built-ins while leading you into a large formal dining room opening into the kitchen and breakfast room. The master suite is located on the main floor for convenience and privacy. Upstairs you'll find two additional bedrooms with angled ceilings, a full bathroom and a large attic storage area.

Width: 45' 0" • Depth: 67' 2"
Main Floor: 1,412 sq. ft. • Upper Floor: 494 sq. ft.
Total Living: 1,906 sq. ft. • Main Ceiling: 9 ft. • Upper Ceiling: 8 ft.
Bedrooms: 3 • Baths: 2 1/2
Foundation: Crawl, Slab, Opt. Basement, Opt. Daylight Basement
Plan Options: page 282 • **Price Tier:** B

Designers Choice
BEST SELLER
NELSON DESIGN GROUP

BUILDING SYSTEM
NGI
Next Generation Industries
COMPATABLE

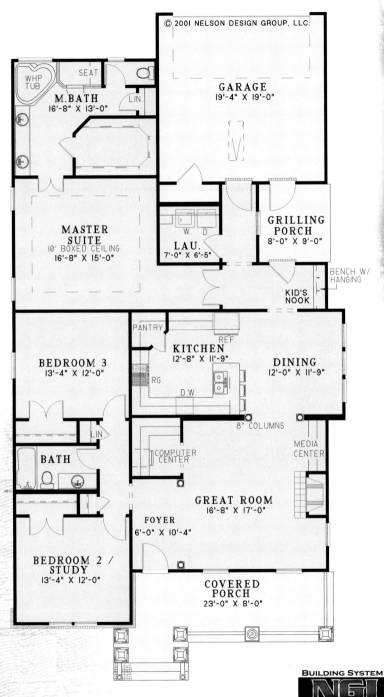

© 2001 NELSON DESIGN GROUP, LLC.

GARAGE
19'-4" X 19'-0"

M. BATH
16'-8" X 13'-0"

WHP TUB

SEAT

LIN

MASTER SUITE
10' BOXED CEILING
16'-8" X 15'-0"

W. D

LAU.
7'-0" X 6'-5"

GRILLING PORCH
8'-0" X 9'-0"

BENCH W/ HANGING

KID'S NOOK

PANTRY

REF.

KITCHEN
12'-8" X 11'-9"

DINING
12'-0" X 11'-9"

BEDROOM 3
13'-4" X 12'-0"

RG.

D.W.

8" COLUMNS

COMPUTER CENTER

MEDIA CENTER

LIN

BATH

GREAT ROOM
16'-8" X 17'-0"

FOYER
6'-0" X 10'-4"

BEDROOM 2 / STUDY
13'-4" X 12'-0"

COVERED PORCH
23'-0" X 8'-0"

596 Elm

The detailing of this Nelson Design Group home warmly invites friends and family into a home reflective of the Craftsman Era. A covered porch leads to a foyer separating the guest bedrooms from the rest of the home. The great room entry has eight-inch columns, media center, a cozy fireplace and a hidden computer center. A spacious kitchen with bar seating adjoins the dining room and has a wall of windows for plenty of natural lighting. Conveniently located near the garage entry is a kid's nook with bench to help keep areas clutter free. A ten-foot boxed ceiling, a large walk-in closet, whirlpool tub and a separate shower with seat enhance the master suite for the ultimate privacy and relaxation.

Width: 37' 0" • Depth: 74' 4" • Total Living: 1,933 sq. ft.
Main Ceiling: 9 ft. • Bedrooms: 3 • Baths: 2
Foundation: Crawl and Slab • Plan Options: page 282
Price Tier: B

Main Floor

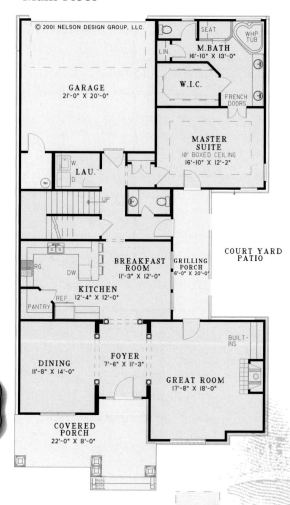

© 2001 NELSON DESIGN GROUP, LLC.

SEAT

WHP TUB

M. BATH
16'-10" X 13'-0"

LIN.

GARAGE
21'-0" X 20'-0"

W.I.C.

FRENCH DOORS

MASTER SUITE
10' BOXED CEILING
16'-10" X 12'-2"

LAU.
W
D

UP

COURT YARD PATIO

BREAKFAST ROOM
11'-3" X 12'-0"

GRILLING PORCH
16'-0" X 20'-0"

KITCHEN
12'-4" X 12'-0"

RG

DW

PANTRY

REF.

BUILT-INS

DINING
11'-8" X 14'-0"

FOYER
7'-6" X 11'-3"

GREAT ROOM
17'-8" X 18'-0"

COVERED PORCH
22'-0" X 8'-0"

590 Willow

BEST SELLER
Designers Choice
NELSON DESIGN GROUP

Gables, columns and architectural detailing give this Nelson Design Group home a warm feeling reminiscent of your grandmother's home.
A cozy porch gently welcomes you into a foyer lined with columns and separating the formal dining room from a large great room with fireplace. The kitchen and breakfast room is centrally located and views a lovely courtyard patio perfect for entertaining. Your perfect hideaway awaits you in a spacious master suite with large walk-in closet and bathroom packed with amenities. The upstairs as two bedrooms each with private access to a full bathroom as well as future bonus space when desired.

Width: 38' 10" • Depth: 70' 4"
Main Floor: 1,654 sq. ft. • Upper Floor: 492 sq. ft.
Total Living: 2,146 sq. ft. • Main Ceiling: 9 ft. • Upper Ceiling: 8 ft.
Bedrooms: 3 • Baths: 2 1/2
Foundation: Crawl, Slab, Opt. Basement and Opt. Daylight Basement
Plan Options: page 282 • **Price Tier:** C

BUILDING SYSTEM
NGI
Next Generation Industries
COMPATABLE

Upper Floor

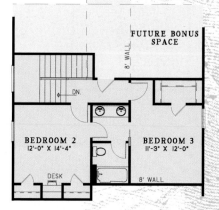

FUTURE BONUS SPACE

8' WALL

DN.

BEDROOM 2
12'-0" X 14'-4"

BEDROOM 3
11'-3" X 12'-0"

DESK

8' WALL

To Order Call 1.800.590.2423   **Similar plans can be viewed and ordered at www.nelsondesigngroup.com**

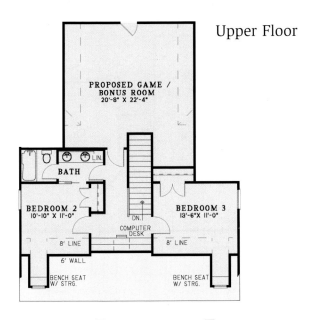

Upper Floor

PROPOSED GAME /
BONUS ROOM
20'-8" X 22'-4"

BATH

LIN

BEDROOM 2
10'-10" X 11'-0"

DN.

COMPUTER
DESK

BEDROOM 3
13'-6" X 11'-0"

8' LINE

8' LINE

6' WALL

BENCH SEAT
W/ STRG.

BENCH SEAT
W/ STRG.

Main Floor

© 2001 NELSON DESIGN GROUP, LLC.

WHP TUB

M. BATH
16'-0" X 11'-0"

LIN

SEAT

FRENCH DOORS

GARAGE
18'-4" X 19'-6"

BENCH W/ HANGING

MASTER SUITE
OPTIONAL 10' BOXED
CEILING IN LIEU OF BONUS
ROOM ABOVE
16'-0" X 14'-10"

KID'S NOOK

LAU
6'-2" X 6'-0"

W

STORAGE BINS

GRILLING PORCH
6'-0" X 17'-6"

BREAKFAST ROOM
12'-4" X 11'-6"

UP

42" HIGH BAR

GREAT RM.
16'-0" X 16'-8"

D. W.

KITCHEN
13'-6" X 12'-10"

PANTRY

RG.

WET BAR

REF.

REF.

8" RND. COLUMNS

OFFICE / STUDY
13'-0" X 10'-0"

FOYER
7'-6" X 11'-0"

DINING
13'-2" X 12'-0"

COVERED PORCH
24'-4" X 8'-0"

BUILDING SYSTEM
NGI
Next Generation Industries
COMPATABLE

594 Holly

This Nelson Design Group home has dormers with copper roofing and a covered porch for lovely street appeal. The large great room with built-in wet bar and a large fireplace is centrally located for a family oriented atmosphere. A large breakfast room accesses the covered grilling porch – perfect for entertaining. After a long day retire to your master bedroom with French door entry to your elegant master bathroom complete with whirlpool tub, separate shower and large walk-in closet. The upstairs has a built-in computer desk for study time, two bedrooms, a full bath, and a large optional game/bonus room.

Width: 37' 8" • Depth: 71' 6"
Main Floor: 1,708 sq. ft. • Upper Floor: 529 sq. ft.
Total Living: 2,237 sq. ft.* • *Optional Bonus: 436 sq. ft.
Main Ceiling: 9 ft. • Upper Ceiling: 8 ft.
Bedrooms: 3 • Baths: 2 1/2
Foundation: Crawl, Slab, Opt. Basement, Opt. Daylight Basement
Plan Options: page 282 • **Price Tier:** C

587 Wisteria

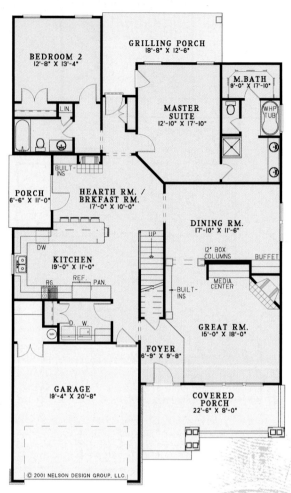

Main Floor

ATTIC STORAGE

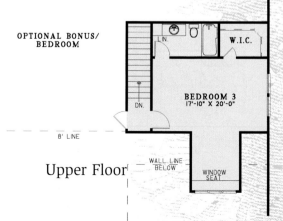

OPTIONAL BONUS/ BEDROOM

Upper Floor

Nelson Design Group has created a beautiful design that resembles a home that your grandfather might have built. Double columns atop brick pillars enhance the front covered porch. An open foyer leads through a great room with corner fireplace and built-in media center. A formal dining room accesses the cozy hearth room and kitchen divided by a bar counter for additional seating. Also on the main floor are the master suite, an additional bedroom and a full bathroom. Foyer stairs lead up to a large room with private bath as well as an optional bonus area.

Width: 42' 0" • Depth: 70' 10"
Main Floor: 1,903 sq. ft. • Upper Floor: 385 sq. ft.
Total Living: 2,288 sq. ft. • Main Ceiling: 9 ft. • Upper Ceiling: 8 ft.
Bedrooms: 3 • Baths: 3
Foundation: Crawl, Slab, Opt. Basement, Opt. Daylight Basement
Plan Options: page 282 • **Price Tier: C**

BUILDING SYSTEM
NGI
Next Generation Industries
COMPATABLE

To Order Call 1.800.590.2423   **Similar plans can be viewed and ordered at www.nelsondesigngroup.com**

THE URBAN
COLLECTION

These narrow lot Traditional Neighborhood Designs represent a growing trend in the New Urbanism movement. Cities are becoming stronger by building historically inspired homes in existing neighborhoods thus preserving communities of 50 to 100 years old. Our Urban Collection offers eight plans ranging in square footage from 1,200 to 1,600 with modern living spaces and amenities that families demand. Rear entry garages and private grilling porches are among the many features while offering the safety of a close environment. These plans preserve the integrity of our city neighborhoods and offer an innovative living environment.

Nelson Design Group LLC

RESIDENTIAL & COMMERCIAL PLANNERS - DESIGNERS

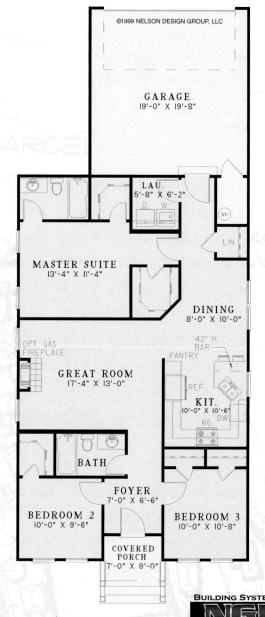

©1999 NELSON DESIGN GROUP, LLC

GARAGE
19'-0" X 19'-8"

LAU.
5'-8" X 6'-2"

MASTER SUITE
13'-4" X 11'-4"

DINING
8'-0" X 10'-0"

OPT. GAS FIREPLACE

42" H. BAR

PANTRY

GREAT ROOM
17'-4" X 13'-0"

KIT.
10'-0" X 10'-6"

BATH

FOYER
7'-0" X 6'-6"

BEDROOM 2
10'-0" X 9'-6"

BEDROOM 3
10'-0" X 10'-8"

COVERED PORCH
7'-0" X 8'-0"

398 Urban Lane
Urban Collection I

Picture yourself greeting your family and friends on the covered entry porch of this Nelson Design Group home. The warmth of this split bedroom design will enchant you and your guests as they enter the foyer. The attractive great room offers you the perfect place to relax and enjoy the company of loved ones in front of the fireplace. Dinner will be delicious and convenient with easy access to the kitchen from the dining room. As evening falls and the guests leave you will find seclusion in the master suite complete with spacious his and her walk-in closets and private bath. This southern traditional style design has all the amenities you've come to expect.

Width: 28' 4"

Depth: 66' 0"

Total Living: 1,260 sq. ft.

Main Ceiling: 9 ft.

Price Tier: A

Bedrooms: 3

Baths: 2

Foundation: Crawl, Slab

Plan Options: page 282

BUILDING SYSTEM
NGI
Next Generation Industries
COMPATABLE

To Order Call 1.800.590.2423   Similar plans can be viewed and ordered at www.nelsondesigngroup.com

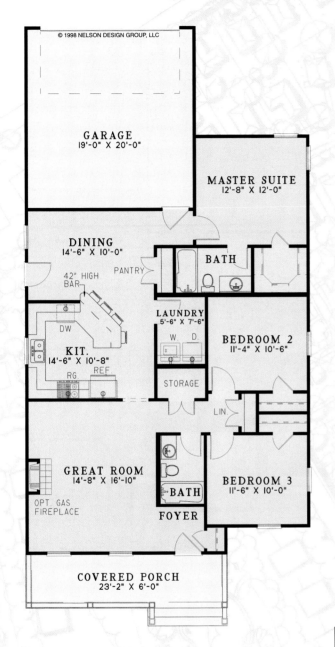

© 1998 NELSON DESIGN GROUP, LLC

GARAGE
19'-0" X 20'-0"

MASTER SUITE
12'-8" X 12'-0"

DINING
14'-6" X 10'-0"

PANTRY

42" HIGH BAR

BATH

DW

KIT.
14'-6" X 10'-8"

RG   REF

LAUNDRY
5'-6" X 7'-6"

W. D.

BEDROOM 2
11'-4" X 10'-6"

STORAGE

LIN.

GREAT ROOM
14'-8" X 16'-10"

BATH

BEDROOM 3
11'-6" X 10'-0"

OPT. GAS FIREPLACE

FOYER

COVERED PORCH
23'-2" X 6'-0"

Width: 32' 8"

Depth: 64' 10"

Total Living: 1,342 sq. ft.

Main Ceiling: 9 ft.

Price Tier: A

Bedrooms: 3

Baths: 2

Foundation: Crawl, Slab,
Optional Basement,
Optional Daylight Basement

Plan Options: page 282

BUILDING SYSTEM
NGI
Next Generation Industries
COMPATABLE

400 Urban Lane
Urban Collection I

Imagine yourself coming home to this southern traditional Nelson Design Group home. Upon entering the foyer, you can relax away the day in your charming great room with optional fireplace. You will have ample room in the kitchen and dining room to spend some quality time with your family. Helping the kids with their homework or finishing that report for work can be easy with one bedroom converted to a study. As the evening sets in, you will be able to relax in the privacy of the master suite with private bath and spacious walk in closet. This delightful neighborhood design has all the pleasantries you're looking for in your future home.

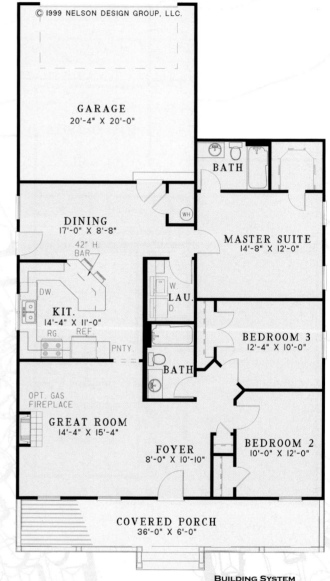

© 1999 NELSON DESIGN GROUP, LLC.

GARAGE
20'-4" X 20'-0"

BATH

DINING
17'-0" X 8'-8"

42" H. BAR

WH

MASTER SUITE
14'-8" X 12'-0"

DW.

KIT.
14'-4" X 11'-0"

RG. REF.

W LAU. D

PNTY.

BATH

BEDROOM 3
12'-4" X 10'-0"

OPT. GAS FIREPLACE

GREAT ROOM
14'-4" X 15'-4"

FOYER
8'-0" X 10'-10"

BEDROOM 2
10'-0" X 12'-0"

COVERED PORCH
36'-0" X 6'-0"

397 Urban Lane
Urban Collection I

Sit back and breathe deeply on the covered porch of this traditional southern style Nelson Design Group home. The great room, with fireplace, is the perfect place to converse with your loved ones and friends. Easy access from the dining room to the kitchen makes serving your family a delight on those warm Sunday afternoons. This traditional neighborhood design offers a double bedroom area with full bath that is ideal for the kids or overnight guests. After a full day of activity you can seclude yourself in the master suite with private bath and huge walk-in closet.

Width: 36' 0"

Depth: 62' 4"

Total Living: 1,381 sq. ft.

Main Ceiling: 9 ft.

Price Tier: A

Bedrooms: 3

Baths: 2

Foundation: Crawl, Slab, Optional Basement, Optional Daylight Basement

Plan Options: page 282

BUILDING SYSTEM
NGI
Next Generation Industries
COMPATABLE

© 1999 NELSON DESIGN GROUP, LLC

GARAGE
20'-4" X 20'-0"

WH

GRILLING PORCH
10'-10" X 13'-0"

BATH
LIN

MASTER SUITE
15'-4" X 12'-4"

STRG BINS

KID'S NOOK

BATH

NOOK
10'-2" X 7'-8"

KITCHEN
9'-10" X 7'-8"
DW.
REF.   RG.

LIN

BEDROOM 2
12'-6" X 11'-0"

LAU.
8'-8" X 5'-8"
W   D

GREAT ROOM
16'-0" X 16'-6"

OPT GAS FIREPLACE

BEDROOM 3
12'-6" X 10'-4"

COVERED PORCH
26'-0" X 8'-0"

Width: 39' 0"

Depth: 70' 6"

Total Living: 1,401 sq. ft.

Main Ceiling: 9 ft.

Price Tier: A

Bedrooms: 3

Baths: 2

Foundation: Crawl, Slab

Plan Options: page 282

BUILDING SYSTEM
NGI
Next Generation Industries
COMPATABLE

401 Urban Lane
Urban Collection I

This Nelson Design Group home has classic southern traditional charm. Picture yourself gazing in the distance on the front covered porch of your new home as the sun sets. Traveling inside, you'll feel right at home in the spacious great room with optional fireplace. You'll start family traditions in the cozy breakfast nook with access to the kid's nook which includes built-in storage bins. The rear side grilling porch, with access to the master suite will make entertaining a breeze on those warm summer weekends. As night falls, you'll find peace in your master suite with private bath and large walk-in closet. Two bedrooms with large walk-in closets complete the design.

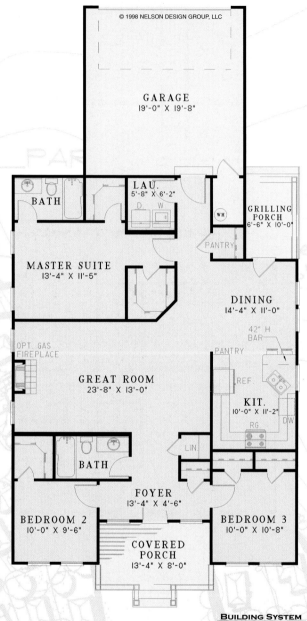

© 1998 NELSON DESIGN GROUP, LLC

GARAGE
19'-0" X 19'-8"

LAU.
5'-8" X 6'-2"

BATH

GRILLING
PORCH
6'-6" X 10'-0"

PANTRY

MASTER SUITE
13'-4" X 11'-5"

DINING
14'-4" X 11'-0"

42" H
BAR

OPT. GAS
FIREPLACE

PANTRY

GREAT ROOM
23'-8" X 13'-0"

REF.

KIT.
10'-0" X 11'-2"

RG.

DW

LIN.

BATH

FOYER
13'-4" X 4'-6"

BEDROOM 2
10'-0" X 9'-6"

BEDROOM 3
10'-0" X 10'-8"

COVERED
PORCH
13'-4" X 8'-0"

402 Urban Lane
Urban Collection I

This adorable Nelson Design Group home is the perfect starter home for you and your new family. Imagine coming home after a long day and basking in the afternoon sun on the cozy covered porch, while watching the kids play. After entering the charming foyer, you'll travel into the spacious great room, which will serve as the heart of your home. Spending time in front of the fireplace will warm the hearts of family and friends. Dining will be fun for the whole family with easy access to the grilling porch. After the kids are in bed, you'll be able to find solitude in your master suite with private bath and his and her closets. This split bedroom traditional style design has all the amenities you'll need to call it home.

Width: 34' 8"

Depth: 71' 0"

Total Living: 1,442 sq. ft.

Main Ceiling: 9 ft.

Price Tier: A

Bedrooms: 3

Baths: 2

Foundation: Crawl, Slab

Plan Options: page 282

BUILDING SYSTEM
NGI
Next Generation Industries
COMPATABLE

To Order Call 1.800.590.2423   Similar plans can be viewed and ordered at www.nelsondesigngroup.com

Main Floor

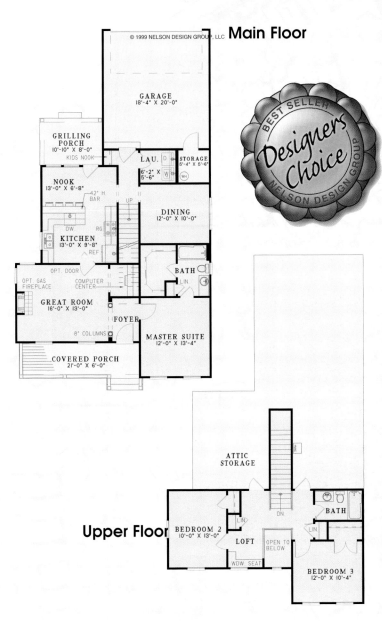

© 1999 NELSON DESIGN GROUP, LLC

GARAGE
18'-4" X 20'-0"

GRILLING PORCH
10'-10" X 8'-0"
KIDS NOOK

LAU.
STORAGE
5'-4" X 5'-6"

NOOK
13'-0" X 6'-8"
42" H. BAR
UP

DINING
12'-0" X 10'-0"

DW   RG
KITCHEN
13'-0" X 9'-8"
REF.

BATH
LIN.

OPT. DOOR
OPT. GAS FIREPLACE
COMPUTER CENTER

GREAT ROOM
16'-0" X 13'-0"

FOYER

8" COLUMNS

MASTER SUITE
12'-0" X 13'-4"

COVERED PORCH
21'-0" X 6'-0"

Upper Floor

ATTIC STORAGE

DN

BATH
LIN.

BEDROOM 2
10'-0" X 13'-0"
LIN.

LOFT
OPEN TO BELOW

WDW. SEAT

BEDROOM 3
12'-0" X 10'-4"

Width: 34' 4"
Depth: 61' 6"
Main Floor: 1,063 sq. ft.
Upper Floor: 496 sq. ft.
Total Living: 1,559 sq. ft.
Price Tier: B

Main Ceiling: 9 ft.
Upper Ceiling: 8 ft.
Bedrooms: 3
Baths: 2
Foundation: Crawl, Slab,
Optional Basement,
Optional Daylight Basement

Plan Options: page 282

BUILDING SYSTEM
NGI
Next Generation Industries
COMPATABLE

❀ **399 Urban Lane**
Urban Collection I

The simple elegance of this Nelson Design Group home will capture your imagination. As you enter the foyer, you'll admire the graceful appeal of the eight-inch columns that invite you into the spacious great room. The warmth of this room will provide the perfect place to create lasting memories with family and friends. Starting the day will be fun for everyone in the charming breakfast nook with access to the rear grilling porch. After everyone is off to work or play, you'll be able to relax upstairs, maybe read your favorite book on the window seat, or retreat to the master suite with private bath complete with a huge walk in closet. This home also features two large bedrooms, loft area, and has ample storage space to suit your needs.

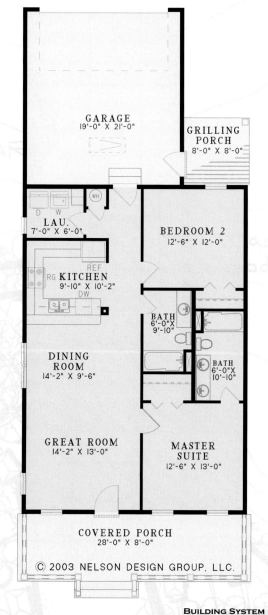

GARAGE
19'-0" X 21'-0"

GRILLING PORCH
8'-0" X 8'-0"

LAU.
7'-0" X 6'-0"

BEDROOM 2
12'-6" X 12'-0"

KITCHEN
9'-10" X 10'-2"

BATH
6'-0" X 9'-10"

BATH
6'-0" X 10'-10"

DINING ROOM
14'-2" X 9'-6"

GREAT ROOM
14'-2" X 13'-0"

MASTER SUITE
12'-6" X 13'-0"

COVERED PORCH
28'-0" X 8'-0"

© 2003 NELSON DESIGN GROUP, LLC.

794 Urban Lane
Urban Collection II

Sit back and breathe deeply on the covered front porch of this traditional style home. Begin a new tradition preparing steaks on the backyard grilling porch, spending summer evenings together with your family and friends. Move the group indoors to the cozy great room and dining room for drinks and laughter afterwards. As evening draws closer, you'll be able to find solitude in your master suite with private bath.

Width: 28' 0"

Depth: 69' 6"

Total Living: 1,120 sq. ft.

Main Ceiling: 9 ft.

Price Tier: A

Bedrooms: 2

Baths: 2

Foundation: Crawl, Slab,

Plan Options: page 282

BUILDING SYSTEM
NGI
Next Generation Industries
COMPATABLE

To Order Call 1.800.590.2423   Similar plans can be viewed and ordered at www.nelsondesigngroup.com

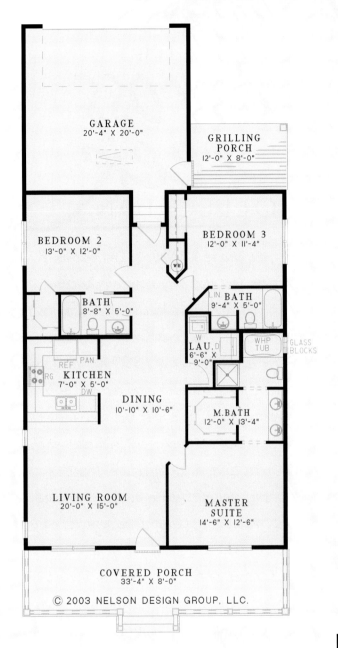

GARAGE
20'-4" X 20'-0"

GRILLING PORCH
12'-0" X 8'-0"

BEDROOM 2
13'-0" X 12'-0"

BEDROOM 3
12'-0" X 11'-4"

WH

BATH
8'-8" X 5'-0"

LIN BATH
9'-4" X 5'-0"

REF PAN
KITCHEN
7'-0" X 5'-0"
RG
DW

W LAU. D
6'-6" X 9'-0"

WHP TUB

GLASS BLOCKS

DINING
10'-10" X 10'-6"

M.BATH
12'-0" X 13'-4"

LIVING ROOM
20'-0" X 15'-0"

MASTER SUITE
14'-6" X 12'-6"

COVERED PORCH
33'-4" X 8'-0"

© 2003 NELSON DESIGN GROUP, LLC.

Width: 33' 4"

Depth: 72' 10"

Total Living: 1,462 sq. ft.

Main Ceiling: 9 ft.

Price Tier: A

Bedrooms: 3

Baths: 3

Foundation: Crawl, Slab

Plan Options: page 282

BUILDING SYSTEM
NGI
Next Generation Industries
COMPATABLE

795 Urban Lane
Urban Collection II

Imagine coming home and basking in the afternoon sun or watching a gorgeous sunset on the covered front porch. The spacious living room just inside the front door flows easily into the dining area, adjacent to the kitchen. When days get warmer, prepare dinner outside on the backyard grilling porch, accessible from the garage. Everyone will love having his or her own private bathroom before retiring to bed. The master suite includes a large walk-in closet, split vanities and a whirlpool bath to help you relax at the end of a long day.

THE
Cross
Creek
COLLECTION

When you choose a Nelson Design Group collection, you not only create beautiful homes, you achieve ideal master planned communities. The Cross Creek Collection features living spaces of 1,300 to 1,700 square feet with front loading garages gently tiered for street appeal. Each of the six plans - with brick or siding exterior - complement each other, resulting in an effective Traditional European design theme and a complete neighborhood — making development easy for you. All plans are designed to fit a narrow lot of 50 feet to 60 feet. Nelson Design Group also offers complementary collections with the same traditional appeal and quality as our Cross Creek Collection. Visit our website to view these collections.

Nelson Design Group LLC

RESIDENTIAL & COMMERCIAL PLANNERS - DESIGNERS

GRILLING PORCH
12'-0" X 6'-0"

MASTER BATH
15'-8" X 11'-4"

WHP TUB

LIN

STORAGE

BRKFAST RM.
11'-4" X 12'-0"

MASTER SUITE
10' BOXED CEILING
15'-8" X 13'-8"

GARAGE
19'-8" X 23'-4"

© 1999 NELSON DESIGN GROUP, LLC

KITCHEN
RG. 11'-4" X 11'-2"

DW

REF

D.

W.

WH

BEDROOM 2
11'-4" X 11'-0"

LIN

LIN

BATH

GAS FIREPLACE

GREAT RM.
10' BOXED CEILING
15'-8" X 16'-6"

COVERED PORCH
16'-0" X 8'-0"
10" COLUMNS

BEDROOM 3 / OFFICE
11'-4" X 12'-0"

Elevation B

299 Cross Creek

If you can picture yourself hosting an elegant dinner party surrounded by friends and family, then step into this Nelson Design Group home. After greeting guests on the covered porch, guide them into the spacious great room. Here, mingling can begin and maybe drinks around the romantic gas fireplace. Conveniently accessible to the kitchen, you can slip away to check on the excellent cuisine you are preparing. A connecting breakfast room can serve as more space for guests or a quiet place just for you. A door opening to a grilling porch allows you to even prepare grilled meats with ease. When all the excitement is over, enjoy the privacy of the master suite or relax in a whirlpool bath.

Width: 48' 0"

Depth: 63' 4"

Total Living: 1,452 sq. ft.

Main Ceiling: 9 ft.

Price Tier: A

Bedrooms: 3

Baths: 2

Foundation: Crawl, Slab, Optional Basement, Optional Daylight Basement

Plan Options: page 282

BUILDING SYSTEM
NGI
Next Generation Industries
COMPATABLE

Elevation A

Elevation B

STRG.
8'-2" X 5'-6"

LAU.
7'-0" X 5'-6"

NOOK
9'-0" X 7'-0"

MASTER SUITE
10'-0" BOXED CEILING
12'-0" X 13'-8"

GARAGE
20'-0" X 20'-0"

KITCHEN
14'-8" X 12'-4"

PANTRY

REF

DW

RG

© 1998 NELSON DESIGN GROUP, LLC

DINING ROOM
10'-8" X 10'-0"

M.BATH
12'-0" X 11'-6"

LIN

WHP TUB

SHWR

GLASS BLOCKS

8" COLUMNS

BEDROOM 3
12'-0" X 10'-8"

GREAT ROOM
10'-0" BOXED CEILING
14'-8" X 20'-0"

LIN

BATH

SITTING AREA
9'-0" X 4'-0"

FOYER

BEDROOM 2
12'-0" X 10'-4"

PRCH

298 Cross Creek

Elegance radiates through this Nelson Design Group home. Through a traditional foyer, enter a tasteful sitting area — perfect for greeting guests before continuing into the great room with intricate ten-foot boxed ceiling. Set off by magnificently crafted wooden columns, the dining room area provides an excellent atmosphere for graceful dinner parties — business or pleasure. A wonderfully open kitchen with island and bright bay window nook will ensure you have all the tools you need.

Width: 48' 0"
Depth: 60' 4"
Total Living: 1,598 sq. ft.
Main Ceiling: 9 ft.
Price Tier: B

Bedrooms: 3
Baths: 2
Foundation: Crawl, Slab
Plan Options: page 282

BUILDING SYSTEM
NGI
Next Generation Industries
COMPATABLE

Elevation A

MASTER BATH
15'-8" X 8'-4"

WHP TUB

LIN

MASTER SUITE
10' BOXED CEILING
15'-8" X 12'-0"

GRILLING PORCH
11'-4" X 8'-0"

BRKFAST RM.
11'-0" X 8'-10"

LAU.
7'-6" X 6'-6"

W
D
W.B.

WH

STORAGE
6'-8" X 5'-6"

BED RM. 2
10'-6" X 12'-4"

BED RM. 3
10'-6" X 13'-10"

LIN

DW

REF.

RG

KITCHEN
11'-0" X 13'-8"

PANTRY

GARAGE
19'-0" X 20'-0"

© 1998 NELSON DESIGN GROUP, LLC

FOYER

GREAT RM.
10' BOXED CEILING
15'-0" X 18'-4"

GAS FIREPLACE

ENTRY PORCH

8" COLUMNS

DINING RM.
10' CEILING
10'-8" X 11'-6"

10" COLUMNS

Elevation B

Width: 52' 8"

Depth: 60' 6"

Total Living: 1,627 sq. ft.

Main Ceiling: 9 ft.

Price Tier: B

Bedrooms: 3

Baths: 2

Foundation: Crawl, Slab

Plan Options: page 282

BUILDING SYSTEM
NGI
Next Generation Industries
COMPATABLE

302 Cross Creek

Entering through majestic columns into the traditional foyer, you instantly feel the grandeur of this Nelson Design Group home. Imagine an evening of exquisite cuisine as you entertain your close friends and colleagues in the elegant dining room enhanced by ten-foot ceilings and beautifully crafted columns. A grilling porch, located off the spacious kitchen and breakfast room, provides the ease needed to serve your favorite recipes. Following the festivities, retreat to a private master suite and relax in your whirlpool bath.

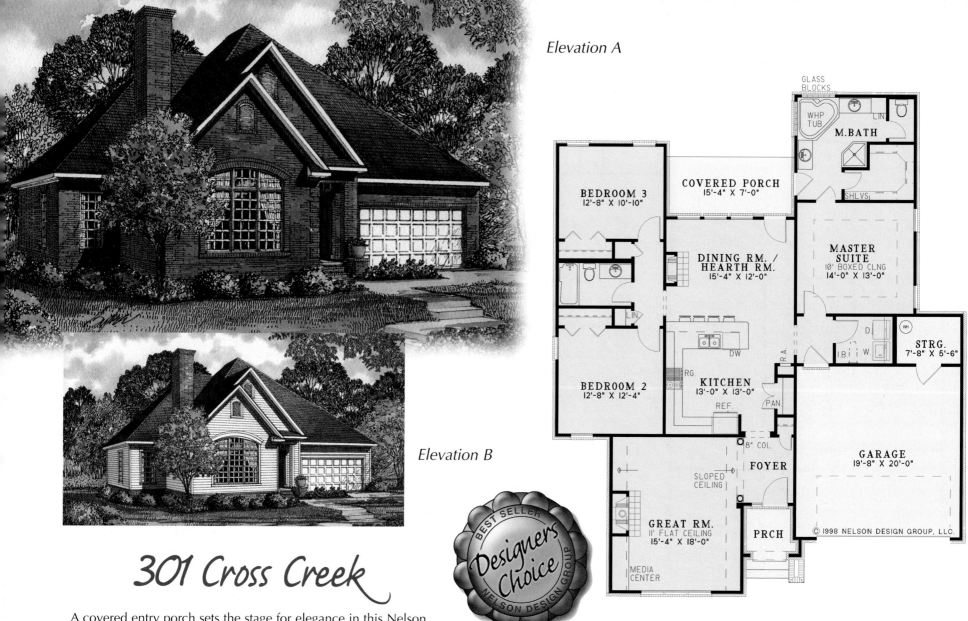

Elevation A

Elevation B

GLASS BLOCKS

WHP TUB

M.BATH

LIN

COVERED PORCH
15'-4" X 7'-0"

BEDROOM 3
12'-8" X 10'-10"

SHLVS

MASTER SUITE
10' BOXED CLNG
14'-0" X 13'-0"

DINING RM. / HEARTH RM.
15'-4" X 12'-0"

LIN

STRG.
7'-8" X 5'-6"

D. WH

KITCHEN
13'-0" X 13'-0"

DW

I.B. W.

BEDROOM 2
12'-8" X 12'-4"

RG

REF.

R.A.

PAN

8" COL.

GARAGE
19'-8" X 20'-0"

FOYER

SLOPED CEILING

GREAT RM.
11' FLAT CEILING
15'-4" X 18'-0"

PRCH

© 1998 NELSON DESIGN GROUP, LLC.

MEDIA CENTER

301 Cross Creek

A covered entry porch sets the stage for elegance in this Nelson Design Group home. Travel through the foyer and enter a spacious great room with unique sloped ceilings, complete with built-in media center, for hours of family entertainment. Take advantage of the distinguished dining and hearth room with a lovely fireplace. Continue entertaining on your covered rear porch over conversation and a breath-taking view.

BEST SELLER
Designers Choice
NELSON DESIGN GROUP

Width: 49' 0"

Depth: 58' 6"

Total Living: 1,654 sq. ft.

Main Ceiling: 9 ft.

Price Tier: B

Bedrooms: 3

Baths: 2

Foundation: Crawl, Slab, Basement, Daylight Basement

Plan Options: page 282

BUILDING SYSTEM
NGI
Next Generation Industries
COMPATABLE

Main Floor

GLASS BLOCKS

WHP TUB

MASTER BATH 15'-6" X 9'-0"

LIN

GRILLING PORCH 14'-0" X 6'-0"

LAU.

WH

STORAGE 10'-0" X 6'-0"

KITCHEN 11'-0" X 10'-0"

NOOK 7'-0" X 9'-0"

DW

D

W

RG.

ISLAND

REF.

MASTER SUITE 11'-6" X 14'-0"

GARAGE 19'-8" X 19'-4"

© 1998 NELSON DESIGN GROUP, LLC

GAS FIREPLACE

8" COLUMNS

UP

DINING 10'-2" X 14'-0"

GREAT RM. 15'-6" X 16'-0"

FOYER

PORCH

Upper Floor

BONUS AREA 17'-8" X 16'-0" 380 SQ.FT.

LIN

DN.

BED RM. 2 16'-4" X 9'-2"

BED RM. 3 9'-8" X 12'-2"

8' LINE

Elevation A

Elevation B

300 Cross Creek

Become enchanted by European beauty as you enter this Nelson Design Group home. Nine-foot ceilings create a marvelous openness throughout the entire plan especially in the great room. Spend hours entertaining friends and family, before journeying to the elegant dining room for a spectacular meal followed by conversation over coffee. A clever grilling porch just off the kitchen area provides ample room and convenience to prepare the cuisine. After the party ends, retreat to your private master suite or relax in the whirlpool tub of your master bath. A large bonus room and two bedrooms, with adjoining bath on the upper level, make an excellent children's suite.

Width: 47' 0"
Depth: 50' 0"
Main Floor: 1,155 sq. ft.
Upper Floor: 529 sq. ft.
Total Living: 1,684 sq. ft.*
*Bonus: 380 sq. ft.
Price Tier: B

Main Ceiling: 9 ft.
Upper Ceiling: 8 ft.
Bedrooms: 3
Baths: 2 1/2
Foundation: Crawl, Slab, Opt. Basement, Opt. Daylight Basement
Plan Options: page 282

BUILDING SYSTEM NGI Next Generation Industries COMPATABLE

To Order Call 1.800.590.2423   Similar plans can be viewed and ordered at www.nelsondesigngroup.com

73

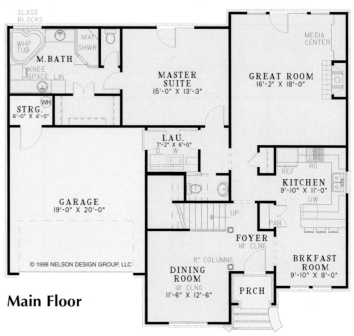

Elevation A

Main Floor

GLASS BLOCKS

WHP TUB

M.BATH

KNEE SPACE LIN

STRG. 6'-0" X 4'-0"

WH

SEAT SHWR

MASTER SUITE 15'-0" X 13'-3"

MEDIA CENTER

GREAT ROOM 16'-2" X 18'-0"

GARAGE 19'-0" X 20'-0"

LAU. 7'-2" X 6'-0"

REF RG

KITCHEN 9'-10" X 11'-0"

DW

UP

PAN

FOYER 10' CLNG

BRKFAST ROOM 9'-10" X 8'-0"

© 1998 NELSON DESIGN GROUP, LLC

8" COLUMNS

DINING ROOM 10' CLNG 11'-6" X 12'-6"

PRCH

4" WALL

BED RM. 2 11'-0" X 10'-8"

HVAC

BED RM. 3 9'-3" X 11'-0"

DN

ATTIC STORAGE

Upper Floor

5" WALL

Elevation B

303 Cross Creek

The lovely covered entry porch of this Nelson Design Group home leads you into a traditional foyer — perfect for greeting guests before an elegant dinner party. Through graceful wooden columns, enter the dining area with ten-foot ceiling, creating the perfect dining ambiance. Following dinner, retreat with guests to a spacious great room for conversation over coffee and dessert. After a full night of entertaining, retreat to the comfort and privacy of a secluded master suite. The children will be fast asleep on the upper level in the two bedrooms with walk-through bath.

Width: 48' 0"	Main Ceiling: 9 ft.
Depth: 43' 0"	Upper Ceiling: 8 ft.
Main Floor: 1,356 sq. ft.	Bedrooms: 3
Upper Floor: 441 sq. ft.	Baths: 2 1/2
Total Living: 1,797 sq. ft.	Foundation: Crawl, Slab, Basement, Daylight Basement
Price Tier: B	Plan Options: page 282

BUILDING SYSTEM
NGI
Next Generation Industries
COMPATABLE

The Village at Wellington

This collection has been put together to ease the selection of a home plan with minimal yet efficient space. Enjoy charming traditional front porches and gently recessed garages for better street appeal. All fourteen plans in this collection range between 1,000 to 1,600 square feet and are perfect for narrow lots and Traditional Neighborhood Design. Take a moment and stroll through some of our Village at Wellington plans for a beautifully designed home plan to suit your needs and visit our website for our complete portfolio of home plans.

Nelson Design Group LLC

RESIDENTIAL & COMMERCIAL PLANNERS - DESIGNERS

GARAGE
17'-8" X 20'-0"

© 1998 NELSON DESIGN GROUP, LLC

MASTER SUITE
11'-0" X 14'-8"
10' BOXED CEILING

BEDROOM 2
10'-6" X 11'-3"

BEDROOM 3 / OFFICE
10'-6" X 9'-3"

DINING RM.
10'-2" X 11'-10"

8" BOXED COLUMNS

GREAT RM.
14'-6" X 17'-0"
GAS FIREPLACE

10' BOXED CEILING

PAN

FOYER

KIT.
10'-6" X 15'-10"

COVERED PORCH
15'-0" X 8'-0"

NOOK

DW.   REF.

RG.

WH   LIN   D.   W.

289 Wellington Lane

Impressive boxed columns surround the covered porch of this Nelson Design Group home. As you enter the foyer, you notice a spacious great room with fireplace that will be a wonderful gathering place for family and friends to begin an evening of entertainment. Serve your elegant cuisine in the dining room detailed with eight inch boxed columns with a view to the kitchen with a quaint breakfast nook. After your guests leave, you can retire to your master suite with ample room available in the large walk-in closet.

Width: 44' 0"	Bedrooms: 3
Depth: 54' 8"	Baths: 2
Total Living: 1,281 sq. ft.	Foundation: Crawl, Slab
Main Ceiling: 9 ft.	Plan Options: page 282
Price Tier: A	

BUILDING SYSTEM
NGI
Next Generation Industries
COMPATABLE

NOOK
7'-0" X 8'-0"

GRILLING PORCH

STORAGE

BED RM. 2
11'-0" X 13'-0"

PAN.

REF.

KIT.
10'-4" X 14'-8"

RG.

GARAGE
17'-8" X 23'-4"

DW.

LIN

© 1998 NELSON DESIGN GROUP, LLC

BED RM. 3
10'-8" X 11'-6"

R.A.

DINING
10'-0" X 9'-0"

OPT. GAS FIREPLACE

GREAT RM.
14'-0" X 16'-0"

MASTER SUITE
10' BOXED CEILING
13'-0" X 13'-0"

COVERED PORCH
14'-4" X 5'-0"

Width: 46' 0"

Depth: 54' 10"

Total Living: 1,317 sq. ft.

Main Ceiling: 9 ft.

Price Tier: A

Bedrooms: 3

Baths: 2

Foundation: Crawl, Slab, Basement, Daylight Basement

Plan Options: page 282

BUILDING SYSTEM
NGI
Next Generation Industries
COMPATABLE

291 Wellington Lane

This split bedroom Nelson Design Group home will turn your dreams into reality. Imagine greeting your family and friends on the front porch adorned with ten-inch columns. Upon entering the home you'll notice the expansive great room with fireplace, open to the dining room and kitchen. This will make entertaining guests a cinch. The master suite will be your haven with it's spacious ten foot boxed ceiling and full bath. The second and third bedrooms offer the kids their own part of the home with a full bath complete with his and her vanities, as well as ample closet space.

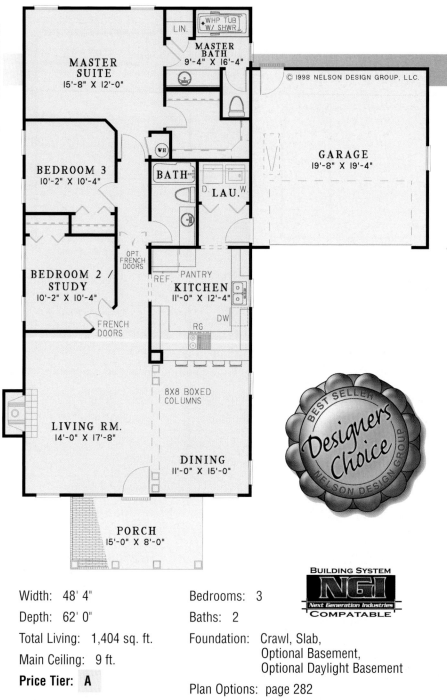

© 1998 NELSON DESIGN GROUP, LLC.

MASTER SUITE
15'-8" X 12'-0"

MASTER BATH
9'-4" X 16'-4"

WHP TUB W/ SHWR

LIN.

GARAGE
19'-8" X 19'-4"

BEDROOM 3
10'-2" X 10'-4"

BATH

WH

D LAU. W

BEDROOM 2 / STUDY
10'-2" X 10'-4"

OPT. FRENCH DOORS

REF. PANTRY

KITCHEN
11'-0" X 12'-4"

RG

DW

FRENCH DOORS

8X8 BOXED COLUMNS

LIVING RM.
14'-0" X 17'-8"

DINING
11'-0" X 15'-0"

PORCH
15'-0" X 8'-0"

Designers Choice
BEST SELLER · NELSON DESIGN GROUP

271 Wellington Lane

A charming southern traditional home reminiscent of grandmother's house exemplifies this Nelson Design Group home. Impressive boxed columns embrace the entry to the spacious dining room, while beautiful French doors open to the study. Breakfast tradition can begin in your home in the cozy kitchen with view to the dining room. To the rear of the home, you'll find a spacious master suite with ample closet space. Conclude a busy day with a long soak in your whirlpool bath.

Width: 48' 4"

Depth: 62' 0"

Total Living: 1,404 sq. ft.

Main Ceiling: 9 ft.

Price Tier: A

Bedrooms: 3

Baths: 2

Foundation: Crawl, Slab, Optional Basement, Optional Daylight Basement

Plan Options: page 282

BUILDING SYSTEM
NGI
Next Generation Industries
COMPATABLE

GRILLING PORCH
11'-8" X 6'-0"

HEARTH RM.
11'-4" X 12'-0"

OPT. GAS FIREPLACE

MASTER SUITE
14'-8" X 13'-8"
10' BOXED CEILING

WHP TUB
SHWR LIN.

GARAGE
17'-8" X 20'-0"

© 1999 NELSON DESIGN GROUP, LLC

KIT.
11'-4" X 11'-2"
DW
RG.
REF.

D.
W.
WH

BEDROOM 2
11'-4" X 11'-0"

GREAT RM.
14'-8" X 16'-6"
10' BOXED CEILING

GAS FIREPLACE

LIN.
LIN.

BATH

COVERED PORCH
15'-0" X 8'-0"

10' COLUMNS

BEDROOM 3 / STUDY
11'-4" X 12'-0"

Width: 45' 0"
Depth: 64' 10"
Total Living: 1,425 sq. ft.
Main Ceiling: 9 ft.
Price Tier: A

Bedrooms: 3
Baths: 2
Foundation: Crawl, Slab,
Optional Basement,
Optional Daylight Basement
Plan Options: page 282

BUILDING SYSTEM
NGI
Next Generation Industries
COMPATABLE

290 Wellington Lane

Enjoy peaceful fall evenings watching the sun set in this Nelson Design Group home. When it gets too cold, you can warm yourself in the comfortable great room, complete with fireplace. Begin each day with coffee and the morning paper in the hearth room with fluid access to the kitchen. The family chef will love displaying their skills during an afternoon cookout on the rear grilling porch. After the day has come to a close, you will find it most relaxing to soothe those aches away in the privacy of your master bath.

Main Floor

GARAGE
17'-8" X 19'-4"

©1998 NELSON DESIGN GROUP, LLC

STORAGE
WH

GRILLING PORCH
5'-4" X 7'-4"

BRKFAST RM.
9'-2" X 13'-2"

D
W

DESK
DW
KITCHEN
12'-6" X 11'-6"
REF
RG
PAN

WHP TUB

M.BATH
15'-6" X 11'-6"

GREAT RM.
12'-6" X 15'-0"

UP

M.BED RM.
11'-8" X 15'-0"

COVERED PORCH
29'-0" X 8'-0"

18" COLUMNS

BED RM. 2
12'-6" X 11'-0"

DN

LIN.

BED RM. 3
11'-8" X 11'-0"

DESK

DESK

8' LINE

293 Wellington Lane

A charming front porch attracts everyone to this traditional Nelson Design Group home. Entertaining will be easy on your convenient grilling porch which allows you to prepare dinner with ease. After dinner, your guests can gather in the spacious great room for games and laughter. After the guests leave, you can retire to your private master suite and bath which features an enticing whirlpool bath as well as his and her walk-in closets. Upstairs, the children will be tucked away in their own bedrooms.

Upper Floor

Width: 47' 0"
Depth: 55' 2"
Main Floor: 980 sq. ft.
Upper Floor: 561 sq. ft.
Total Living: 1,541 sq. ft.
Price Tier: B

Main Ceiling: 9 ft.
Upper Ceiling: 8 ft.
Bedrooms: 3
Baths: 2
Foundation: Crawl, Slab, Basement, Daylight Basement
Plan Options: page 282

BUILDING SYSTEM
NGI
Next Generation Industries
COMPATABLE

RENAISSANCE

A FRENCH COUNTRY NEIGHBORHOOD

A "rebirth" of the small country cottage and stone house combining grace, comfort and warmth describes the Renaissance Collection. This collection of French Country plans range in square footage of 1,800 to 2,300. Country living entails pure enjoyment and love for the countryside, so we've added grilling porches and an abundance of windows to bring the outside into the home. Distinctive elements of boxed ceilings and columns grace these six French Country designs. Enjoy the return of a simple yet elegant life style.

Nelson Design Group LLC

RESIDENTIAL & COMMERCIAL PLANNERS - DESIGNERS

545 Calais Drive

Beautiful stone and siding give warmth to this French Country design. Elegance is achieved in our Nelson Design Group home by using boxed columns and ten-foot ceilings. The foyer and dining rooms are lined with columns and adjoin the great room, all with high ceilings. The kitchen and breakfast room are great for entertaining and have access to the grilling porch. This split bedroom plan has a master suite with large walk-in closet, whirlpool tub, shower and private area. A bonus room above the garage, is available with stair access near the master suite. Two bedrooms and a large bathroom are located on the other side of the great room giving privacy to the entire family.

Width: 52' 0"	Main Ceiling: 9 ft.
Depth: 69' 6"	Bonus Ceiling: 8 ft.
Total Living: 1,869 sq. ft.*	Bedrooms: 3
*Optional Bonus: 288 sq. ft.	Baths: 2
Price Tier: B	Foundation: Crawl, Slab, Optional Basement, Optional Daylight Basement
Plan Options: page 282	

BUILDING SYSTEM
NGI
Next Generation Industries
COMPATABLE

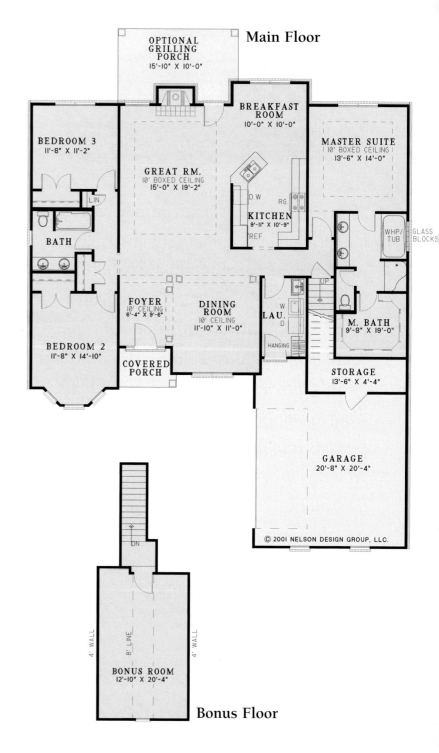

Main Floor

Bonus Floor

© 2001 NELSON DESIGN GROUP, LLC.

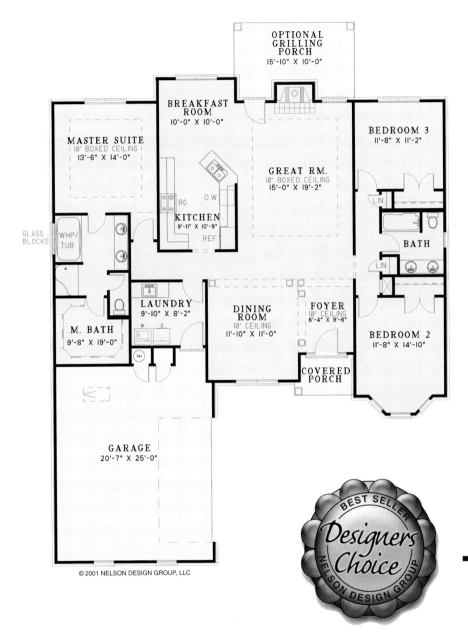

OPTIONAL
GRILLING
PORCH
15'-10" X 10'-0"

BREAKFAST
ROOM
10'-0" X 10'-0"

MASTER SUITE
10' BOXED CEILING
13'-6" X 14'-0"

GREAT RM.
10' BOXED CEILING
15'-0" X 19'-2"

BEDROOM 3
11'-8" X 11'-2"

RG
D.W.
KITCHEN
9'-11" X 10'-9"
REF.

LIN.

GLASS
BLOCKS

WHP/
TUB

BATH

LIN.

M. BATH
9'-8" X 19'-0"

LAUNDRY
9'-10" X 8'-2"

DINING
ROOM
10' CEILING
11'-10" X 11'-0"

FOYER
10' CEILING
6'-4" X 9'-6"

W D
WH

BEDROOM 2
11'-8" X 14'-10"

COVERED
PORCH

GARAGE
20'-7" X 25'-0"

© 2001 NELSON DESIGN GROUP, LLC

BEST SELLER
Designers
Choice
NELSON DESIGN GROUP

523 Fontenay Drive

Upon entering the foyer of this Nelson Design Group home, you'll notice the magnificent boxed columns surrounding the dining room. Ten-foot ceilings enhance the foyer, dining and great rooms giving this split bedroom plan a very open effect. Entertaining becomes simple for the grill master on the grilling porch accessible from the great room. As night falls, retreat to your master bath by relaxing in your whirlpool tub. The courtyard entry garage enhances the street appeal of this beautiful French country home.

Width: 52' 0"	Bedrooms: 3
Depth: 69' 6"	Baths: 2
Total Living: 1,882 sq. ft.	Foundation: Crawl, Slab, Optional Basement, Optional Daylight Basement
Main Ceiling: 9 ft.	
Price Tier: B	Plan Options: page 282

BUILDING SYSTEM
NGI
Next Generation Industries
COMPATABLE

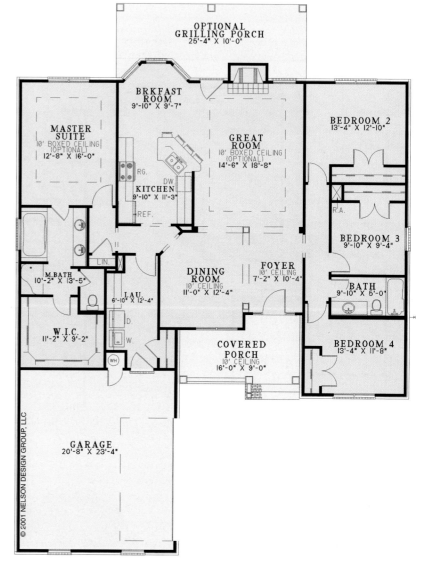

522 Calais Drive

This enchanting Nelson Design Group home incorporates the best in floor planning all in one level. The great room – which is convenient for those family gatherings that need extra room – is highlighted by a fireplace and a ten-foot boxed ceiling. Easy access from the kitchen to the dining room makes hosting a dinner party more convenient. Entertain friends and family during the summer out on the rear grilling porch. As evening approaches, retreat to your master bath complete with large walk-in closet, double vanities and whirlpool bath.

Width: 52' 0"

Depth: 71' 6"

Total Living: 1,930 sq. ft.

Main Ceiling: 9 ft.

Price Tier: B

Bedrooms: 4

Baths: 2

Foundation: Crawl, Slab, Optional Basement, Optional Daylight Basement

Plan Options: page 282

BUILDING SYSTEM
NGi
Next Generation Industries
COMPATABLE

GRILLING PORCH
16'-4" X 10'-0"

OPT. FIRE PLACE

BEDROOM 3
11'-4" X 11'-0"

BREAKFAST ROOM
11'-4" X 9'-6"

GREAT ROOM
10' BOXED CLG.
15'-8" X 21'-0"

MASTER SUITE
10' BOXED CLG.
12'-0" X 18'-0"

LIN.

REF.

RG.

D.W

LIN.

BATH
8'-0" X 8'-0"

KITCHEN
11'-0" X 11'-0"

PAN.

8' BOXED COLUMNS

WHP TUB

BEDROOM 2
11'-4" X 11'-0"

D.

BROOM CLST.

FOYER
10' CLG.
7'-0" X 10'-8"

DINING ROOM
10' CLG.
10'-9" X 14'-8"

LIN.

M.BATH
12'-3" X 15'-8"

W.

LAU.
8'-0" X 11'-0"

STORAGE

WH

PORCH
7'-0" X 3'-6"

GARAGE
20'-0" X 21'-0"

© 2001 NELSON DESIGN GROUP, LLC.

519 Chantilly Circle

Welcome your dinner guests into this elegant Nelson Design Group home enhanced by ten-foot ceilings and an open floor plan. Once in the foyer, notice the boxed columns separating the dining room and great room. The great room has a fireplace and door accessing the rear grilling porch which makes for entertaining ease. Two bedrooms and a full bath are located on one side of the house, allowing the master suite total privacy. This large master bedroom has plenty of wall space for large furniture and a master bathroom with whirlpool tub, double vanity, separate shower with seat, toilet room and a walk-in closet. Enjoy this beautiful home with plenty of room for your family.

Width: 52' 0"
Depth: 71' 2"
Total Living: 1,931 sq. ft.
Main Ceiling: 9 ft.
Price Tier: B

Bedrooms: 3
Baths: 2
Foundation: Crawl, Slab, Optional Basement, Optional Daylight Basement
Plan Options: page 282

BUILDING SYSTEM
NGI
Next Generation Industries
COMPATABLE

Main Floor

520 Fontenay Drive

Drive into a courtyard entry garage and retreat to your French Country home. Nelson Design Group has designed a beautiful floor plan that is very family oriented beginning with a porch and foyer with ten-foot ceilings. Enter the foyer and travel into a massive great room adjoining the breakfast room with access to a grilling porch. The kitchen bar area makes grilling easy and gives extra seating for large family gatherings. The master suite enhanced by a ten-foot ceiling, is located on the main level and has 'his and her' closets leading to the master bathroom full of amenities. As you travel upstairs, you'll find three bedrooms and a full bath with optional bonus area.

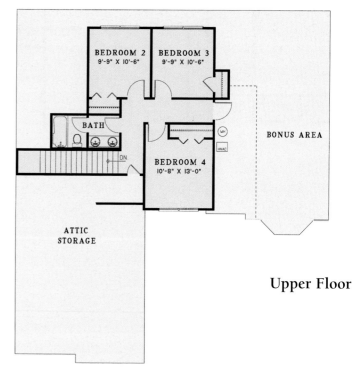

Upper Floor

Width: 50' 6"	Main Ceiling: 9 ft.
Depth: 54' 8"	Upper Ceiling: 8 ft.
Main Floor: 1,495 sq. ft.	Bedrooms: 4
Upper Floor: 546 sq. ft.	Baths: 2 1/2
Total Living: 2,041 sq. ft.	Foundation: Crawl, Slab, Optional Basement, Optional Daylight Basement
Price Tier: C	Plan Options: page 282

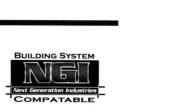

BUILDING SYSTEM
NGI
Next Generation Industries
COMPATABLE

To Order Call 1.800.590.2423   To view the rest of this collection visit www.nelsondesigngroup.com

Main Floor

GRILLING PORCH
19'-4" X 8'-0"

W.I.C.

MASTER SUITE
16'-8" X 14'-9"

GREAT ROOM
18'-2" X 18'-0"

M. BATH
13'-10" X 14'-9"

WHP. TUB

WH

LIN

LAU.

OPEN PASS-THRU

D W R.A.

REF. R.G.

KITCHEN
13'-10" X 11'-4"

D.W

PAN

GARAGE
19'-0" X 22'-3"

UP

8" RND COLUMNS

FOYER
6'-4" X 7'-6"

BREAKFAST ROOM
11'-4" X 10'-0"

DINING RM.
10' CEILING
12'-0" X 13'-6"

 © 2001 NELSON DESIGN GROUP, LLC.

Upper Floor

BEDROOM 4
11'-7" X 13'-0"

BEDROOM 3
11'-0" X 12'-8"

R.A.

BATH

BEDROOM 2
9'-6" X 11'-0"

DN.

ATTIC STORAGE

536 Chantilly Circle

The focal point of this French Country plan is a large stone wrapped window extending a feeling of warmth in the neighborhood. This lovely Nelson Design Group home has a great room with fireplace and access to a rear grilling porch. The kitchen has a pass-thru to the great room and adjoins a large breakfast room with a bar counter. The master suite is on the main floor and has a large bathroom with walk-in closet and numerous amenities. Travel upstairs and find three bedrooms and a full bathroom. Attic storage is easily accessed for seasonal usage.

Width: 50' 2"	Main Ceiling: 9 ft.
Depth: 52' 0"	Upper Ceiling: 8 ft.
Main Floor: 1,563 sq. ft.	Bedrooms: 4
Upper Floor: 727 sq. ft.	Baths: 2 1/2
Total Living: 2,290 sq. ft.	Foundation: Crawl, Slab
Price Tier: C	Plan Options: page 282

BUILDING SYSTEM
NGI
Next Generation Industries
COMPATABLE

The Multi Family Collection

The Multi-Family Collection features over fifty designs with a variety of exterior styles including Traditional, French Country, Southern Traditional and European Traditional. With a combined living space of 2,000 to 4,500 square feet, every family is easily accommodated. These creations of modular units were originally designed as individual homes that had the possibility of being built as one unit. The collaboration of smaller homes into duplexes, triplexes and fourplexes was designed to convey the true feelings and emotions of buying your starter home or retirement home. A Traditional home environment is truly exemplified with front porches, rear grilling porches and garages. The Multi-Family Collection offers all the accommodations and amenities of a single home with the benefits and savings afforded from a consolidated, low-maintenance environment.

Nelson Design Group
LLC

RESIDENTIAL & COMMERCIAL PLANNERS - DESIGNERS

488 Cambridge Court

This two bedroom duplex plan allows neighbors privacy as well as a shared rear porch for afternoon conversation. An enormous living room opens to the kitchen and gives you many options for furniture arrangement. A handy storage room located on the rear porch will allow outdoor equipment easily accessed.

Width: 54' 6"
Depth: 38' 4"
Home 1: 818 sq. ft.
Home 2: 818 sq. ft.
Combined Living: 1,636 sq. ft.

Main Ceiling: 8 ft.
Bedrooms: 4
Baths: 2
Foundation: Crawl, Slab
Plan Options: page 282

Price Tier: B

BUILDING SYSTEM
NGI
Next Generation Industries
COMPATABLE

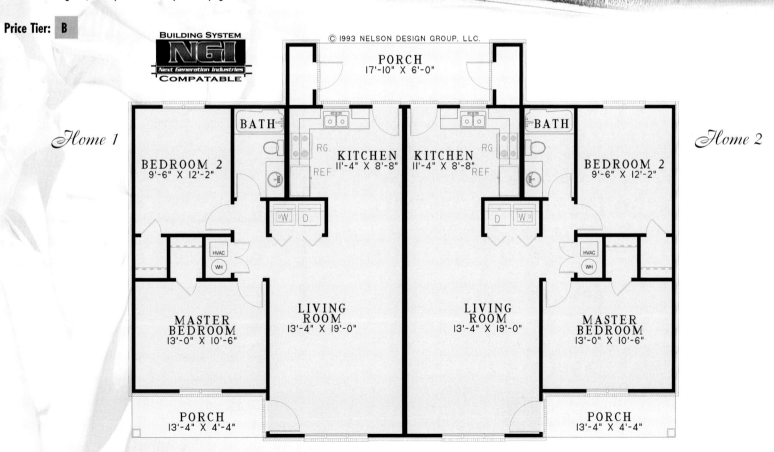

© 1993 NELSON DESIGN GROUP, LLC.

Home 1

Home 2

PORCH
17'-10" X 6'-0"

BATH

BEDROOM 2
9'-6" X 12'-2"

KITCHEN
11'-4" X 8'-8"

RG.

REF

W   D

HVAC
WH

MASTER
BEDROOM
13'-0" X 10'-6"

LIVING
ROOM
13'-4" X 19'-0"

KITCHEN
11'-4" X 8'-8"

RG

REF

BATH

BEDROOM 2
9'-6" X 12'-2"

D   W

HVAC
WH

LIVING
ROOM
13'-4" X 19'-0"

MASTER
BEDROOM
13'-0" X 10'-6"

PORCH
13'-4" X 4'-4"

PORCH
13'-4" X 4'-4"

489 Carriage Hill

This contemporary duplex plan will add class to any neighborhood. Brick columns and a hip roof enhance this two-bedroom plan complete with a large kitchen and small laundry closet. The great room is spacious and has a small sitting area by the front window. On the rear patio you'll be able to have a drink with friends and watch the sun set.

Width: 37' 0"
Depth: 56' 10"
Home 1: 922 sq. ft.
Home 2: 922 sq. ft.
Combined Living: 1,844 sq. ft.

Main Ceiling: 8 ft.
Bedrooms: 4
Baths: 2
Foundation: Crawl, Slab
Plan Options: page 282

Price Tier: B

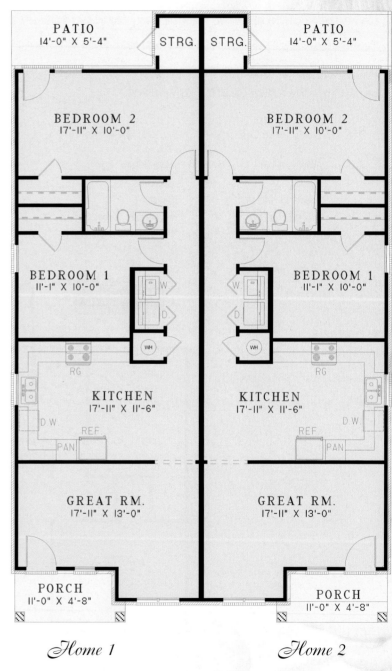

Home 1   *Home 2*

782 *Auburn Place*

This three bedroom duplex is perfect for couples and families beginning to grow. The expansive great room opens to the kitchen area with a convenient grilling porch nearby. The private suite provides you access to the bath. Ample storage space in this home is an absolute bonus feature.

Width: 96' 8"
Depth: 37' 6"
Home 1: 965 sq. ft.
Home 2: 965 sq. ft.
Combined Living: 1,930 sq. ft.

Main Ceiling: 8 ft.
Bedrooms: 6
Baths: 2
Foundation: Crawl, Slab
Plan Options: page 282

Price Tier: **B**

BUILDING SYSTEM
NGI
Next Generation Industries
COMPATABLE

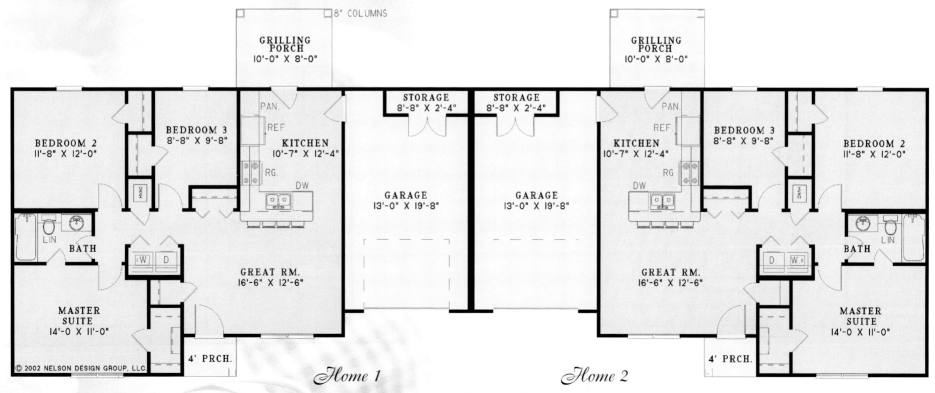

Home 1   *Home 2*

To Order Call 1.800.590.2423   **To view the rest of this collection visit www.nelsondesigngroup.com**

490 Hidden Hill Cove

We have created a southern traditional duplex plan with the appearance of a two story single family home. The front door leads to a foyer concealing two separate living quarters. Each living quarter has a great room with large closet that can be used as a computer nook; a spacious kitchen with dining area and a rear access to a patio with storage room. Travel upstairs and find a full bath, large storage closet and two bedrooms - one with a walk-in closet and French doors to the balcony.

Width: 33' 2"
Depth: 39' 2"
Main: 516 sq. ft.
Upper: 489 sq. ft.
Total Home 1: 1,005 sq. ft.
Combined Living: 2,010 sq. ft.

Main Ceiling: 10 ft.
Upper Ceiling: 9 ft.
Bedrooms: 4
Baths: 2, 2 1/2
Foundation: Crawl, Slab, Basement, Daylight Basement
Plan Options: page 282

Price Tier: C

Home 1

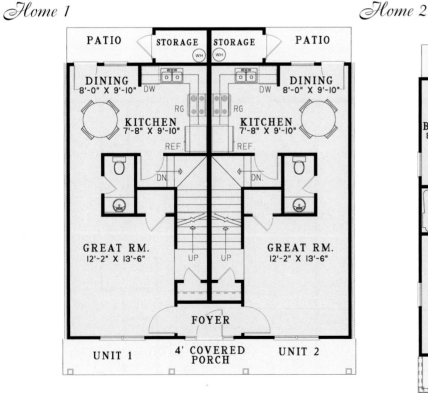

Home 2

To Order Call 1.800.590.2423   **To view the rest of this collection visit www.nelsondesigngroup.com**

662 Rosewood

This elegant Nelson Design Group duplex features a magnificaent interior design. Each home plan offers an open floor plan for the main rooms of the design. A glowing corner fireplace will provide a much needed way to wind down from the day's end. The quaint dining room will provide an awesome rear view. The secluded master suite provides a wonderful sanctuary including the private bath. A convenient laundry area and hidden porch are key features completing this design.

Width: 81' 4"
Depth: 55' 10"
Home 1:   1,271 sq. ft.
Home 2:   1,271 sq. ft.
Combined Living: 2,542 sq. ft.

Main Ceiling: 9 ft.
Bedrooms: 4
Baths: 4
Foundation: Crawl, Slab
Plan Options: page 282

Price Tier: D

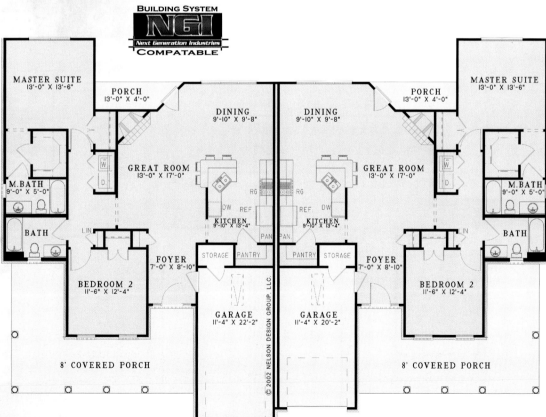

Home 1

Home 2

658 Centre Grove Circle

This traditional style Nelson Design Group duplex has a cozy front porch and offers numerous options. One of the living quarters has a master suite, a second bedroom and sun room while the other home has a large great room and formal dining room in place of the second bedroom. These open floor plans have blended kitchen and breakfast areas with handy breakfast bars and plenty of kitchen storage. The laundry area is conveniently located in the hall and near an additional bathroom. Both master suites are privately placed at the rear of the home and have large walk-in closets and private bathrooms.

Width: 82' 4"	Main Ceiling: 9 ft.
Depth: 53' 10"	Bedrooms: 3
Home 1: 1,398 sq. ft.	Baths: 3 1/2
Home 2: 1,180 sq. ft.	Foundation: Crawl, Slab
Combined Living: 2,578 sq. ft.	Plan Options: page 282

Price Tier: D

BUILDING SYSTEM
NGI NEXT GENERATION INDUSTRIES
COMPATABLE

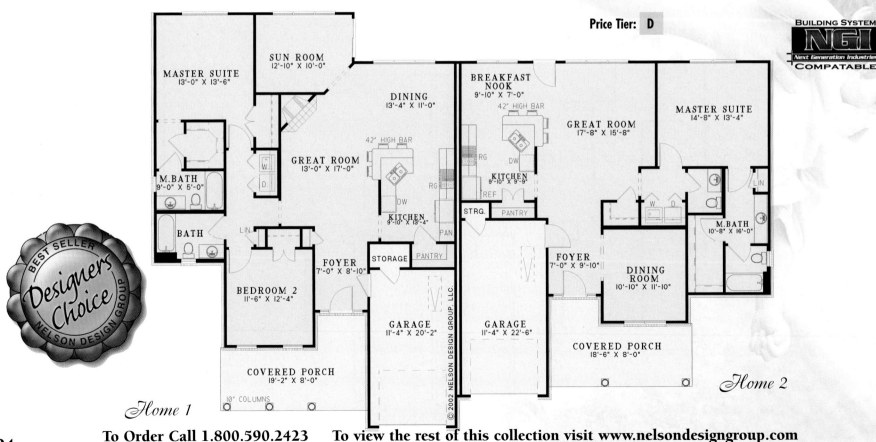

Home 1

Home 2

Designers Choice — BEST SELLER — NELSON DESIGN GROUP

© 2002 NELSON DESIGN GROUP, LLC.

To Order Call 1.800.590.2423   **To view the rest of this collection visit www.nelsondesigngroup.com**

455 Cambridge Court

This beautiful duplex hosts year round gatherings. The expansive great room gathers friends and family about the fireplace on those crisp autumn eves. The dining room affords a beautiful view of spring blossoms as the family gathers around the island snack bar from the kitchen. The master suite boasts access to the rear covered porch on those romantic summer evenings while an expansive walk-in closet, shower and corner whirlpool tub stands ready for you in the bath. Finally, the children drift to dream on Christmas Eve in their own rooms sharing full bath access.

Width: 90' 0"
Depth: 60' 4"
Home 1: 1,481 sq. ft.
Home 2: 1,472 sq. ft.
Combined Living: 2,953 sq. ft.

Price Tier: D

Main Ceiling: 9 ft.
Bedrooms: 6
Baths: 4
Foundation: Crawl, Slab,
Optional Basement,
Optional Daylight Basement,
Plan Options: page 282

BUILDING SYSTEM
NGI
Next Generation Industries
COMPATABLE

Home 1

Home 2

527 Ivy Green

Optimum convenience abounds in this Nelson Design Group duplex. The great room offers a warm fireplace and sloped ceilings. The kitchen offers island bar open to the breakfast room accessing the rear-screened porch. The master bath features 'his and her' walk-in closets, glass shower, double vanities and a whirlpool tub. The remaining two bedrooms share access to a full bath in the hall. You will find an additional storage room in the garage.

Width: 130' 0"	Main Ceiling: 9 ft.
Depth: 51' 0"	Bedrooms: 6
Home 1: 1,870 sq. ft.	Baths: 4
Home 2: 1,870 sq. ft.	Foundation: Crawl, Slab
Combined Living: 3,740 sq. ft.	Plan Options: page 282

Price Tier: F

BUILDING SYSTEM
NGI
Next Generation Industries
COMPATABLE

© 2001 NELSON DESIGN GROUP, LLC.

Home 1   *Home 2*

660 Rosewood

Nelson Design Group has created this multi-family home plan with three traditional living quarters — making the perfect investment! The central unit is smaller and designed with a single person or couple in mind while the remaining two bedroom homes include a relaxing sun room opening into the blended kitchen and dining room with a cozy fireplace to enjoy. The open kitchen features a spacious pantry and an island with handy breakfast bar and extra seating. The private master suites are placed at the rear of the home and have a large walk-in closet and private bathroom.

Width: 123' 2"
Depth: 53' 10"
Home 1: 1,398 sq. ft.
Home 2: 1,180 sq. ft.
Home 3: 1,398 sq. ft.
Combined Living: 3,976 sq. ft.

Main Ceiling: 9 ft.
Bedrooms: 5
Baths: 5, 1-1/2
Foundation: Crawl, Slab
Plan Options: page 282

Price Tier: F

BUILDING SYSTEM
NGI
Next Generation Industries
COMPATABLE

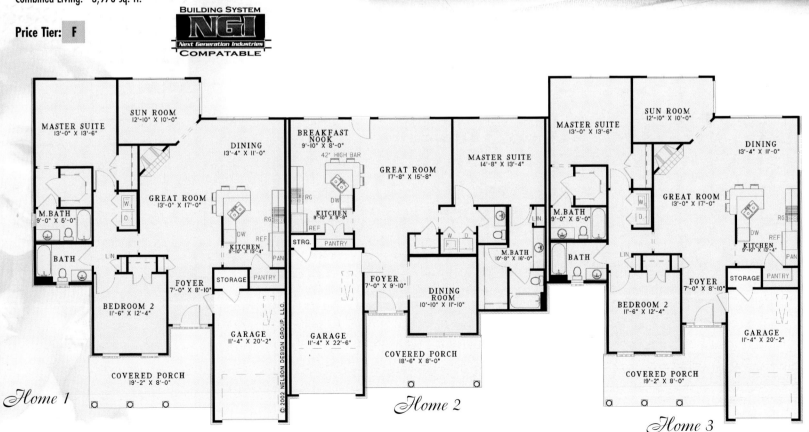

Home 1

Home 2

Home 3

661 Heather Ridge

A Traditional Neighborhood Design triplex – perfect for golf course settings. All units created in mirror imaging with unique features such as the corner fireplace in the open great room and the convenient sun room off the dining room. The private master suite with bath will be most appreciated when unwinding at the day's end.

Width: 122' 2"
Depth: 55' 10"
Home 1: 1,398 sq. ft.
Home 2: 1,398 sq. ft.
Home 3: 1,398 sq. ft.
Combined Living: 4,194 sq. ft.

Main Ceiling: 9 ft.
Bedrooms: 6
Baths: 6
Foundation: Crawl, Slab
Plan Options: page 282

Price Tier: **G**

BUILDING SYSTEM
NGI
Next Generation Industries
COMPATABLE

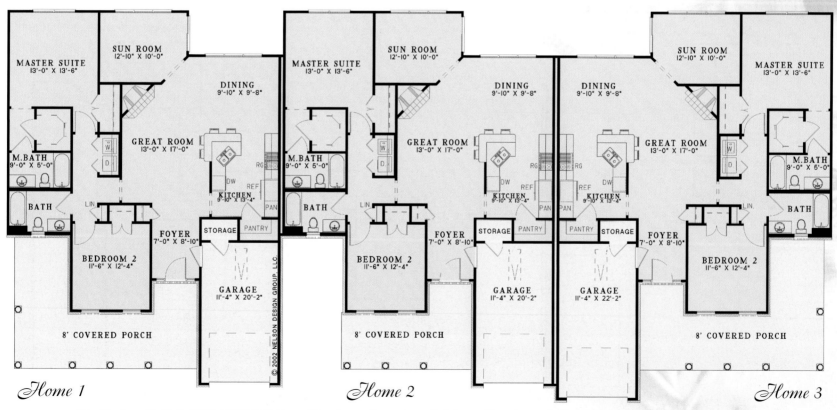

Home 1   *Home 2*   *Home 3*

To Order Call 1.800.590.2423   **To view the rest of this collection visit www.nelsondesigngroup.com**

The *Waterfront* Collection

Eleven beautiful designs that emphasize the rear view of the plan. Enjoy a waterfront or lake view through large windows while vaulted ceilings provide ample natural lighting. These plans range between 1,200 to 6,500 square feet and include beautiful fireplaces, loft areas and massive decks, perfect for entertaining. These designs are family oriented and luxurious while allowing full enjoyment of your natural setting. View the remaining plans in this collection on our website.

Nelson Design Group
LLC

RESIDENTIAL & COMMERCIAL PLANNERS - DESIGNERS

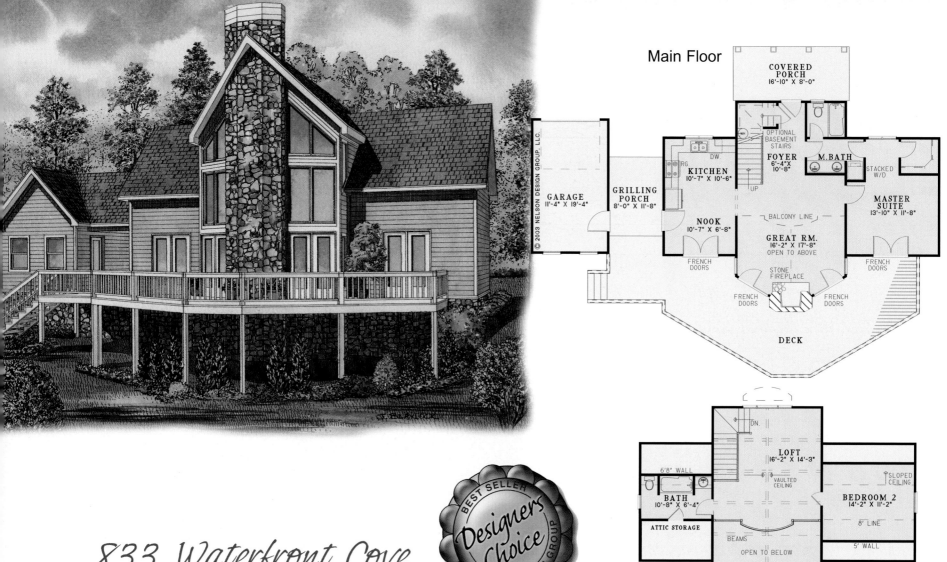

Main Floor

COVERED PORCH
16'-10" X 8'-0"

OPTIONAL BASEMENT STAIRS

GARAGE
11'-4" X 19'-4"

GRILLING PORCH
8'-0" X 11'-8"

KITCHEN
10'-7" X 10'-6"

FOYER
6'-4" X 10'-8"

M. BATH

STACKED W/D

NOOK
10'-7" X 6'-8"

BALCONY LINE

MASTER SUITE
13'-10" X 11'-8"

GREAT RM.
16'-2" X 17'-8"
OPEN TO ABOVE

FRENCH DOORS

FRENCH DOORS

STONE FIREPLACE

FRENCH DOORS

FRENCH DOORS

DECK

LOFT
16'-2" X 14'-3"

6'8" WALL

VAULTED CEILING

SLOPED CEILING

BATH
10'-8" X 6'-4"

BEDROOM 2
14'-2" X 11'-2"

ATTIC STORAGE

8' LINE

BEAMS

OPEN TO BELOW

5' WALL

Upper Floor

© 2003 NELSON DESIGN GROUP, LLC.

833 Waterfront Cove

BEST SELLER · Designers Choice · NELSON DESIGN GROUP

This glorious waterfront plan is perfect for summers of entertaining and cozy winters with family and friends. Upon entry, you will have a direct view of the great room with a rock fireplace centered among a full wall of windows and French doors leading to the rear deck. The kitchen has a quaint breakfast nook with French doors and a nearby covered grilling porch for entertaining. For privacy, the master suite is located on the main level and has a laundry area in the master bathroom for added convenience. Travel upstairs to find a spacious loft area centered between a bathroom and bedroom while enjoying a breathtaking view from the balcony.

Width: 62' 0"	Main Ceiling: 8 ft.
Depth: 39' 2"	Upper Ceiling: 8 ft.
Main Floor: 917 sq. ft.	Bedrooms: 2
Upper Floor: 491 sq. ft.	Baths: 2
Total Living: 1,408 sq. ft.	Foundation: Crawl, Slab,
Price Tier: A	Optional Basement, Optional Daylight Basement

BUILDING SYSTEM
NGi
Next Generation Industries
COMPATABLE

Plan Options: page 282

Front Elevation

Main Floor

© 1998 NELSON DESIGN GROUP, LLC

DECK
26'-8" X 8'-0"

MASTER
SUITE
15'-8" X 14'-6"

MASTER
BATH
10'-0" X 21'-8"

LIN

SEAT
GLASS
SHWR

LIN

PANTRY
REF.

KNEE
SPACE

WHP
TUB

VAULTED
CEILING

KITCHEN
12'-4" X 11'-0"

RG

DW TC

D

W

U.P.

DINING
12'-0" X 12'-0"

GREAT ROOM
26'-0" X 20'-0"

MEDIA
CENTER

8' DECK

Upper Floor

BEDROOM 2
9'-10" X 14'-0"

BEDROOM 3
9'-10" X 14'-0"

BATH

LOFT
26'-0" X 8'-8"

OPEN TO BELOW

VAULTED
CEILING

Rear Elevation

231 Waterfront Cove

Vacation throughout the year in this Nelson Design Group home. You will be delighted with the open great room with vaulted ceiling and full window view of the lake or mountains. A media center and fireplace add efficiency as well as enjoyment. Enjoy cozy evenings locked away in your secluded master suite and bath which include double vanities, glass shower and large whirlpool tub. The loft area features two bedrooms which share a full bath. This home is heavenly for a family and weekend guests.

Width: 47' 0"	Main Ceiling: 8 ft.
Depth: 63' 0"	Upper Ceiling: 8 ft.
Main Floor: 1,413 sq. ft.	Bedrooms: 3
Upper Floor: 641 sq. ft.	Baths: 2 1/2
Total Living: 2,054 sq. ft.	Foundation: Crawl, Slab, Basement, Daylight Basement
Price Tier: C	Plan Options: page 282

BUILDING SYSTEM
NGI
Next Generation Industries
COMPATABLE

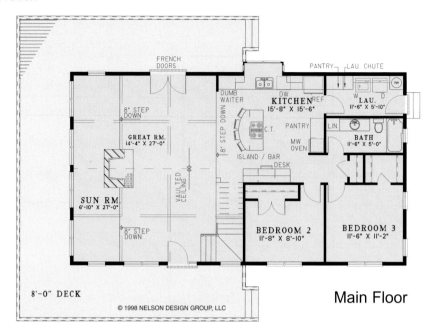

Front Elevation

Main Floor

© 1998 NELSON DESIGN GROUP, LLC

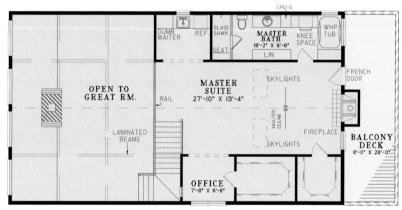

Upper Floor

Rear Elevation

Designed For:

Pioneer

sound.vision.soul

Pioneer Sound System

Designed For:

JBL

RESIDENTIAL SYSTEMS
COMPLETE HOME
ENTERTAINMENT NETWORKS
& DISTRIBUTED AUDIO

JBL
Home Theater

173 Waterfront Cove

A vacation home with the master suite upstairs makes this Nelson Design Group home desirable. The eight foot wrap around deck with access to both sides of the great room is perfect for entertaining weekend guests. Breakfast is made easy with an island bar, ideal for those big breakfasts outdoorsmen enjoy. The master suite comes complete with skylights, vaulted ceilings and a fireplace, just right for those romantic evenings for the two of you. You also have a private access to the rear balcony deck through French doors.

Width: 50' 0"	Main Ceiling: 8 ft.
Depth: 28' 0"	Upper Ceiling: 8 ft.
Main Floor: 1,400 sq. ft.	Bedrooms: 3
Upper Floor: 743 sq. ft.	Baths: 2
Total Living: 2,143 sq. ft.	Foundation: Crawl, Slab,
Price Tier: C	Optional Basement,
	Optional Daylight Basement
	Plan Options: page 282

BUILDING SYSTEM
NGI
Next Generation Industries
COMPATABLE

Main Floor

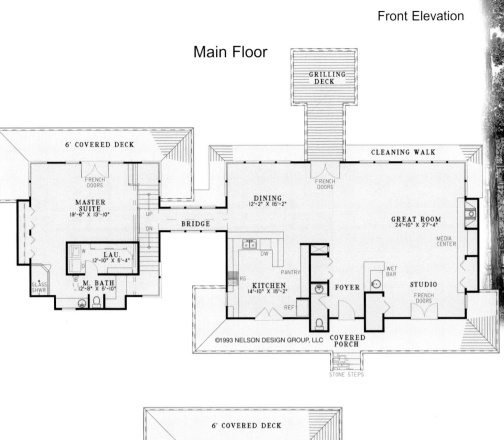

6' COVERED DECK

FRENCH DOORS

MASTER SUITE
19'-6" X 13'-10"

UP

DN

BRIDGE

LAU.
12'-10" X 5'-4"

GLASS SHWR

M. BATH
12'-8" X 5'-10"

CLEANING WALK

FRENCH DOORS

DINING
12'-2" X 15'-2"

GREAT ROOM
24'-10" X 27'-4"

MEDIA CENTER

DW

PANTRY

KITCHEN
14'-10" X 15'-2"

REF

FOYER

WET BAR

STUDIO

FRENCH DOORS

©1993 NELSON DESIGN GROUP, LLC

COVERED PORCH

STONE STEPS

GRILLING DECK

Lower Floor

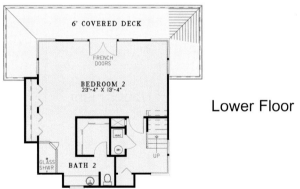

6' COVERED DECK

FRENCH DOORS

BEDROOM 2
23'-4" X 13'-4"

GLASS SHWR

BATH 2

UP

HVAC

Rear Elevation

311 Waterfront Cove

Stone steps and a covered porch welcome you to this Nelson Design Group treehouse style home. French doors open to the studio with a wet bar providing relaxation while enjoying the great room fireplace. Your guests will enjoy the openness of the dining room and kitchen created by the vaulted ceilings above. A peninsula grilling deck allows you to prepare your meals with ease. Separated from the living areas by a bridge, your master suite includes corner glass shower and walk-in closet with a convenient laundry area. The lower level has an identical bedroom suite with French door access to the rear deck.

Width: 91' 10"	Main Ceiling: Vaulted
Depth: 54' 0"	Lower Ceiling: 10 ft.
Main Floor: 1,976 sq. ft.	Bedrooms: 2
Lower Floor: 634 sq. ft.	Baths: 2 1/2
Total Living: 2,610 sq. ft.	Foundation: Crawl, Basement, Daylight Basement
Price Tier: D	

BUILDING SYSTEM
NGi Next Generation Industries
COMPATABLE

Plan Options: page 282

© 1998 NELSON DESIGN GROUP, LLC

DECK
30'-8" X 20'-0"

COVERED
8' PORCH

STEP DOWN

COVERED
8' PORCH

BEDROOM 4
19'-8" X 18'-6"

WHP
TUB

LIN

SEAT

16" VANITY LIN

BEDROOM 1
13'-8" X 15'-2"

REF

RG

VAULTED
CEILING

GREAT RM.
29'-4" X 20'-4"

EXPOSED WOOD
TRUSSES

ISLAND
BAR

KITCHEN
13'-6" X 18'-4"

DW

STEP DOWN

DESK

LIN

FOYER

HANG
ROD

LAU.
D W

BEDROOM 3
13'-8" X 19'-0"

SEAT

BEDROOM 2
13'-10" X 15'-2"

BUILT-
IN CHEST

STRG.

Main Floor

CARPORT
30'-0" X 20'-0"

VAULTED
CEILING

OPEN TO BELOW   EXPOSED WOOD
TRUSSES

OPEN TO BELOW

8' LINE

LOFT
18'-0" X 18'-6"

Upper Floor

Rear Elevation

226 Waterfront Cove

This Nelson Design Group plan is a vacation dream home come true. As you enter the foyer, you are exposed to the spacious great room with large rock fireplace - perfect for entertaining family and friends. If more room is needed for the party, lead them into your kitchen with large island bar. Your guests will enjoy climbing the spiral staircase to the loft above with a great view of the lake. You will find plenty of space and privacy in all of your bedrooms, complete with their own baths. The fourth bedroom and bath includes a whirlpool bath and glass shower for relaxing comfort.

Width: 73' 0"	Main Ceiling: 8 ft.
Depth: 69' 4"	Upper Ceiling: 8 ft.
Main Floor: 2,687 sq. ft.	Bedrooms: 4
Upper Floor: 342 sq. ft.	Baths: 5
Total Living: 3,029 sq. ft.	Foundation: Crawl, Slab,
Price Tier: E	Optional Basement,
	Optional Daylight Basement

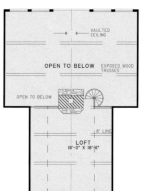

BUILDING SYSTEM
NGI
Next Generation Industries
COMPATABLE

Plan Options: page 282

Sage Meadows
COLLECTION

When you choose a Nelson Design Group collection, you not only create beautiful homes, you achieve ideal master planned communities. The Sage Meadows Collection of French Country designs features living spaces of 1,100 to 1,600 square feet — advantageous for rear access and open views for lake or golf course settings. Each of the twelve plans complement each other, resulting in an effective overall design theme and a complete neighborhood — making development easy for you. All plans are designed to fit a narrow lot of 50 feet to 60 feet. Nelson Design Group also offers complementary collections with the same traditional appeal and quality as our Sage Meadows Collection at our website.

Nelson Design Group LLC

RESIDENTIAL & COMMERCIAL PLANNERS - DESIGNERS

288 Sage Meadows

Imagine the luxury of waking to a warm spring morning, walking out an atrium door from your master suite onto a rear covered porch overlooking a beautiful lake or golf course. With this Nelson Design Group home, the dream is a reality. The covered porch makes entertaining friends easy with convenient access to the great room — complete with gas fireplace and ten-foot boxed ceilings.

Width: 41' 10"
Depth: 59' 8"
Total Living: 1,287 sq. ft.
Main Ceiling: 9 ft.
Price Tier: A

Bedrooms: 2
Baths: 2
Foundation: Crawl, Slab, Basement, Daylight Basement
Plan Options: page 282

BUILDING SYSTEM
NGi
Next Generation Industries
COMPATABLE

279 Sage Meadows

279

279A

GRILLING PORCH
14'-6" X 8'-0"

FRENCH DOORS

MASTER SUITE
11'-4" X 15'-0"

FRENCH DOORS

10' BOXED CEILING

LIN.

GREAT ROOM
13'-8" X 17'-6"

M.BATH
11'-4" X 12'-4"

GLASS BLOCKS

10' BOXED CEILING

GLASS SHWR

WHP TUB

D

W LAU.
6'-10" X 6'-6"

8X8 BOXED COLUMNS

GOLF CART
8'-0" X 6'-10"

DINING
13'-8" X 10'-0"

OPT. FRENCH DOORS

BEDROOM 3 / DEN / STUDY
11'-4" X 11'-0"

KIT.
8'-10" X 13'-0"

GARAGE
19'-8" X 20'-0"

PAN

FOYER
4'-6" X 8'-3"

© 1998 NELSON DESIGN GROUP, LLC

RG

DW

REF

PAN

PORCH

BEDROOM 2
11'-4" X 11'-0"

279B

Throughout this Nelson Design Group home, you'll feel the openness achieved by the grandeur of nine-foot ceilings. A covered rear porch makes entertaining friends and family a breeze, and perfect for a delicious summer barbecue. Elegant French doors lead you back inside where you'll enjoy conversation in your spacious great room, conveniently accessible to the dining area and kitchen. An additional third bedroom can be converted to a den or study to accommodate everyone.

Width: 46' 0"	Bedrooms: 3
Depth: 60' 4"	Baths: 2
Total Living: 1,359 sq. ft.	Foundation: Crawl, Slab
Main Ceiling: 9 ft.	Plan Options: page 282
Price Tier: A	

Designed For:

JBL

RESIDENTIAL SYSTEMS
COMPLETE HOME ENTERTAINMENT NETWORKS & DISTRIBUTED AUDIO

JBL
Home Theater

BUILDING SYSTEM
NGI
Next Generation Industries
COMPATABLE

282 Sage Meadows

MASTER SUITE
14'-10" X 12'-0"
OPT. 10' BOXED CEILING

COVERED PORCH
10'-6" X 8'-8"

BRKFAST RM.
12'-0" X 9'-4"

GLASS SHWR

M.BATH
11'-0" X 8'-4"

WHP TUB

LIN

GLASS BLOCKS

BED RM. 3
11'-0" X 10'-0"

GAS FIREPLACE

GREAT RM.
16'-0" X 17'-4"
OPT. 10' BOXED CEILING

KIT
10'-0" X 9'-6"

RG

REF

PAN

LAU.
7'-6" X 5'-6"

W.

D

FOYER
10' CEILING

© 1998 NELSON DESIGN GROUP, LLC

GOLF CART

BED RM. 2
11'-0" X 10'-0"

COVERED ENTRY

GARAGE
19'-4" X 25'-6"

Enter this French Country Nelson Design Group home and find a traditional covered entry porch with marvelous ten-foot ceilings. Following through the foyer, you're led into a spacious great room where you can spend cold winter nights in front of a warm fire. In addition, convenient access from the master suite to the covered rear porch provides the atmosphere for private romantic summer evenings.

Designed For:

JBL
RESIDENTIAL SYSTEMS
COMPLETE HOME ENTERTAINMENT NETWORKS & DISTRIBUTED AUDIO

JBL
Home Theater

Designed For:

Pioneer
sound.vision.soul
Pioneer Sound System

Width: 38' 4"

Depth: 68' 6"

Total Living: 1,379 sq. ft.

Main Ceiling: 9 ft.

Price Tier: A

Bedrooms: 3

Baths: 2

Foundation: Crawl, Slab

Plan Options: page 282

BUILDING SYSTEM
NGI
Next Generation Industries
COMPATABLE

To Order Call 1.800.590.2423   To view the rest of this collection visit www.nelsondesigngroup.com

281 Sage Meadows

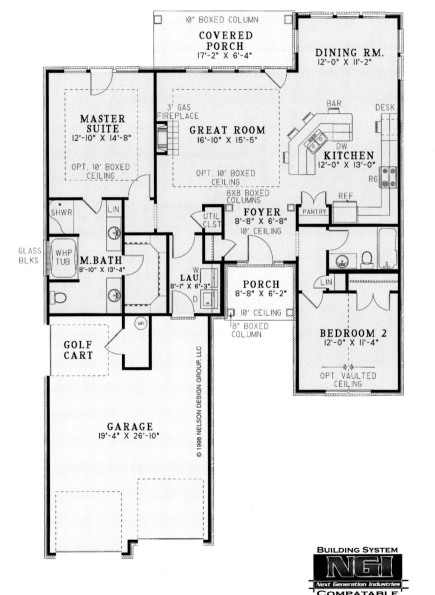

After a great game, drive your golf cart right off the course and up to your spacious two-car garage with side golf cart entry in this French Country Nelson Design Group home. Or come up the front walk and enter a beautiful porch with ten-foot ceiling and boxed columns leading to an open foyer and great room where you'll enjoy hours of relaxation and entertainment. Share conversation or sit in silent awe as you watch the calming lake from your rear covered porch.

Width: 43' 0"

Depth: 63' 6"

Total Living: 1,387 sq. ft.

Main Ceiling: 9 ft.

Price Tier: **A**

Bedrooms: 2

Baths: 2

Foundation: Crawl, Slab,
Optional Basement,
Optional Daylight Basement

Plan Options: page 282

286 Sage Meadows

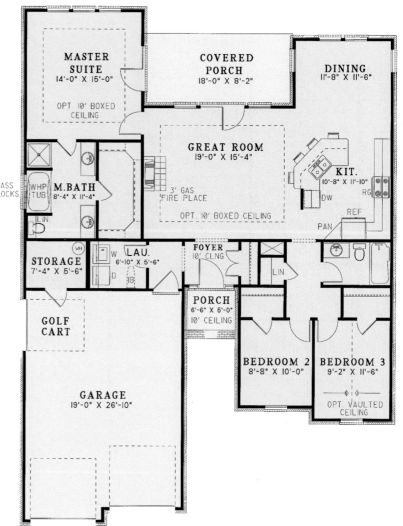

Whether entering through the traditional covered porch with ten-foot ceiling or the wonderful two-car garage with offset doors and side golf cart storage, this French Country Nelson Design Group home has plenty to offer. Passing through the foyer, you'll find an expansive great room complete with a gas fireplace and atrium doors leading to a rear covered porch, the ideal setting for grilling and entertaining. Enjoy the convenience of preparing meals in a spacious kitchen with angular island and eat-at bar. After a long day of work or play, relax in your private master suite with a beautiful view and access to the rear porch.

Width: 45' 0"

Depth: 60' 4"

Total Living: 1,472 sq. ft.

Main Ceiling: 9 ft.

Price Tier: A

Bedrooms: 3

Baths: 2

Foundation: Crawl, Slab

Plan Options: page 282

BUILDING SYSTEM
NGI
Next Generation Industries
COMPATABLE

283 Sage Meadows

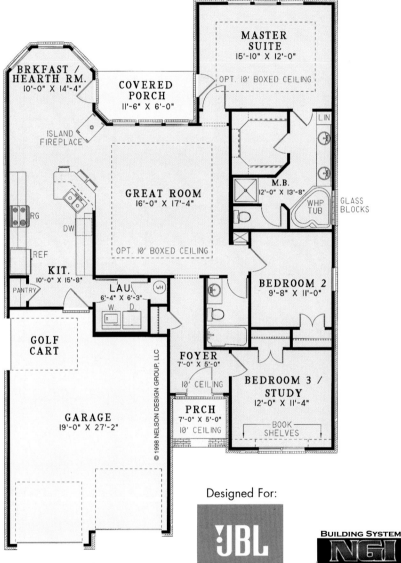

BRKFAST / HEARTH RM.
10'-0" X 14'-4"

COVERED PORCH
11'-6" X 6'-0"

MASTER SUITE
15'-10" X 12'-0"
OPT. 10' BOXED CEILING

ISLAND FIREPLACE

LIN

GREAT ROOM
16'-0" X 17'-4"
OPT. 10' BOXED CEILING

M.B.
12'-0" X 13'-8"

WHP TUB

GLASS BLOCKS

RG
DW
REF

KIT.
10'-0" X 15'-8"
PANTRY

LAU
6'-4" X 6'-3"
W   D

WH

BEDROOM 2
9'-8" X 11'-0"

GOLF CART

FOYER
7'-0" X 5'-0"
10' CEILING

BEDROOM 3 / STUDY
12'-0" X 11'-4"

GARAGE
19'-0" X 27'-2"

PRCH
7'-0" X 5'-0"
10' CEILING

BOOK SHELVES

© 1998 NELSON DESIGN GROUP, LLC

At the heart of this Nelson Design Group home is an impressive great room with ten-foot ceilings and peninsula fireplace. Off the great room, your family will enjoy meals together any time of day in the expansive kitchen. With an island, eat-at open bar, and breakfast nook complete with bay windows, you won't hear any excuses for not finding time to eat. A secluded private entrance with French doors from the master suite to a rear covered porch allows you the opportunity to "get away" from it all.

Width: 39' 4"	Bedrooms: 3
Depth: 63' 2"	Baths: 2
Total Living: 1,480 sq. ft.	Foundation: Crawl, Slab
Main Ceiling: 9 ft.	Plan Options: page 282
Price Tier: A	

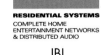
To Order Call 1.800.590.2423   **To view the rest of this collection visit www.nelsondesigngroup.com**

284 Sage Meadows

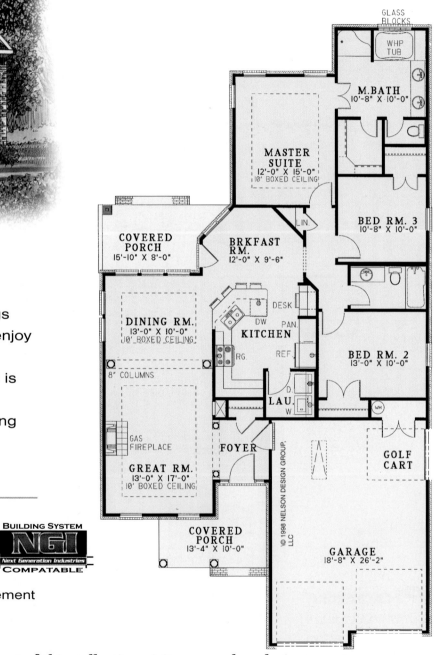

As you enter this Nelson Design Group home, you are welcomed onto a lovely covered porch with ten-foot ceilings and led directly into the traditional foyer. From there you'll enjoy a combination great room and dining area divided only by magnificent wooden columns. An easily accessible kitchen is accented by a breakfast nook complete with windows and entry to a rear covered grilling porch. Spend hours delighting friends and family with your grilling expertise.

Width: 39' 6"
Depth: 72' 5"
Total Living: 1,504 sq. ft.
Main Ceiling: 9 ft.
Price Tier: B

Bedrooms: 3
Baths: 2
Foundation: Crawl, Slab, Optional Basement, Optional Daylight Basement
Plan Options: page 282

BUILDING SYSTEM
NGI
Next Generation Industries
COMPATABLE

THE RiverBend™ COLLECTION

The River Bend Collection™ of cottage cabins, designed by Nelson Design Group, includes numerous unique designs perfect for second residences and relaxing getaways. Each River Bend Collection™ design has a living space of 1,200 to 1,500 square feet. There's a River Bend home perfect for your favorite setting. Enjoy fly fishing for rainbows, casting for lunker bass, deer hunting or a secluded weekend. Our spacious, feature-filled designs allow you to enjoy the great outdoors with all the comforts of home. Make memories that last a lifetime from your River Bend cottage cabin hideaway.

Nelson Design Group LLC

RESIDENTIAL & COMMERCIAL PLANNERS - DESIGNERS

NDG421

RIVER VIEW
River Bend Collection I

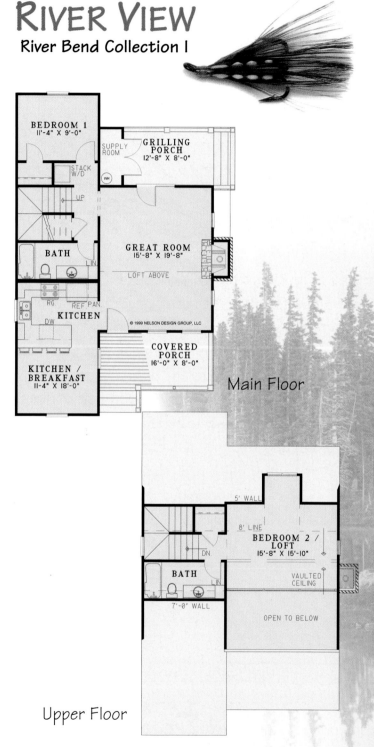

BEDROOM 1
11'-4" X 9'-0"

SUPPLY ROOM

STACK W/D

GRILLING PORCH
12'-8" X 8'-0"

UP

BATH

GREAT ROOM
15'-8" X 19'-8"

LOFT ABOVE

LIN

© 1999 NELSON DESIGN GROUP, LLC

RG. REF PAN

KITCHEN

DW

COVERED PORCH
16'-0" X 8'-0"

KITCHEN / BREAKFAST
11'-4" X 18'-0"

Main Floor

5' WALL

8' LINE

BEDROOM 2 / LOFT
15'-8" X 15'-10"

DN.

BATH

LIN

VAULTED CEILING

7'-0" WALL

OPEN TO BELOW

Upper Floor

Width:	30' 4"	
Depth:	44' 6"	
Main Floor:	859 sq. ft.	
Upper Floor:	319 sq. ft.	
Total Living:	1,178 sq. ft.	
Price Tier:	**A**	
Plan Options:	page 282	

Main Ceiling:	8 ft.
Upper Ceiling:	8 ft.
Bedrooms:	2
Baths:	2
Foundation:	Crawl, Slab, Optional Basement, Optional Daylight Basement

BUILDING SYSTEM
NGi
Next Generation Industries
COMPATABLE

Mom and Dad waved from the front porch as the children splashed in the water. It was always so wonderful coming up to their vacation spot on the River Bend. The mornings were composed of gathering flowers that sprang up along the banks of the river and important trout fishing lessons from Dad. Afternoons consisted of picnics on the riverbank and long walks in the woods. Evenings were spent beside the fireplace where each family member shared stories of the day's adventures. This was the view of life that they enjoyed...the one that took place at River View.

BLUFF'S EDGE

River Bend Collection I

Main Floor

BEDROOM 1
12'-0" X 11'-0"

SUPPLY ROOM

GRILLING PORCH
22'-6" X 8'-0"

CLEANING TABLE

PAN

STACKED W/D

DINING
10'-6" X 11'-4"

DW
KITCHEN
11'-8" X 11'-4"

REF

BEDROOM 2
11'-0" X 11'-0"

VAULTED CEILING

GREAT ROOM
22'-0" X 14'-4"

UP

© 1999 NELSON DESIGN GROUP, LLC

COVERED PORCH
18'-0" X 8'-0"

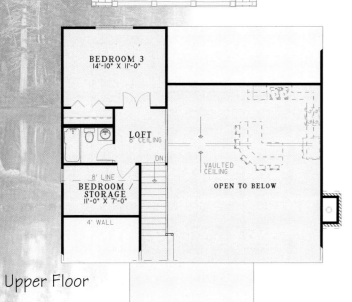

Upper Floor

BEDROOM 3
14'-10" X 11'-0"

LOFT
8' CEILING

8' LINE

BEDROOM / STORAGE
11'-0" X 7'-0"

4' WALL

DN

VAULTED CEILING

OPEN TO BELOW

NDG419

Width:	40' 4"	Main Ceiling:	8 ft.	
Depth:	41' 6"	Upper Ceiling:	8 ft.	
Main Floor:	1,070 sq. ft.	Bedrooms:	3	
Upper Floor:	304 sq. ft.	Baths:	2	
Total Living:	1,374 sq. ft.	Foundation:	Crawl, Slab, Optional Basement, Optional Daylight Basement	
Price Tier:	A			
Plan Options:	page 282			

BUILDING SYSTEM
NGI
Next Generation Industries
COMPATABLE

They reveled in the beauty of the forests' foliage as they hiked from the top of the mountain. Evergreens extended their arms to be touched by the sun's rays. Animals scampered about the ground and the trees. The family hiked from the cabin many times, but the views never ceased to take their breath away. The cabin sat on the edge of a bluff overlooking River Bend. The family vacations at Bluff's Edge were always a much anticipated time for family and friends.

PEBBLE CREEK
River Bend Collection I

NDG414

Main Floor

Main Floor plan labels:
- KITCHEN 9'-4" X 10'-10"
- REF
- PANTRY
- RG
- DW
- GRILLING PORCH 11'-8" X 6'-0"
- DINING 10'-0" X 13'-6"
- SUPPLY ROOM
- WH
- BATH
- STACK W/D
- DEN 15'-6" X 18'-10"
- BEDROOM 1 11'-4" X 11'-0"
- UP
- COVERED PORCH 20'-0" X 8'-0"
- © 1999 NELSON DESIGN GROUP, LLC

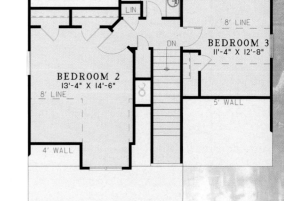

Upper Floor plan labels:
- BATH
- LIN
- 5' WALL
- 8' LINE
- DN
- BEDROOM 3 11'-4" X 12'-8"
- BEDROOM 2 13'-4" X 14'-6"
- 8' LINE
- 5' WALL
- 4' WALL

Upper Floor

Width:	31' 8"	Main Ceiling:	8 ft.
Depth:	38' 4"	Upper Ceiling:	8 ft.
Main Floor:	890 sq. ft.	Bedrooms:	3
Upper Floor:	507 sq. ft.	Baths:	2
Total Living:	1,397 sq. ft.	Foundation:	Crawl, Slab, Optional Basement, Optional Daylight Basement
Price Tier:	**A**		
Plan Options:	page 282		

BUILDING SYSTEM
NGI
Next Generation Industries
COMPATABLE

As the smooth stones skipped across the clear water, the children giggled with delight. Both remembered how Mom and Dad had taught them how to skip rocks - it was all in the wrist. There were many smooth, flat stones perfect for skipping that lined River Bend. At night, everyone would sit along the side of the river and talk about the adventures of the day. Adventures were always abundant...at Pebble Creek.

To Order Call 1.800.590.2423   Similar plans can be viewed and ordered at www.nelsondesigngroup.com

HUNTER'S DEN
River Bend Collection I

GRILLING PORCH 11'-8" X 6'-0"

KITCHEN 9'-4" X 10'-10"

REF. PANTRY

RG.

DW

DINING 10'-0" X 13'-6"

SUPPLY ROOM

BATH

STACK W/D

DEN 15'-6" X 18'-10"

© 1999 NELSON DESIGN GROUP LLC

UP

BEDROOM 1 11'-4" X 11'-0"

8' COVERED PORCH

Main Floor

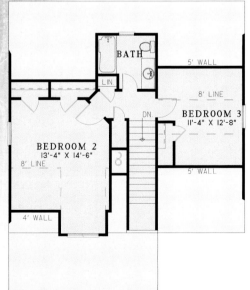

BATH

LIN

5' WALL

8' LINE

DN

BEDROOM 3 11'-4" X 12'-8"

BEDROOM 2 13'-4" X 14'-6"

8' LINE

5' WALL

4' WALL

Upper Floor

NDG416

Width:	39' 8"	Main Ceiling:	8 ft.
Depth:	38' 4"	Upper Ceiling:	8 ft.
Main Floor:	890 sq. ft.	Bedrooms:	3
Upper Floor:	507 sq. ft.	Baths:	2
Total Living:	1,397 sq. ft.	Foundation:	Crawl, Slab,
Price Tier:	**A**		Optional Basement,
Plan Options:	page 282		Optional Daylight Basement

BUILDING SYSTEM NGI Next Generation Industries **COMPATABLE**

A fter a brisk fall day, hunters gather here to reminisce over the day's events. Each brother has his own rendition of how big the deer that they encountered, really was. The days at Hunter's Den are like the leaves on a breeze, floating by with such peacefulness. As the men exchange stories on the front porch, their minds recall a time of when their parents had first built their getaway. Each brother remembered the hikes in the woods and exciting hunting trips with dad that all began here...at Hunter's Den.

To Order Call 1.800.590.2423   **Similar plans can be viewed and ordered at www.nelsondesigngroup.com**

NDG420

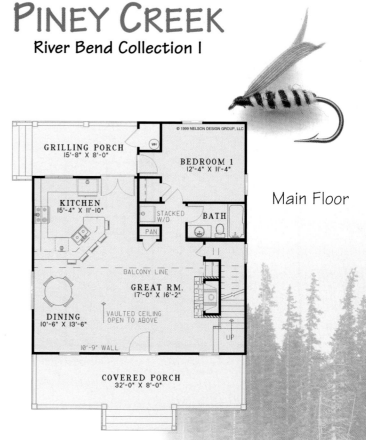

PINEY CREEK
River Bend Collection I

Main Floor

Main Floor plan labels:
- GRILLING PORCH 15'-8" X 8'-0"
- BEDROOM 1 12'-4" X 11'-4"
- KITCHEN 15'-4" X 11'-10"
- STACKED W/D
- BATH
- PAN
- BALCONY LINE
- GREAT RM. 17'-0" X 16'-2"
- DINING 10'-6" X 13'-6"
- VAULTED CEILING OPEN TO ABOVE
- UP
- 10'-9" WALL
- COVERED PORCH 32'-0" X 8'-0"
- © 1999 NELSON DESIGN GROUP, LLC

Width:	32' 0"	Main Ceiling:	8 ft.
Depth:	42' 0"	Upper Ceiling:	8 ft.
Main Floor:	948 sq. ft.	Bedrooms:	2
Upper Floor:	452 sq. ft.	Baths:	2
Total Living:	1,400 sq. ft.	Foundation:	Crawl, Slab,
Price Tier:	**A**		Optional Basement,
Plan Options:	page 282		Optional Daylight Basement

BUILDING SYSTEM NGI Next Generation Industries **COMPATABLE**

As he helped her up to the steps of the cabin, the couple began reminiscing about the many summers they had spent there. The summer afternoons when their children and grandchildren came to visit were undeniably the most treasured. Watching as they caught their first fish, floated on intertubes and picked flowers in the field always brought a smile to their faces. As they looked out across River Bend, they imagined many generations of their family spending their summers here...at Piney Creek.

Upper Floor plan labels:
- BEDROOM 2 11'-4" X 11'-8"
- STORAGE
- BATH
- SLEEPING LOFT 21'-0" X 8'-0"
- DN.
- VAULTED CEILING

Upper Floor

To Order Call 1.800.590.2423   **Similar plans can be viewed and ordered at www.nelsondesigngroup.com**

STONE BROOK

River Bend Collection I

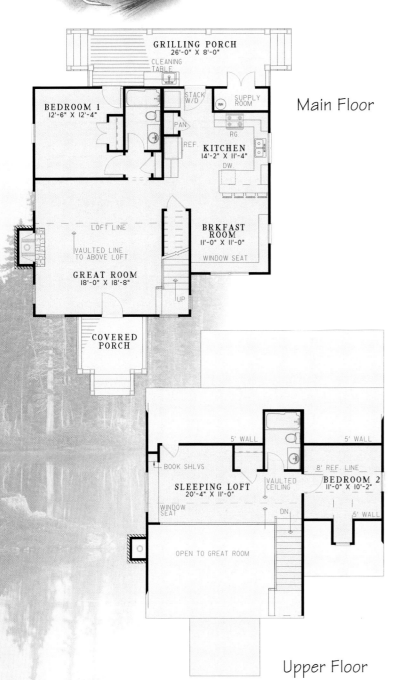

GRILLING PORCH
26'-0" X 8'-0"

CLEANING TABLE

STACK W/D

SUPPLY ROOM

WH

PAN

RG

REF.

BEDROOM 1
12'-6" X 12'-4"

KITCHEN
14'-2" X 11'-4"

DW

Main Floor

LOFT LINE

VAULTED LINE TO ABOVE LOFT

BRKFAST ROOM
11'-0" X 11'-0"

WINDOW SEAT

GREAT ROOM
18'-0" X 18'-8"

UP

COVERED PORCH

5' WALL   5' WALL

BOOK SHLVS

8' REF. LINE

SLEEPING LOFT
20'-4" X 11'-0"

VAULTED CEILING

BEDROOM 2
11'-0" X 10'-2"

WINDOW SEAT

DN

5' WALL

OPEN TO GREAT ROOM

Upper Floor

NDG422

Width:	36' 2"	Main Ceiling:	8 ft.
Depth:	48' 0"	Upper Ceiling:	8 ft.
Main Floor:	1,016 sq. ft.	Bedrooms:	2
Upper Floor:	409 sq. ft.	Baths:	2
Total Living:	1,425 sq. ft.	Foundation:	Crawl, Slab,
Price Tier:	**A**		Optional Basement,
Plan Options:	page 282		Optional Daylight Basement

BUILDING SYSTEM
NGi
Next Generation Industries
COMPATABLE

As she walked down the stairs from the loft, she could see the sun rising like a fire. Across the horizon, when she sat on the window seat and stared out into the dawning of a new day, she could see the water rippling onto the shore to greet the stones for the first time that day. Catching a glimpse of movement, her eyes focused on her husband displaying a stringer of fish caught that morning in River Bend. This would be the first of many memorable weekends and vacations...at Stone Brook.

CANOE POINT
River Bend Collection I

NDG418

Main Floor

Width:	44' 2"	
Depth:	39' 0"	
Main Floor:	1,140 sq. ft.	
Upper Floor:	332 sq. ft.	
Total Living:	1,472 sq. ft.*	
*Bonus:	199 sq. ft.	
Price Tier:	**A**	
Plan Options:	page 282	

Main Ceiling:	8 ft.
Upper Ceiling:	8 ft.
Bedrooms:	4
Baths:	2
Foundation:	Crawl, Slab, Optional Basement, Optional Daylight Basement

BUILDING SYSTEM
NGi
Next Generation Industries
COMPATABLE

They sat on the front porch and watched as the canoes floated by. People always enjoyed canoeing at this point of River Bend because of its thrilling rapids. Watching the canoes was a family event because of the variety of expressions on the canoeists faces and the screams of excitement as they battled the rapids. Mom would make scorecards for everyone to hold up to rate the thrill-seekers on their skills. Canoe Point was a memorable place that was familiar to all.

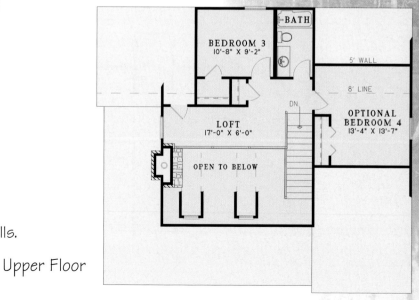

Upper Floor

To Order Call 1.800.590.2423 **Similar plans can be viewed and ordered at www.nelsondesigngroup.com**

TABLE ROCK
River Bend Collection I

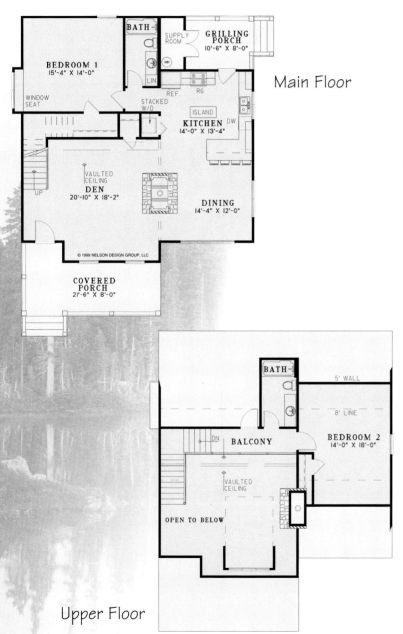

Main Floor

© 1999 NELSON DESIGN GROUP, LLC

BEDROOM 1
15'-4" X 14'-0"

WINDOW SEAT

BATH

SUPPLY ROOM

GRILLING PORCH
10'-6" X 8'-0"

LIN

REF.

RG

STACKED W/D

ISLAND

KITCHEN
14'-0" X 13'-4"

DW

VAULTED CEILING
DEN
20'-10" X 18'-2"

UP

DINING
14'-4" X 12'-0"

COVERED PORCH
21'-6" X 8'-0"

Upper Floor

BATH

5' WALL

8' LINE

DN

BALCONY

BEDROOM 2
14'-0" X 18'-0"

VAULTED CEILING

OPEN TO BELOW

NDG423

Width:	37' 2"	Main Ceiling:	8 ft.
Depth:	45' 0"	Upper Ceiling:	8 ft.
Main Floor:	1,159 sq. ft.	Bedrooms:	2
Upper Floor:	383 sq. ft.	Baths:	2
Total Living:	1,542 sq. ft.	Foundation:	Crawl, Slab,
Price Tier:	**B**		Optional Basement,
Plan Options:	page 282		Optional Daylight Basement

BUILDING SYSTEM
NGI
Next Generation Industries
COMPATABLE

They giggled with delight as the fish began to nibble on their toes as they dipped their feet into the water. The children always loved the lazy summers at Grandma's and Grandpa's cabin. They loved the early morning swims in River Bend's cool waters and the lemonade that Grandma served in the afternoons. What they especially enjoyed, was laying on the large flat rock that allowed the rivers water to gently splash over its surface providing cool relief from the summer's heat. The days here at Table Rock would always be home to their fondest memories.

CREEK SIDE
River Bend Collection I

Main Floor

GRILLING PORCH
32'-0" X 8'-0"

CLEANING TABLE

SUPPLY ROOM

KITCHEN
12'-2" X 11'-4"

BEDROOM 2
11'-0" X 8'-8"

DINING
9'-0" X 14'-2"

BATH

Vaulted Ceiling

GREAT ROOM
20'-0" X 17'-6"

STACK W/D

UP

BEDROOM 1
11'-0" X 11'-6"

COVERED PORCH
32'-0" X 8'-0"

© 1999 NELSON DESIGN GROUP, LLC

NDG415

Width:	34' 4"	Main Ceiling:	8 ft.
Depth:	48' 4"	Upper Ceiling:	8 ft.
Main Floor:	1,031 sq. ft.	Bedrooms:	3
Upper Floor:	513 sq. ft.	Baths:	2
Total Living:	1,544 sq. ft.	Foundation:	Crawl, Slab,
Price Tier:	**B**		Optional Basement,
Plan Options:	page 282		Optional Daylight Basement

BUILDING SYSTEM
NGI
Next Generation Industries
COMPATABLE

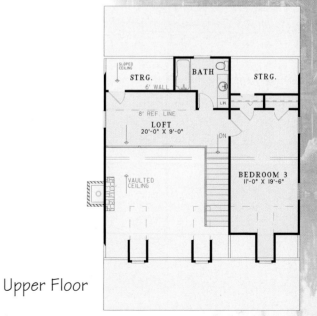

SLOPED CEILING

STRG.

BATH

STRG.

6' WALL

8' REF. LINE

LOFT
20'-0" X 9'-0"

DN

Vaulted Ceiling

BEDROOM 3
11'-0" X 19'-6"

Upper Floor

He began thinking where he was as he cast the fly rod upstream. A dream world. Not just any ole' dream world, but his dream world. Everything was as he had always imagined and hoped for. The cold, crisp waters of River Bend tickled his legs with its voice. Across the river, a trout leaped to an unknown destination. The porch of the cabin beckoned him to come and relax in the cool shade. The sun showered it's rays onto the water causing him to catch a glimpse of his own reflection. He was always a happy man when he was at his dream getaway called Creek Side.

LAKE SIDE
River Bend Collection I

Main Floor

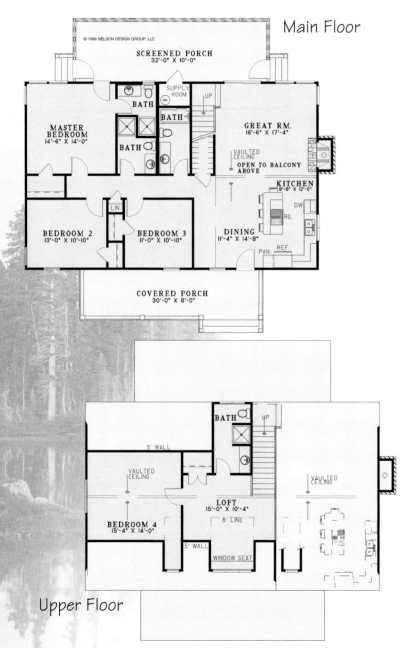

© 1999 NELSON DESIGN GROUP, LLC

SCREENED PORCH
32'-0" X 10'-0"

SUPPLY ROOM
UP

BATH

BATH

GREAT RM.
16'-6" X 17'-4"

MASTER BEDROOM
14'-6" X 14'-0"

BATH

VAULTED CEILING
OPEN TO BALCONY ABOVE

KITCHEN
8'-8" X 12'-0"

DW

LIN

BEDROOM 2
13'-0" X 10'-10"

BEDROOM 3
11'-0" X 10'-10"

DINING
11'-4" X 14'-8"

PAN. REF.

COVERED PORCH
30'-0" X 8'-0"

Upper Floor

BATH
UP

5' WALL

VAULTED CEILING

VAULTED CEILING

LOFT
15'-0" X 10'-4"

8' LINE

BEDROOM 4
15'-4" X 14'-0"

5' WALL

WINDOW SEAT

NDG417

Width:	50' 4"	Main Ceiling:	8 ft.
Depth:	48' 0"	Upper Ceiling:	8 ft.
Main Floor:	1,440 sq. ft.	Bedrooms:	4
Upper Floor:	530 sq. ft.	Baths:	4
Total Living:	1,970 sq. ft.	Foundation:	Crawl, Slab,
Price Tier:	**B**		Optional Basement,
Plan Options:	page 282		Optional Daylight Basement

BUILDING SYSTEM
NGI
Next Generation Industries
COMPATABLE

They woke up early that summer morning to watch the sun rise over the mountains. As they sat on the porch drinking coffee, they began talking about the future. This was only the first of many vacations at their new retreat. They began dreaming of the fishing lessons with their children and the nighttime storytelling beside the fireplace. This was a place in which to build traditions. Traditions that would last throughout the generations. Traditions that would begin here...at Lake Side.

CANYON STREAM
River Bend Collection II

Main Floor

Upper Floor

© 2002 NELSON DESIGN GROUP, LLC.

BEDROOM 1 11'-4" X 12'-10"

SCREENED PORCH 12'-4" X 8'-0"

GARAGE 26'-8" X 21'-4"

BATH 9'-0" X 5'-0"

GLASS BLOCKS

GREAT ROOM 15'-8" X 19'-8"

KITCHEN 11'-8" X 12'-0"

VAULTED CEILING OPEN TO LOFT ABOVE

DINING AREA 11'-4" X 9'-6"

COVERED PORCH 16'-0" X 8'-0"

BEDROOM 2 / LOFT 15'-8" X 11'-7"

VAULTED CEILING

BATH 11'-4" X 5'-0"

OPEN TO BELOW

VAULTED CEILING

NDG623

Width:	56' 6"	Main Ceiling:	9 ft.
Depth:	51' 0"	Upper Ceiling:	8 ft.
Main Floor:	972 sq. ft.	Bedrooms:	2
Upper Floor:	322 sq. ft.	Baths:	2
Total Living:	1,294 sq. ft.	Foundation:	Crawl, Slab,
Price Tier:	**A**		Optional Basement,
Plan Options:	page 282		Optional Daylight Basement

BUILDING SYSTEM
NGi
Next Generation Industries
COMPATABLE

Mom and Dad always liked to spend time together at our family cabin. This past summer Dad told mom he was building a garage for our fishing and hunting gear – but we knew different. It was Mom and Dad's 30th wedding anniversary and Dad had a special gift for her...a bright red convertible! Our Mom who loves sitting in a fishing boat on the lake all day loved that shiny new car. Now, after a long workweek in the city Mom can't wait to drive that little car to our favorite family getaway.... at Canyon Stream.

To Order Call 1.800.590.2423   **Similar plans can be viewed and ordered at www.nelsondesigngroup.com**

CAROL'S CABIN
River Bend Collection II

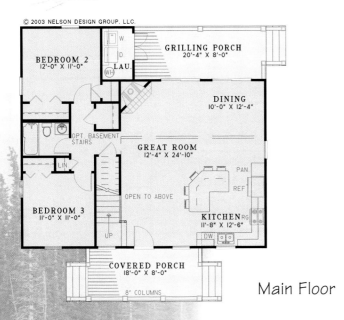

© 2003 NELSON DESIGN GROUP, LLC.

BEDROOM 2
12'-0" X 11'-0"

GRILLING PORCH
20'-4" X 8'-0"

W
D
LAU.
WH

OPT. BASEMENT STAIRS

DINING
10'-0" X 12'-4"

GREAT ROOM
12'-4" X 24'-10"

OPEN TO ABOVE

LIN

BEDROOM 3
11'-0" X 11'-0"

UP

PAN.
REF

KITCHEN
11'-8" X 12'-6"

DW
RG

COVERED PORCH
18'-0" X 8'-0"

8" COLUMNS

Main Floor

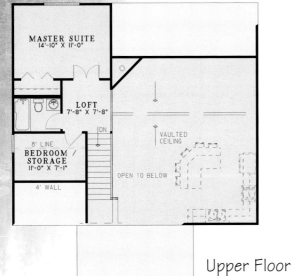

MASTER SUITE
14'-10" X 11'-0"

LOFT
7'-8" X 7'-8"

VAULTED CEILING

8' LINE

DN

BEDROOM / STORAGE
11'-0" X 7'-1"

4' WALL

OPEN TO BELOW

Upper Floor

NDG649

Width:	38' 0"	Main Ceiling:	8 ft.
Depth:	41' 6"	Upper Ceiling:	8 ft.
Main Floor:	1,070 sq. ft.	Bedrooms:	4
Upper Floor:	388 sq. ft.	Baths:	2
Total Living:	1,458 sq. ft.	Foundation:	Crawl, Slab,
Price Tier:	A		Optional Basement,
Plan Options:	page 282		Optional Daylight Basement

BUILDING SYSTEM
NGI
Next Generation Industries
COMPATABLE

My great grandparents built this cabin back in the fifties and we still spend our summers and fall weekends there enjoying the lake and playing cards at night. My granddad told me about the time my great-grandfather caught a wild turkey and let it go inside the cabin. Good think it was blind in one eye - he finally caught it an hour later but couldn't find grandma awhile! And the old stone fireplace is actually made of the rock they found on their fishing trips. This family cabin we call Carol's Cabin is full of wonderful memories that we'll never forget.

MOSS COVE
River Bend Collection II

© 2002 NELSON DESIGN GROUP, LLC.

SCREENED PORCH
15'-2" X 10'-4"

DINING
11'-8" X 11'-6"

KITCHEN
12'-10" X 11'-6"

REF · DW · OVEN MW

GARAGE
21'-4" X 21'-4"

CT

42" BAR

PAN

WH

BATH
9'-2" X 6'-2"

D · W

LIN

GREAT ROOM
22'-2" X 21'-4"

BEDROOM 1
11'-0" X 13'-6"

UP

VAULTED CEILING
OPEN TO ABOVE

NDG624

COVERED PORCH
38'-0" X 8'-0"

Main Floor

Width:	64' 0"	Main Ceiling:	9 ft.
Depth:	41' 6"	Upper Ceiling:	8 ft.
Main Floor:	1,156 sq. ft.	Bedrooms:	2
Upper Floor:	747 sq. ft.	Baths:	2
Total Living:	1,903 sq. ft.	Foundation:	Crawl, Slab,
Price Tier:	**B**		Optional Basement,
Plan Options:	page 282		Optional Daylight Basement

BUILDING SYSTEM
NGi Next Generation Industries
COMPATABLE

BEDROOM 2
14'-10" X 11'-8"

5' WALL

8' LINE

BATH
11'-0" X 14'-8"

DN

SLEEPING LOFT
22'-2" X 14'-7"

ATTIC ACC.

8' LINE

FRENCH DOORS

RAILING

5' WALL

OPEN TO BELOW

Upper Floor

My fondest memories are spending the fall weekends with my best friend at our cabin at Moss Cove. Billy and I used to scare my brothers at night by throwing pine needles on them as they tried to fall asleep. We had the best place to camp out in the upstairs loft and Mom would let us stay up all night — if we could. We still to this day play cards on the screened in porch and listen to the crickets chirp. I hope my kids have wonderful memories like I do and someday.... Maybe my grandchildren will reminisce about their campouts in the upstairs loft.

To Order Call 1.800.590.2423   Similar plans can be viewed and ordered at www.nelsondesigngroup.com

THE *Florida* COLLECTION

An oasis of amenities in twelve designs created for a warm climate. These designs range between 1,800 to 3,600 square feet and include open spacious living areas, luxurious master suites and lanais perfect for entertaining. High ceilings and columns are used throughout giving a grand effect while arched openings and a plenitude of windows allow natural light to shine throughout. Visit our website to view the remaining plans not shown here.

Nelson Design Group LLC

RESIDENTIAL & COMMERCIAL PLANNERS - DESIGNERS

The Austin

Total living: 2,388 s.f.
Bedrooms: 4, Baths: 2-1/2
Width: 68' 6" Depth: 64' 8"
Price Category: C

The Armhurst

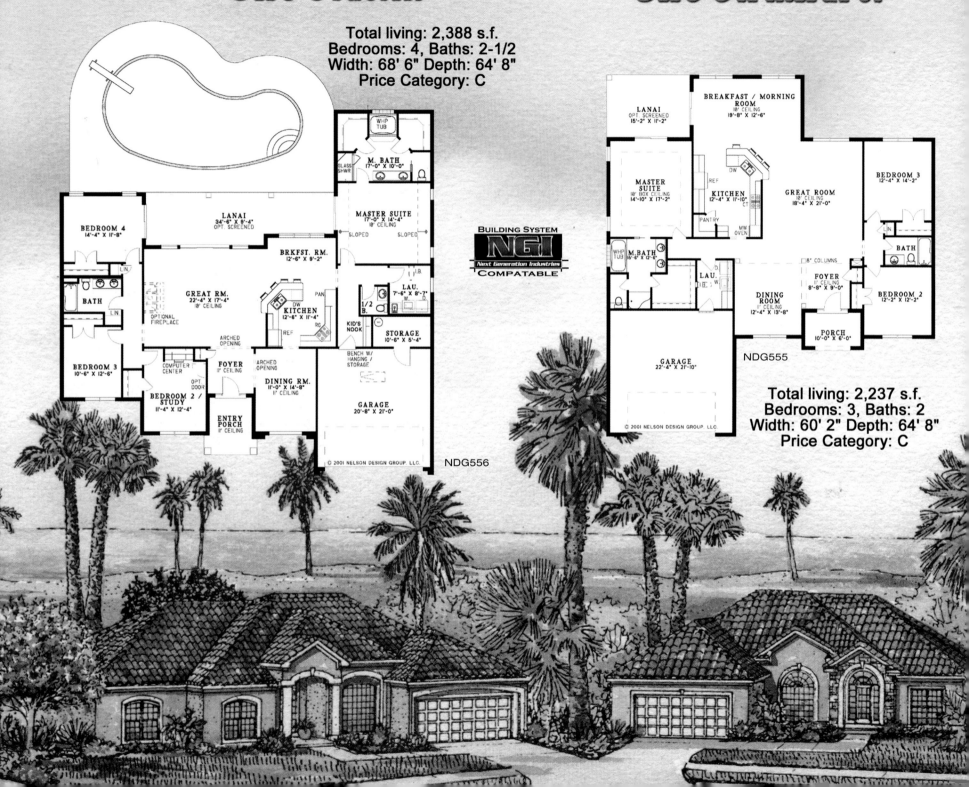

BUILDING SYSTEM
NGI
Next Generation Industries
COMPATABLE

The Austin plan labels:
- WHP TUB
- M. BATH 17'-0" X 10'-0"
- GLASS SHWR
- LANAI 34'-6" X 9'-4" OPT. SCREENED
- MASTER SUITE 17'-0" X 14'-4" 10' CEILING
- SLOPED / SLOPED
- BRKFST. RM. 12'-6" X 9'-2"
- BEDROOM 4 14'-4" X 11'-8"
- GREAT RM. 22'-4" X 17'-4" 10' CEILING
- OPTIONAL FIREPLACE
- DW
- KITCHEN 12'-6" X 11'-4"
- PAN
- LAU. 7'-6" X 8'-7" W. D.
- L.B.
- BATH
- LIN
- 1/2 B.
- KID'S NOOK
- ARCHED OPENING
- REF
- RG
- STORAGE 10'-6" X 5'-4"
- BEDROOM 3 10'-6" X 12'-6"
- COMPUTER CENTER
- FOYER 11' CEILING
- ARCHED OPENING
- DINING RM. 11'-0" X 14'-8" 11' CEILING
- BENCH W/ HANGING / STORAGE
- BEDROOM 2 / STUDY 11'-4" X 12'-4"
- OPT DOOR
- ENTRY PORCH 11' CEILING
- GARAGE 20'-8" X 21'-0"
- © 2001 NELSON DESIGN GROUP, LLC.
- NDG556

The Armhurst plan labels:
- LANAI OPT. SCREENED 15'-2" X 11'-4"
- BREAKFAST / MORNING ROOM 10' CEILING 19'-8" X 12'-6"
- BEDROOM 3 12'-4" X 14'-2"
- MASTER SUITE 10' BOX CEILING 14'-10" X 17'-2"
- REF
- DW
- KITCHEN 12'-4" X 11'-10" CT.
- GREAT ROOM 10' CEILING 18'-4" X 21'-0"
- PANTRY
- MW OVEN
- LIN
- BATH
- WHP TUB
- M. BATH 16'-6" X 12'-6"
- LAU.
- L.B.
- W D
- 8" COLUMNS
- FOYER 11' CEILING 8'-8" X 9'-0"
- BEDROOM 2 12'-2" X 12'-2"
- DINING ROOM 11' CEILING 12'-4" X 13'-8"
- GARAGE 22'-4" X 21'-10"
- PORCH 10'-0" X 6'-0"
- NDG555
- © 2001 NELSON DESIGN GROUP, LLC.

Total living: 2,237 s.f.
Bedrooms: 3, Baths: 2
Width: 60' 2" Depth: 64' 8"
Price Category: C

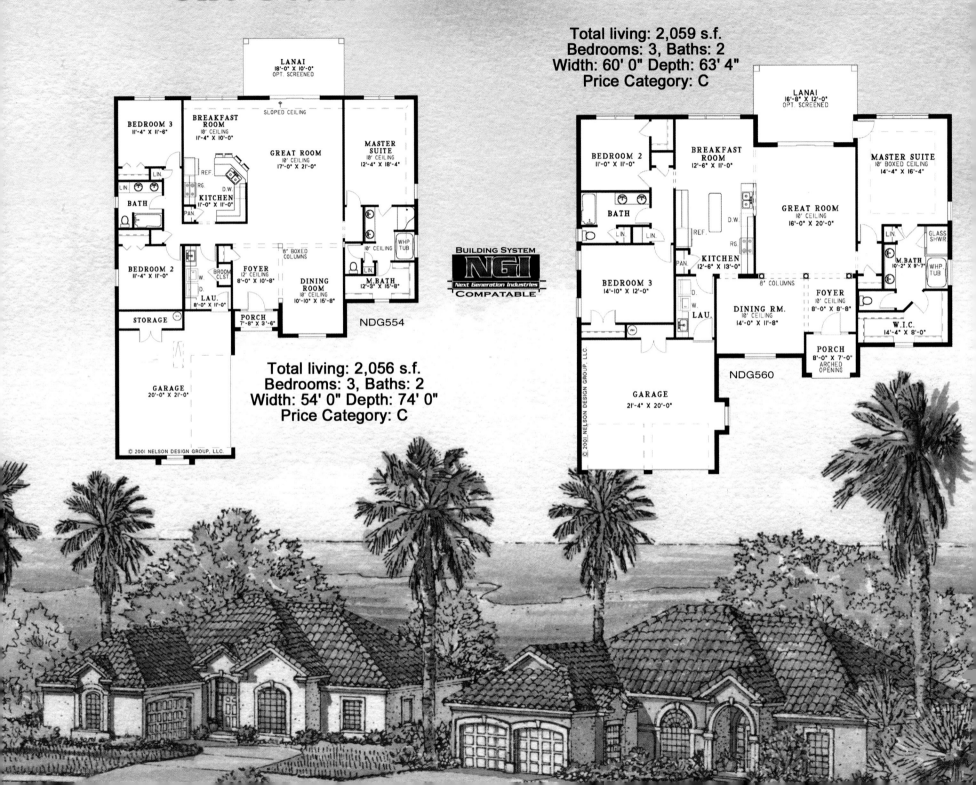

The Devon

LANAI
18'-0" X 10'-0"
OPT. SCREENED

SLOPED CEILING

BEDROOM 3
11'-4" X 11'-6"

BREAKFAST ROOM
10' CEILING
11'-4" X 10'-0"

GREAT ROOM
10' CEILING
17'-0" X 21'-0"

MASTER SUITE
10' CEILING
12'-4" X 18'-4"

LIN.

REF.

RG.

LIN.

D.W.

BATH

KITCHEN
11'-0" X 11'-0"

PAN.

10' CEILING

WHP TUB

BEDROOM 2
11'-4" X 11'-0"

BROOM CLST.

FOYER
12' CEILING
8'-0" X 10'-8"

8" BOXED COLUMNS

DINING ROOM
10' CEILING
10'-10" X 15'-8"

M.BATH
12'-3" X 15'-8"

LIN.

W.

D.

LAU.
8'-0" X 11'-0"

STORAGE

PORCH
7'-8" X 3'-6"

NDG554

GARAGE
20'-0" X 21'-0"

© 2001 NELSON DESIGN GROUP, LLC.

Total living: 2,056 s.f.
Bedrooms: 3, Baths: 2
Width: 54' 0" Depth: 74' 0"
Price Category: C

The Avalon

Total living: 2,059 s.f.
Bedrooms: 3, Baths: 2
Width: 60' 0" Depth: 63' 4"
Price Category: C

LANAI
16'-8" X 12'-0"
OPT. SCREENED

BEDROOM 2
11'-0" X 11'-0"

BREAKFAST ROOM
12'-6" X 11'-0"

MASTER SUITE
10' BOXED CEILING
14'-4" X 16'-4"

BATH

LIN.

LIN.

D.W.

GREAT ROOM
10' CEILING
16'-0" X 20'-0"

LIN.

GLASS SHWR

REF.

RG.

M.BATH
10'-2" X 9'-7"

KITCHEN
12'-6" X 13'-0"

PAN.

8" COLUMNS

WHP TUB

BEDROOM 3
14'-10" X 12'-0"

D.

LAU.

FOYER
10' CEILING
8'-0" X 8'-8"

DINING RM.
10' CEILING
14'-0" X 11'-8"

W.I.C.
14'-4" X 8'-0"

PORCH
8'-0" X 7'-0"
ARCHED OPENING

NDG560

GARAGE
21'-4" X 20'-0"

© 2001 NELSON DESIGN GROUP, LLC.

BUILDING SYSTEM
NGI
Next Generation Industries
COMPATABLE

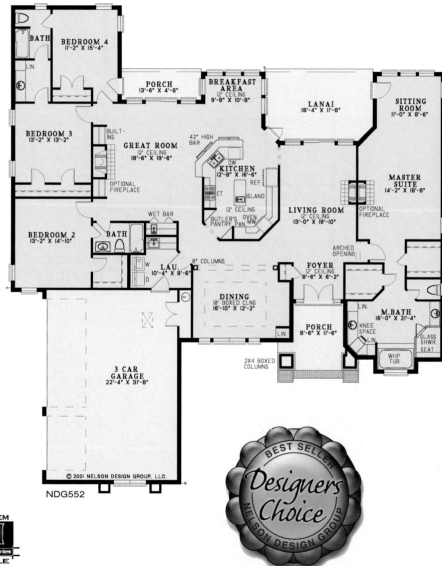

The Evandale
The Florida Collection

*T*his sprawling four-bedroom plan from Nelson Design Group centers on an ultra-functional kitchen accessing all living areas with ease. A handy eat-at bar and island help make this kitchen any gourmet's dream reality. Separate living and great rooms each flaunt gas fireplaces and lots of open space. All three secondary bedrooms feature private bath accesses. The exquisite master suite presents a radiant fireplace, large sitting area, private entrance to the lanai and a massive bath that includes his and her walk-in closets and an oversized whirlpool bath.

Width: 74' 2"	Bedrooms: 4
Depth: 81' 2"	Baths: 3
Total Living: 3,021 sq. ft.	Foundation: Slab
Main Ceiling: 9' 4"	Plan Options: page 282
Price Tier: E	

BUILDING SYSTEM
NGi
Next Generation Industries
COMPATABLE

Designers Choice — BEST SELLER — NELSON DESIGN GROUP

NDG552

To Order Call 1.800.590.2423   **To view the rest of this collection visit www.nelsondesigngroup.com**

E very day, in communities across the country, more and more homebuyers are leaving conventional 'cookie-cutter' developments in search of something special. In increasing numbers, discerning buyers are choosing log homes for their warmth, beauty and natural charm.

When they choose a Jim Barna log home, they get much more – a builder friendly, well engineered building system, low maintenance, energy efficient with a lifetime warranty on all log elements. They also get personalized service, access to experienced log builders and special prices on major home items from financing to fixtures. Maybe that's why BUILDER magazine ranked Jim Barna Log Systems as the #1 log home company in America.*

Welcome to our Neighborhood... of Log Homes

Jim Barna is proud to offer plans and design services through Nelson Design Group by exclusive arrangement. The next 12 pages of plans, plus the other plans included on our websites, represent the latest concepts in comfortable living. For the full collection of collaborative plans and ideas, visit nelsondesigngroup.com or jimbarna.com.

* (Builder Magazine, May 2002)

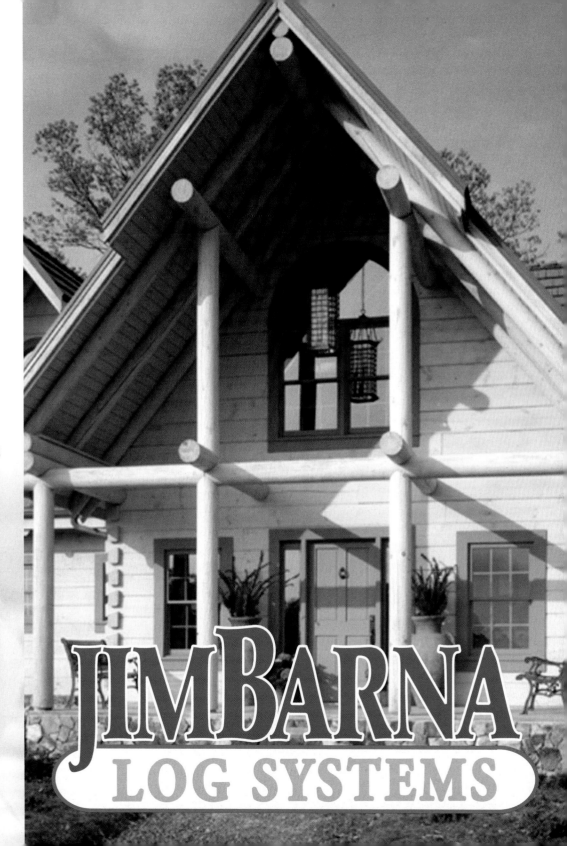

LOG HOMES TODAY'S CHOICE FOR COMFORTABLE LIVING

No longer mere 'cabins,' today's log homes are built around today's families. Using modern milling techniques and specialized construction methods, solid log homes offer unparalleled structural integrity, keeping your family warm, safe and secure in any climate. And, by featuring all natural elements, from log walls to timber beams and trusses and knotty pine ceilings, Jim Barna log homes are the perfect 'stress relief' for today's busy lifestyle. It's no wonder that log homes are one of the fastest growing trends in the current housing market.

LET THE LIGHT SHINE IN

Cabins used to be small, dark and dreary. Not so today. Homes from Jim Barna Log Systems tend to feature open, spacious rooms, often with vaulted ceilings and lots of glass. Large kitchens, great rooms, porches and decks make our homes great for entertaining friends or just enjoying family, and the perfect choice for "indoor/outdoor living." And the large master suites can be as lavish as you like!

SOUND INVESTMENT

Even with all the features we build into our homes, they are more affordable than one might think. In fact, with infinite choices in styles and amenities, we can offer homes in every price point and budget, from vacation cottages and starter homes for growing families to high-end executive and retirement homes. According to a study done by the National Association of Home Builders, log homes are an excellent investment, appreciating in value at nearly twice the rate of conventional 'stick-built' homes. Plus, Jim Barna helps protect your investment with the strongest warranty in the industry - a lifetime warranty on all log elements, and an available 10-year structural warranty from Bonded Builders Home Warranty Association on all other building materials we supply.

Contact your Jim Barna representative for specific details.

BUILDER'S CHOICE – AND CHOICE BUILDERS!

More builders choose Jim Barna Log Systems than any other log home producer. It's not just for the top quality, kiln-dried materials. We offer builders and homebuyers more - more training, more support, and more options. It starts with our special construction school for builders - The Jim Barna Log Home Institute, where builders learn the specialized techniques that give our homes such strength and beauty. We also have a Builder Services Department to give live support to builders during the construction process.

Giving the best builder support brings us the best builders. You can find them on our National Log Builders Registry, where we list the contact information and experience of hundreds of builders who have completed our classes. These builders, from all over the U.S., are listed exclusively for Jim Barna clients needing construction services. No other log home producer can offer such service!

SEE FOR YOURSELF

Discover for yourself the beauty, comfort and affordability of a Jim Barna log home. With so many choices of plans, log styles and options, you're sure to find a home that's just perfect for your family - and your budget. And, with custom design services from Nelson Design Group, we can create an original design just for you.

So, why not take the next step. To speak with a Jim Barna Building Consultant, to find the nearest Jim Barna representative, or to order our full color catalog of plans and information, call 1-800-962-4734. To see our full portfolio of standard plans online, visit either www.jimbarna.com or www.nelsondesigngroup.com. Either way, we look forward to helping you find a new home that is truly something special.

JIMBARNA
LOG SYSTEMS

www.jimbarna.com

builders@jimbarna.com

P.O. Box 4529, Oneida, TN 37841

800-962-4734

NDG1055

The Hemingway

Width: 29' 0"

Depth: 37' 0"

Main Floor: 609 sq. ft.

Upper Floor: 368 sq. ft.

Total Living: 977 sq. ft.

Foundations: Crawl, Optional Basement,
Optional Daylight Basement

Plan Options: page 282

Price Tier: A

Main Floor

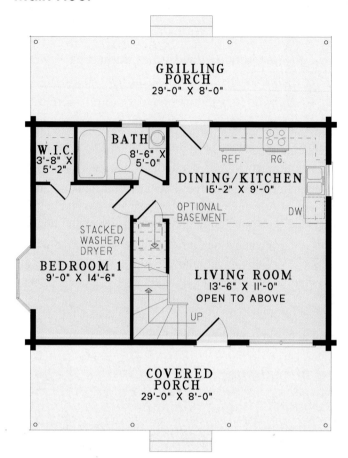

Upper Floor

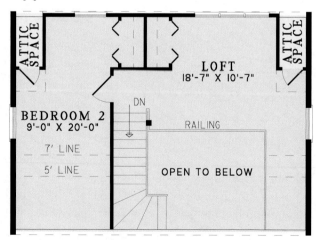

To Order Call 1.800.590.2423   To view the rest of this collection visit www.nelsondesigngroup.com

Main Floor

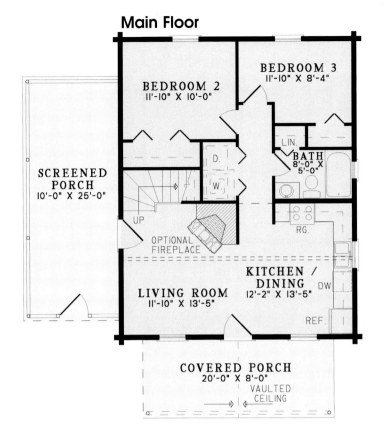

SCREENED PORCH
10'-0" X 25'-0"

BEDROOM 2
11'-10" X 10'-0"

BEDROOM 3
11'-10" X 8'-4"

D.

W.

UP

LIN.

BATH
8'-0" X 5'-0"

OPTIONAL FIREPLACE

RG.

KITCHEN / DINING
12'-2" X 13'-5"

DW

LIVING ROOM
11'-10" X 13'-5"

REF.

COVERED PORCH
20'-0" X 8'-0"
VAULTED CEILING

Upper Floor

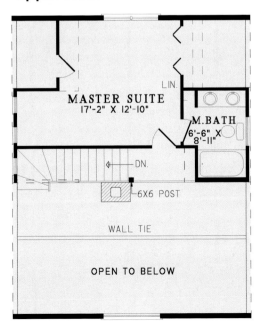

LIN.

MASTER SUITE
17'-2" X 12'-10"

M.BATH
6'-6" X 8'-11"

DN.

6X6 POST

WALL TIE

OPEN TO BELOW

NDG1028

The Spruce Creek

Width: 35' 0"

Depth: 39' 0"

Main Floor: 775 sq. ft.

Upper Floor: 347 sq. ft.

Total Living: 1,122 sq. ft.

Foundation: Crawl, Optional Basement,
Optional Daylight Basement

Plan Options: page 282

Price Tier: A

Main Floor

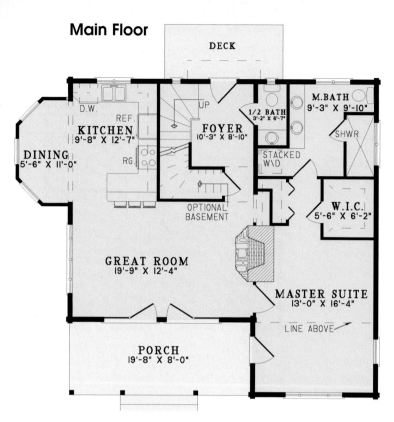

DECK

KITCHEN
9'-8" X 12'-7"

D.W.

REF.

RG.

DINING
5'-6" X 11'-0"

UP

FOYER
10'-3" X 8'-10"

1/2 BATH
3'-2" X 6'-7"

M.BATH
9'-3" X 9'-10"

SHWR

STACKED
W\D

W.I.C.
5'-6" X 6'-2"

OPTIONAL
BASEMENT

GREAT ROOM
19'-9" X 12'-4"

MASTER SUITE
13'-0" X 16'-4"

LINE ABOVE

PORCH
19'-8" X 8'-0"

NDG1007

Upper Floor

OPEN TO
BELOW

STRG

5' WALL

BATH 2
12'-9" X 6'-7"

7' LINE

RAILING

OPEN TO
BELOW

DN

6X6 POST

BEDROOM 2
12'-11" X 15'-1"

7' LINE

5' LINE

OPEN TO
BELOW

WALL TIE

OPEN TO
BELOW

The Baxter

Width: 39' 10"

Depth: 39' 8"

Main Floor: 1,059 sq. ft.

Upper Floor: 390 sq. ft.

Total Living: 1,449 sq. ft.

Foundations: Crawl, Optional Basement,
Optional Daylight Basement

Plan Options: page 282

Price Tier: **A**

To Order Call 1.800.590.2423   To view the rest of this collection visit www.nelsondesigngroup.com

The Westwind I

Width: 52' 0"

Depth: 40' 0"

Main Floor: 1,392 sq. ft.

Upper Floor: 110 sq. ft.

Total Living: 1,502 sq. ft.

Foundation: Crawl, Optional Basement,
Optional Daylight Basement

Plan Options: page 282

Price Tier: B

NDG1024

Main Floor

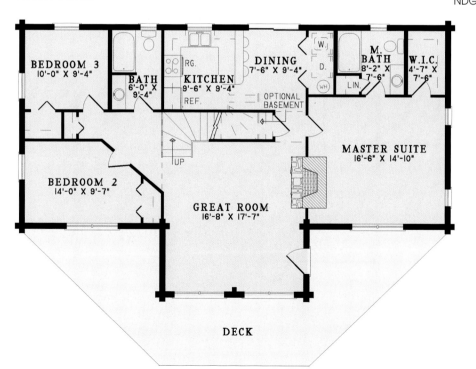

BEDROOM 3
10'-0" X 9'-4"

BATH
6'-0" X 9'-4"

KITCHEN
9'-6" X 9'-4"

RG.

REF.

DINING
7'-6" X 9'-4"

W.
D.

WH

LIN.

M. BATH
8'-2" X 7'-6"

W.I.C.
4'-7" X 7'-6"

OPTIONAL BASEMENT

UP

MASTER SUITE
16'-6" X 14'-10"

BEDROOM 2
14'-0" X 9'-7"

GREAT ROOM
16'-8" X 17'-7"

DECK

Upper Floor

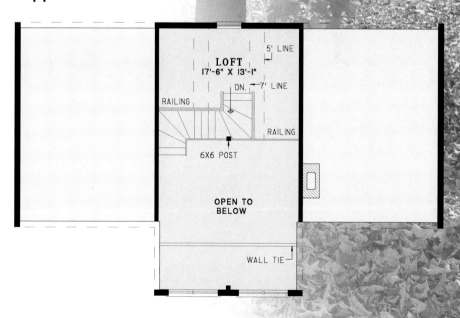

LOFT
17'-6" X 13'-1"

5' LINE

DN.   7' LINE

RAILING

RAILING

6X6 POST

OPEN TO BELOW

WALL TIE

Main Floor

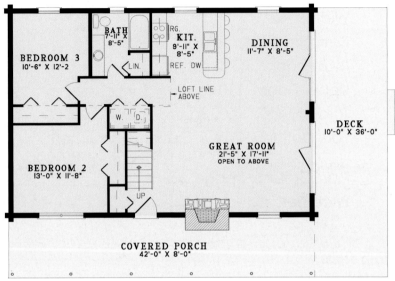

BEDROOM 3
10'-6" X 12'-2"

BATH
7'-11" X
8'-5"

KIT.
9'-11" X
8'-5"
RG.
REF. DW

DINING
11'-7" X 8'-5"

LIN.

LOFT LINE
ABOVE

W. D.

BEDROOM 2
13'-0" X 11'-8"

GREAT ROOM
21'-5" X 17'-11"
OPEN TO ABOVE

DECK
10'-0" X 36'-0"

UP

COVERED PORCH
42'-0" X 8'-0"

NDG1029

Upper Floor

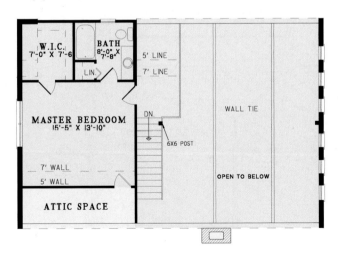

W.I.C.
7'-0" X 7'-6"

BATH
8'-5" X
7'-8"

LIN.

5' LINE

7' LINE

MASTER BEDROOM
15'-5" X 13'-10"

DN.

WALL TIE

6X6 POST

7' WALL

5' WALL

OPEN TO BELOW

ATTIC SPACE

The Shadow Ridge

Width: 52' 0"

Depth: 36' 0"

Main Floor: 1,392 sq. ft.

Upper Floor: 199 sq. ft.

Total Living: 1,591 sq. ft.

Foundation: Crawl, Optional Basement,
Optional Daylight Basement

Plan Options: page 282

Price Tier: B

To Order Call 1.800.590.2423   To view the rest of this collection visit www.nelsondesigngroup.com

Main Floor

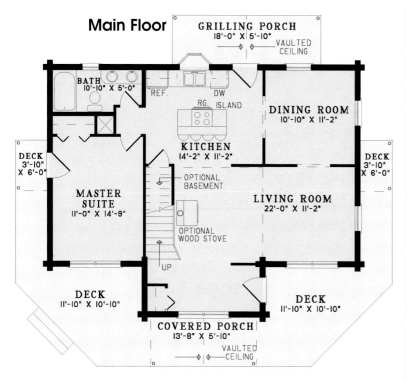

GRILLING PORCH
18'-0" X 5'-10"
VAULTED CEILING

BATH
10'-10" X 5'-0"

REF. DW

RG ISLAND

DINING ROOM
10'-10" X 11'-2"

KITCHEN
14'-2" X 11'-2"

DECK
3'-10"
X 6'-0"

DECK
3'-10"
X 6'-0"

OPTIONAL BASEMENT

MASTER SUITE
11'-0" X 14'-9"

LIVING ROOM
22'-0" X 11'-2"

OPTIONAL WOOD STOVE

UP

DECK
11'-10" X 10'-10"

DECK
11'-10" X 10'-10"

COVERED PORCH
13'-8" X 5'-10"
VAULTED CEILING

Upper Floor

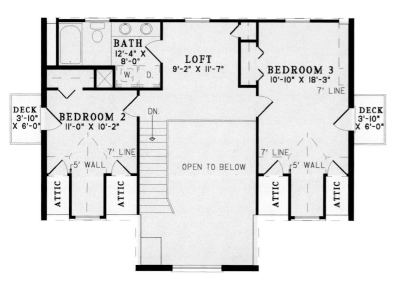

BATH
12'-4" X 8'-0"

LOFT
9'-2" X 11'-7"

BEDROOM 3
10'-10" X 18'-3"

7' LINE

W. D.

DECK
3'-10"
X 6'-0"

BEDROOM 2
11'-0" X 10'-2"

DN.

DECK
3'-10"
X 6'-0"

5' WALL 7' LINE

OPEN TO BELOW

7' LINE

7' LINE 5' WALL

ATTIC ATTIC

ATTIC ATTIC

NDG1065

The Olympiad

Width: 45' 8"

Depth: 41' 8"

Main Floor: 1,002 sq. ft.

Upper Floor: 656 sq. ft.

Total Living: 1,658 sq. ft.

Foundation: Crawl, Optional Basement, Optional Daylight Basement

Plan Options: page 282

Price Tier: B

The Grandview

Width: 51' 8"

Depth: 41' 10"

Main Floor: 1,194 sq. ft.

Upper Floor: 549 sq. ft.

Total Living: 1,743 sq. ft.

Foundation: Crawl, Optional Basement, Optional Daylight Basement

Plan Options: page 282

Price Tier: B

NDG1046

Main Floor

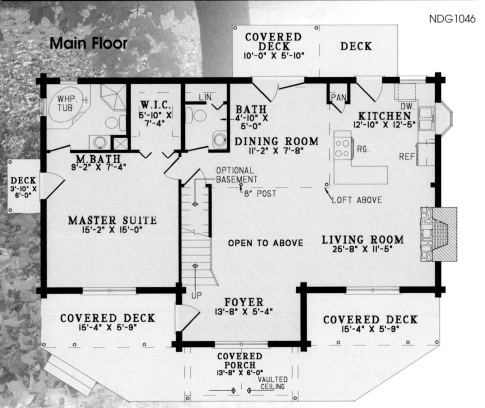

Upper Floor

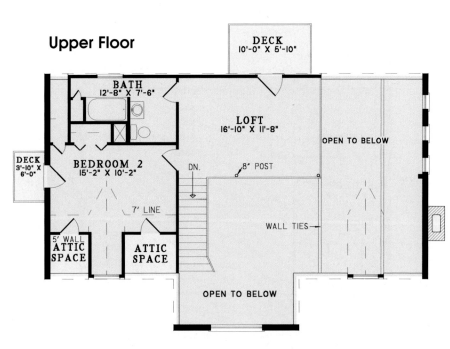

The Winfield

Width: 44' 0"

Depth: 45' 0"

Main Floor: 1,276 sq. ft.

Upper Floor: 534 sq. ft.

Total Living: 1,810 sq. ft.

Foundation: Crawl, Optional Basement,
Optional Daylight Basement

Plan Options: page 282

Price Tier: B

NDG1039

Main Floor

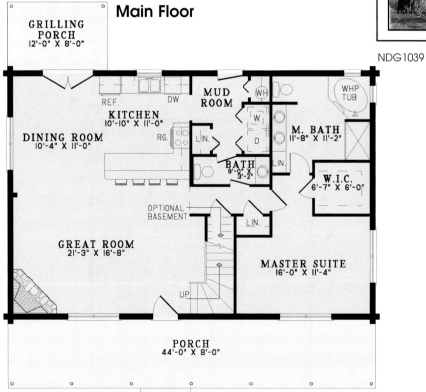

Upper Floor

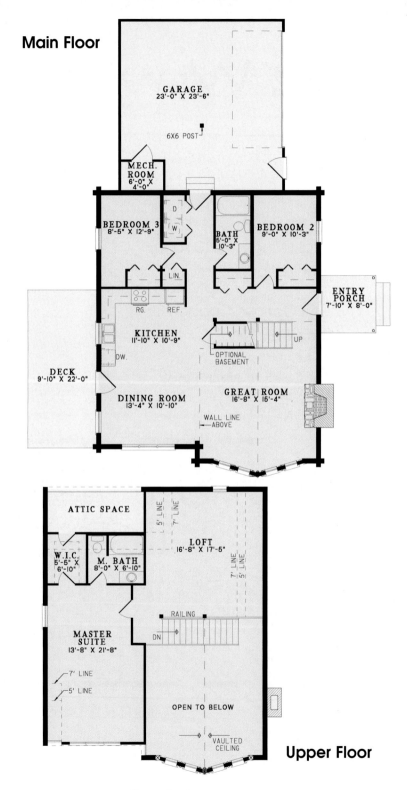

NDG1057

The Highland

Width: 49' 8"

Depth: 63' 8"

Main Floor: 1,202 sq. ft.

Upper Floor: 694 sq. ft.

Total Living: 1,896 sq. ft.

Foundation: Crawl, Optional Basement,
Optional Daylight Basement

Plan Options: page 282

Price Tier: B

Upper Floor

To Order Call 1.800.590.2423   To view the rest of this collection visit www.nelsondesigngroup.com

Main Floor

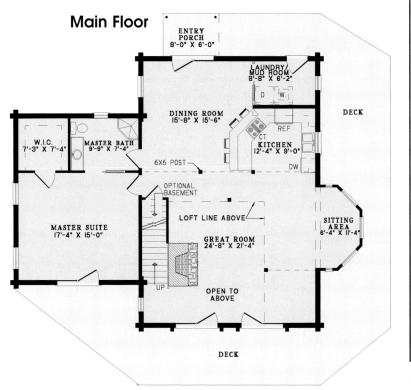

ENTRY PORCH
8'-0" X 6'-0"

LAUNDRY/ MUD ROOM
8'-8" X 6'-2"

D W.

DINING ROOM
15'-8" X 15'-6"

DECK

REF

CT

KITCHEN
12'-4" X 9'-0"

DW

W.I.C.
7'-3" X 7'-4"

MASTER BATH
9'-9" X 7'-4"

6X6 POST

OPTIONAL BASEMENT

LOFT LINE ABOVE

SITTING AREA
6'-4" X 11'-4"

MASTER SUITE
17'-4" X 15'-0"

GREAT ROOM
24'-8" X 21'-4"

UP

OPEN TO ABOVE

DECK

NDG1012

Upper Floor

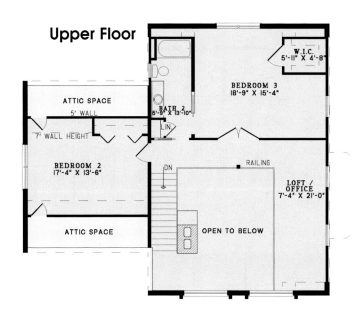

W.I.C.
5'-11" X 4'-8"

ATTIC SPACE

5' WALL

BATH
5'-11" X 13'-10"

BEDROOM 3
18'-9" X 15'-4"

7' WALL HEIGHT

LIN

BEDROOM 2
17'-4" X 13'-6"

DN

RAILING

LOFT / OFFICE
7'-4" X 21'-0"

ATTIC SPACE

OPEN TO BELOW

The Eagle Ridge II

Width: 54' 0"

Depth: 52' 0"

Main Floor: 1,486 sq. ft.

Upper Floor: 903 sq. ft.

Total Living: 2,389 sq. ft.

Foundation: Crawl, Optional Basement, Optional Daylight Basement

Plan Options: page 282

Price Tier: C

NDG1008

Main Floor

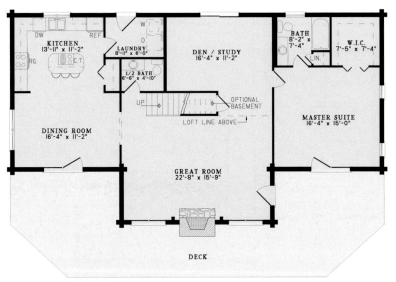

KITCHEN
13'-11" x 11'-2"

LAUNDRY
8'-11" x 6'-0"

DEN / STUDY
16'-4" x 11'-2"

BATH
8'-2" x 7'-4"

W.I.C.
7'-5" x 7'-4"

1/2 BATH
6'-6" x 4'-10"

UP

OPTIONAL
BASEMENT

LOFT LINE ABOVE

MASTER SUITE
16'-4" x 15'-0"

DINING ROOM
16'-4" x 11'-2"

GREAT ROOM
22'-8" x 15'-9"

DECK

Upper Floor

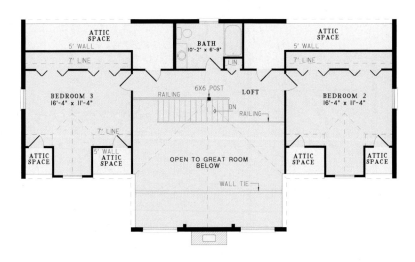

ATTIC
SPACE

ATTIC
SPACE

5' WALL

5' WALL

7' LINE

7' LINE

BATH
10'-2" x 6'-9"

LIN

BEDROOM 3
16'-4" x 11'-4"

RAILING

6X6 POST

LOFT

DN

RAILING

BEDROOM 2
16'-4" x 11'-4"

7' LINE

ATTIC
SPACE

5' WALL
ATTIC
SPACE

OPEN TO GREAT ROOM
BELOW

ATTIC
SPACE

ATTIC
SPACE

WALL TIE

The Westwind III

Width: 58' 0"

Depth: 40' 0"

Main Floor: 1,584 sq. ft.

Upper Floor: 818 sq. ft.

Total Living: 2,402 sq. ft.

Foundation: Crawl, Optional Basement,
Optional Daylight Basement

Plan Options: page 282

Price Tier: C

To Order Call 1.800.590.2423   **To view the rest of this collection visit www.nelsondesigngroup.com**

The Monteagle

Width: 76' 6"

Depth: 57' 0"

Main Floor: 1,707 sq. ft.

Upper Floor: 1,577 sq. ft.

Total Living: 3,284 sq. ft.

Foundation: Crawl, Optional Basement, Optional Daylight Basement

Plan Options: page 282

Price Tier: E

NDG1038

Main Floor

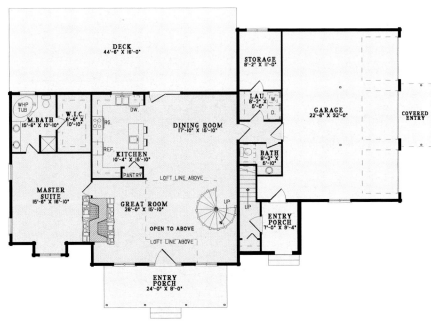

Upper Floor

Here is a glimpse into the New Stone Village and the Olde Towne Collection.

Nelson Design Group offers convenient collections to help you create beautiful homes and achieve ideal master-planned communities. Within each collection, our plans complement one another, resulting in an effective overall design theme and complete neighborhood - making development easy for you.

826 Woodland Drive

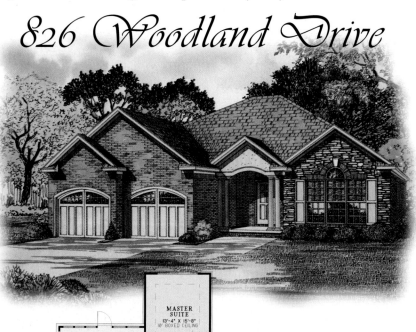

Width: 46' 0"
Depth: 71' 0"
Total Living: 1,855 sq.ft.
Bedrooms: 3
Baths: 2
Main Ceiling: 9 ft.
Foundation: Crawl, Slab, Optional Basement, Optional Daylight Basement

Price Tier: B

Width: 47' 8"
Depth: 65' 2"
Total Living: 1,714 sq. ft.
Bedrooms: 2
Baths: 2
Main Ceiling: 9 ft.
Foundation: Crawl, Slab, Optional Basement, Optional Daylight Basement

Price Tier: B

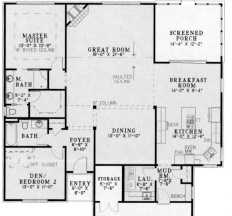

© 2003 NELSON DESIGN GROUP, LLC.

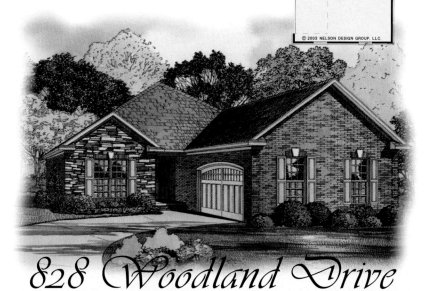

828 Woodland Drive

819 Mulberry Lane

Main Floor

Upper Floor

THE Olde Towne COLLECTION

820 Mulberry Lane

Main Floor

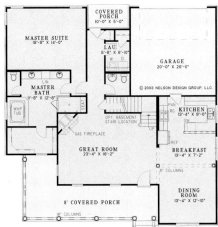

Upper Floor

Width: 50' 0" • Depth: 50' 0"

Main Floor: 1,733 sq. ft. • Upper Floor: 1,269 sq. ft.

Total Living: 3,002 sq. ft. • Bedrooms: 4 • Baths: 3

Main Ceiling: 9 ft. • Upper Ceiling: 8 ft.

Foundation: Crawl, Slab, Optional Basement, Optional Daylight Basement

Price Tier: E

Width: 50' 0" • Depth: 50' 0"

Main Floor: 1,627 sq. ft. • Upper Floor: 670 sq. ft.

Total Living: 2,297 sq. ft.

Main Ceiling: 9 ft. • Upper Ceiling: 8 ft.

Bedrooms: 3 • Baths: 2 1/2

Foundation: Crawl, Slab, Optional Basement, Optional Daylight Basement

Price Tier: C

Stock Plans

For more than 20 years, Nelson Design Group, LLC has been designing *superior* homes for builders and custom plans for clients throughout the country. As a certified member of the American Institute of Building Designers (AIBD), we are nationally known and have been recognized and *highlighted* in publications such as *HomeStyles Publishing, Home Design Alternatives, Builder Magazine* (the official publication of the National Association of Home Builders), *Home Planners, Architectural Designs, Garlinghouse, Good Housekeeping, Old House Journal, House Beautiful, Southern Living Better Homes and Gardens,* and now *Harris Publications* as well as numerous websites including our own.

A successful and *innovative* company is created by providing the best possible product with creative and knowledgeable people to carry each project to completion. Nelson Design Group, LLC Residential & Commercial Planners-Designers is one such success.

Our staff of designers offers the qualities a consumer searching for a home desires — experience, creativity and efficiency. We offer *unique* and diversified designs, as well as Southern Traditionals, Lake Houses, Country Styles and Modern Classics. We can modify any of our plans to suit your needs — saving time and guaranteeing customer *satisfaction.*

The following pages reflect some of the stock plans from our portfolio. Visit our web site at www.nelsondesigngroup.com for additional plans and new plans that are added continuously.

106 Maple Street

GRILLING PORCH
10'-0" X 8'-0"

BEDROOM 2
11'-0" X 11'-8"

BEDROOM 3
8'-8" X 8'-8"

PAN.

REF.

KITCHEN
10'-7" X 11'-8"

RG.

DW

LIN.

HVAC

WH

PAN.

W.   D.

GREAT RM.
16'-6" X 12'-10"

MASTER BEDROOM
14'-0" X 11'-0"

PORCH

BUILDING SYSTEM
NGI
Next Generation Industries
COMPATABLE

Width: 35' 0"
Depth: 36' 6"
Total Living: 930 sq. ft.
Main Ceiling: 8 ft.
Bedrooms: 3
Baths: 1
Foundation: Crawl, Slab
Plan Options: page 282

Price Tier: A

673 Maple Street

Width: 45' 0"
Depth: 47' 0"
Total Living: 1,023 sq. ft.

Price Tier: A

Main Ceiling: 8 ft.
Bedrooms: 3
Baths: 2
Foundation: Crawl, Slab,
Optional Basement,
Optional Daylight Basement
Plan Options: page 282

BUILDING SYSTEM
NGi
Next Generation Industries
COMPATABLE

BEDROOM 3
9'-6" X 10'-0"

MASTER SUITE
11'-0" X 12'-6"

HVAC

BATH

W

D

BEDROOM 2
9'-6" X 10'-6"

LIN.

BATH

WH

STORAGE
10'-0" X 2'-8"

KITCHEN
11'-0" X 9'-0"

RG.

REF

DW

GARAGE
19'-8" X 22'-8"

GREAT RM.
13'-4" X 16'-4"

BREAKFAST ROOM
11'-0" X 7'-4"

COVERED PORCH
16'-0" X 6'-0"

© 1991 NELSON DESIGN GROUP, LLC.

571 Thomas Road

BEST SELLER *Designers Choice* **NELSON DESIGN GROUP**

© 1997 NELSON DESIGN GROUP, LLC.

GRILLING PORCH
14'-0" X 8'-0"

GARAGE
13'-0" X 19'-8"

KITCHEN
11'-4" X 13'-8"

REF
RG
DW

BEDROOM 2
9'-10" X 10'-0"

BEDROOM 3
12'-0" X 10'-0"

VAULTED CEILING

W   D

WH   HVAC

BATH

GREAT ROOM
14'-8" X 14'-2"

MASTER SUITE
13'-4" X 13'-4"

COVERED PORCH
15'-0" X 4'-0"

8" BOXED COLUMNS

Width: 47' 10"
Depth: 41' 6"
Total Living: 1,075 sq. ft.
Main Ceiling: 8 ft.
Bedrooms: 3
Baths: 1 1/2
Foundation: Crawl, Slab, Optional Basement, Optional Daylight Basement
Plan Options: page 282

BUILDING SYSTEM NGI Next Generation Industries **COMPATABLE**

Price Tier: A

675 Cherry Street

Width: 49' 2"
Depth: 50' 2"
Total Living: 1,210 sq. ft.
Main Ceiling: 8 ft.
Bedrooms: 3
Baths: 2
Foundation: Crawl, Slab,
Optional Basement,
Optional Daylight Basement
Plan Options: page 282

Price Tier: A

OPT. GRILLING PORCH
12'-0" X 8'-0"

BATH

MASTER SUITE
12'-2" X 12'-0"

BEDROOM 2
10'-0" X 8'-10"

KITCHEN
11'-8" X 11'-2"

BRKFAST ROOM
8'-8" X 8'-4"

RG   DW

LIN

LIN   REF   HVAC   WH

M.BATH
7'-2" X 8'-10"

LAU.
W   D

GREAT ROOM
18'-0" X 13'-0"

BEDROOM 3
9'-0" X 11'-0"

GARAGE
20'-10" X 20'-0"

COVERED PORCH
18'-4" X 4'-6"

10" COLUMNS

© 1991 NELSON DESIGN GROUP, LLC.

BUILDING SYSTEM
NGI
Next Generation Industries
COMPATABLE

© 1992 NELSON DESIGN GROUP, LLC.

GARAGE
20'-10" X 20'-0"

PATIO

STORAGE
9'-8" X 5'-6"

LAU.
9'-10" X
5'-6"

PAN

D.

W

WH

BENCH
W/ HANGING

**KID'S
NOOK**

M.BATH

LIN.

MASTER SUITE
14'-0" X 11'-0"
9' BOXED CEILING

DW

REF

KITCHEN
11'-2" X 11'-0"
9' CEILING

RG

LIN.

BATH

DINING
10'-2" X 11'-4"
9' CEILING

9' CEILING

LIN.

BEDROOM 2
12'-0" X 10'-6"

BEDROOM 3
11'-0" X 10'-6"
9' CEILING

GREAT ROOM
18'-0" X 14'-0"
10' BOXED CEILING

VAULTED
CEILING

PORCH
33'-4" X 6'-0"
9' CEILING

701 Chestnut Lane

Width: 45' 2"

Depth: 59' 0"

Total Living: 1,235 sq. ft.

Price Tier: A

Main Ceiling: 8 ft.

Bedrooms: 3

Baths: 2

Foundation: Crawl, Slab

Plan Options: page 282

BUILDING SYSTEM
NGI
Next Generation Industries
COMPATABLE

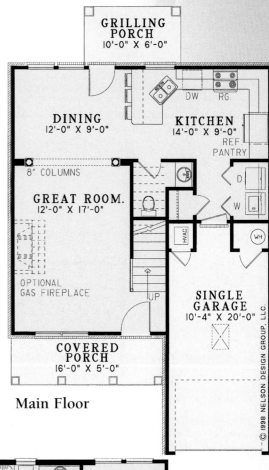

Main Floor

- GRILLING PORCH 10'-0" X 6'-0"
- DINING 12'-0" X 9'-0"
- KITCHEN 14'-0" X 9'-0"
- 8" COLUMNS
- GREAT ROOM. 12'-0" X 17'-0"
- OPTIONAL GAS FIREPLACE
- REF. PANTRY
- HVAC
- WH
- SINGLE GARAGE 10'-4" X 20'-0"
- COVERED PORCH 16'-0" X 5'-0"
- © 1998 NELSON DESIGN GROUP, LLC.

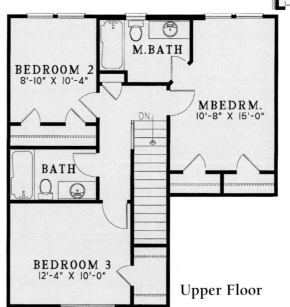

Upper Floor

- M. BATH
- BEDROOM 2 8'-10" X 10'-4"
- MBEDRM. 10'-8" X 15'-0"
- DN.
- BATH
- BEDROOM 3 12'-4" X 10'-0"

188 Maple Street

Width: 27' 0"
Depth: 45' 0"
Main Floor: 609 sq. ft.
Upper Floor: 642 sq. ft.
Total Living: 1,251 sq. ft.

Price Tier: A

Main Ceiling: 8 ft.
Upper Ceiling: 8 ft.
Bedrooms: 3
Baths: 2 1/2
Foundation: Crawl, Slab Basement, Daylight Basement
Plan Options: page 282

BUILDING SYSTEM
NGI
Next Generation Industries
COMPATABLE

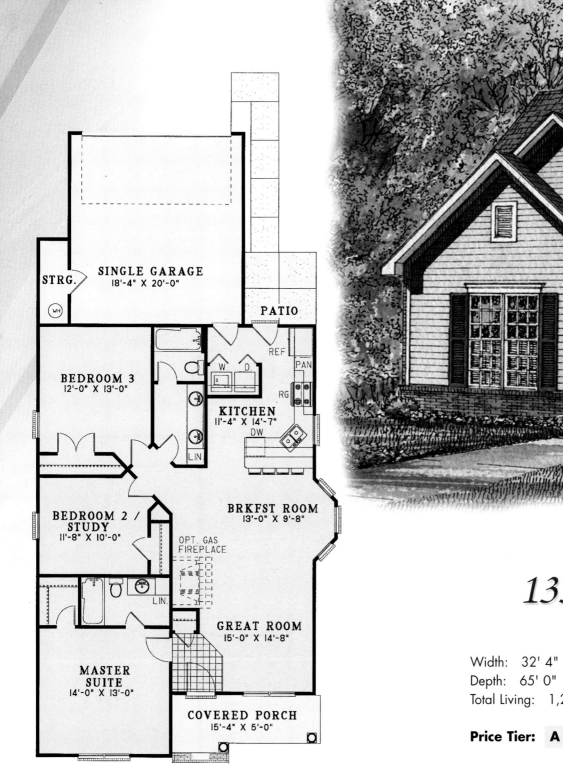

STRG.

SINGLE GARAGE
18'-4" X 20'-0"

PATIO

BEDROOM 3
12'-0" X 13'-0"

REF

PAN

KITCHEN
11'-4" X 14'-7"

W D

RG

DW

LIN.

BEDROOM 2 / STUDY
11'-8" X 10'-0"

BRKFST ROOM
13'-0" X 9'-8"

OPT. GAS FIREPLACE

LIN.

GREAT ROOM
15'-0" X 14'-8"

MASTER SUITE
14'-0" X 13'-0"

COVERED PORCH
15'-4" X 5'-0"

133 Maple Street

Width: 32' 4"

Depth: 65' 0"

Total Living: 1,265 sq. ft.

Main Ceiling: 9 ft.

Bedrooms: 3

Baths: 2

Foundation: Crawl, Slab

Plan Options: page 282

Price Tier: A

533 Maple Street

Width: 51' 0"
Depth: 49' 0"
Total Living: 1,324 sq. ft.

Price Tier: A

Main Ceiling: 8 ft.
Bedrooms: 3
Baths: 2
Foundation: Crawl, Slab, Optional Basement, Optional Daylight Basement
Plan Options: page 282

BUILDING SYSTEM
NGI
Next Generation Industries
COMPATABLE

M. BATH
12'-6" X 5'-0"

W.I.C.

W
D

MASTER SUITE
OPT. 9' BOXED CEILING
13'-4" X 11'-4"

W.I.C.

STORAGE
15'-0" X 3'-0"

DINING
10'-0" X 12'-0"

KITCHEN
10'-0" X 10'-2"

GARAGE
20'-0" X 19'-8"

GREAT ROOM
OPT. 9' BOXED CEILING
17'-4" X 13'-0"

PAN.
REF.

D.W.
R.G.

© 2000 NELSON DESIGN GROUP, LLC.

BATH

FOYER
7'-0" X 6'-6"

BEDROOM 2
10'-0" X 9'-6"

BEDROOM 3
10'-0" X 10'-8"

COVERED PORCH
8'-0" X 6'-0"

© 2000 NELSON DESIGN GROUP, LLC.

GARAGE
19'-4" X 19'-6"

DINING
11'-4" X 17'-10"

LIN.

M.BATH
14'-8" X 11'-6"

WHP TUB

MASTER SUITE
14'-8" X 11'-8"
10' BOXED CEILING

KITCHEN
11'-4" X 11'-2"

DW

RG

REF

D.

W

BEDROOM 3
11'-4" X 8'-8"

LIN.

GREAT RM.
14'-8" X 16'-6"
10' BOXED CEILING

BATH

LIN.

FOYER

COVERED PORCH
15'-0" X 8'-0"

8" COLUMNS

BEDROOM 2
11'-4" X 9'-0"

498 Fir Street

Width: 27' 0"

Depth: 75' 10"

Total Living: 1,370 sq. ft.

Main Ceiling: 9 ft.

Bedrooms: 3

Baths: 2

Foundation: Crawl, Slab

Plan Options: page 282

Price Tier: **A**

BUILDING SYSTEM
NGI
Next Generation Industries
COMPATABLE

GRILLING PORCH
17'-8" X 8'-0"

MASTER SUITE
13'-6" X 13'-6"

9' BOXED CEILING

GREAT ROOM
17'-0" X 13'-6"

GAS FIREPLACE

9' BOXED CEILING

BEDROOM 3
11'-4" X 11'-8"

LIN

BATH

DW   REF.

KITCHEN

RG

DINING
11'-2" X 13'-8"

FOYER

BATH

W   D   **LAU.**   DN

BEDROOM 2
11'-4" X 11'-6"

VAULTED CEILING

COVERED PORCH
16'-0" X 6'-0"

GARAGE
19'-4" X 21'-6"

© 1995 NELSON DESIGN GROUP, LLC.

102-2 Spruce Street

Width: 48' 0"
Depth: 58' 0"
Total Living: 1,401 sq. ft.

Price Tier: A

Main Ceiling: 8 ft.
Bedrooms: 3
Baths: 2
Foundation: Crawl, Slab, Basement, Daylight Basement
Plan Options: page 282

BUILDING SYSTEM
NGI
Next Generation Industries
COMPATABLE

Elevation A

Elevation B

MASTER SUITE
15'-10" X 13'-4"

WHP TUB/ SHWR

M.BATH
5'-10" X 13'-4"

LIN

BEDROOM 2
11'-6" X 10'-0"

DINING ROOM
14'-4" X 7'-8"

LAU.
7'-6" X 5'-6"

D

W

WH

LIN

RG.

DW

KITCHEN
17'-4" X 11'-4"

REF.

HVAC

BATH

GARAGE
19'-0" X 20'-0"

FOYER
9' CEILING
4'-0" X 11'-1"

GREAT ROOM
9' CEILING
15'-0" X 18'-0"

BEDROOM 3
9'-6" X 10'-0"

© 1999 NELSON DESIGN GROUP, LLC.

PORCH

12"X12" BRK COL.

387 Spruce Street

Width: 49' 2"
Depth: 44' 2"
Total Living: 1,466 sq. ft.

Price Tier: A

Main Ceiling: 8 ft.
Bedrooms: 3
Baths: 2
Foundation: Crawl, Slab,
   Optional Basement,
   Optional Daylight Basement
Plan Options: page 282

BUILDING SYSTEM
NGI
Next Generation Industries
COMPATABLE

473 Hannah Lane

Width: 46' 10"

Depth: 54' 10"

Total Living: 1,485 sq. ft.

Price Tier: A

Main Ceiling: 8 ft.

Bedrooms: 3

Baths: 2

Foundation: Crawl, Slab, Optional Basement, Optional Daylight Basement

Plan Options: page 282

BUILDING SYSTEM
NGI
Next Generation Industries
COMPATABLE

7' GRILLING PORCH

MASTER SUITE
9' BOXED CEILING
14'-4" X 12'-4"

BEDROOM 3
11'-0" X 10'-6"

GREAT RM.
9' BOXED CEILING
20'-2" X 15'-2"

8" COLUMNS

M.BATH
10'-0" X 14'-6"

BATH

FOYER

KITCHEN
9'-10" X 11'-8"

DINING RM.
9'-8" X 12'-0"

LAU.
10'-0" X 6'-4"

VAULTED CEILING

PORCH

BEDROOM 2
11'-0" X 10'-0"

GARAGE
20'-10" X 20'-0"

Front Elevation

Rear Elevation

113-1 Chestnut Lane

Width: 51' 6"	Main Ceiling: 8 ft.
Depth: 49' 10"	Bedrooms: 3
Total Living: 1,525 sq. ft.	Baths: 2

Price Tier: B

Foundation: Crawl, Slab, Basement, Daylight Basement

Plan Options: page 282

BUILDING SYSTEM
NGI
Next Generation Industries
COMPATABLE

© 1998 NELSON DESIGN GROUP, LLC

Designed For:

JBL
RESIDENTIAL SYSTEMS
COMPLETE HOME
ENTERTAINMENT NETWORKS
& DISTRIBUTED AUDIO

JBL
Home Theater

Designed For:

Pioneer
sound.vision.soul
Pioneer Sound System

Best Seller
Designers Choice
Nelson Design Group

148 Spruce Street

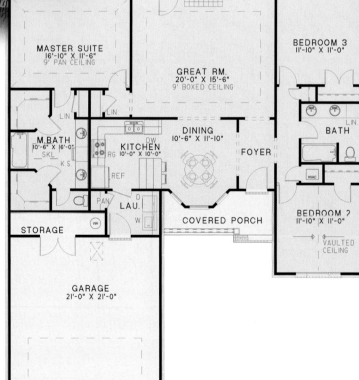

Width: 50' 0"

Depth: 56' 0"

Total Living: 1,538 sq. ft.

Price Tier: B

Main Ceiling: 8 ft.

Bedrooms: 3

Baths: 2

Foundation: Crawl, Slab, Basement, Daylight Basement

Plan Options: page 282

BUILDING SYSTEM
NGI
Next Generation Industries
COMPATABLE

GLASS SHWR

LIN

WHP TUB

M.BATH
8'-0" X 18'-0"

MASTER SUITE
9' PAN CEILING
13'-0" X 14'-0"

DINING
11'-6" X 10'-6"

BAR

GREAT ROOM
15'-4" X 19'-8"
9' BOXED CEILING

RG

DW.

KIT.
10'-6" X 10'-0"

REF

BEDROOM 3
12'-4" X 10'-8"

BATH

HVAC   WH   PAN.

LAU.
9'-4" X 9'-4"

D.

W

PRCH

DN

BEDROOM 2
10'-8" X 12'-0"

VAULTED CEILING

GARAGE
20'-10" X 20'-0"

115B Spruce Street

Width: 48' 6"
Depth: 52' 2"
Total Living: 1,546 sq. ft.

Price Tier: B

Main Ceiling: 8 ft.
Bedrooms: 3
Baths: 2
Foundation: Crawl, Slab, Basement,
             Daylight Basement
Plan Options: page 282

BUILDING SYSTEM
NGI
Next Generation Industries
COMPATABLE

575 Linden Avenue

Width: 50' 10"
Depth: 66' 8"
Total Living: 1,605 sq. ft.

Price Tier: B

Main Ceiling: 8 ft.
Bedrooms: 3
Baths: 2
Foundation: Crawl, Slab,
Optional Basement,
Optional Daylight Basement
Plan Options: page 282

BUILDING SYSTEM
NGI
Next Generation Industries
COMPATABLE

Floor plan labels:
GRILLING PORCH 13'-0" X 10'-0"
MASTER SUITE 17'-8" X 11'-6" 9' BOXED CLG.
VAULTED CEILING
GREAT ROOM 20'-0" X 15'-6"
OPT. FRENCH DOORS
BEDROOM 3 / DEN 11'-10" X 11'-0"
GLASS BLOCKS
WHP TUB
LIN
M. BATH 11'-10" X 19'-10"
KITCHEN 10'-0" X 9'-6"
BRKFAST RM. 10'-6" X 11'-10"
FOYER 5'-0" X 9'-6"
SHELVES
BATH
LAU. 7'-4" X 6'-0"
COVERED PORCH 15'-10" X 6'-0" 9' CLG.
BEDROOM 2 11'-10" X 11'-0"
VAULTED CEILING
WH
GARAGE 21'-10" X 24'-0"

© 2001 NELSON DESIGN GROUP, LLC.

To Order Call 1.800.590.2423   Similar plans can be viewed and ordered at www.nelsondesigngroup.com

707 Dogwood Avenue

Width: 56' 6"
Depth: 49' 2"
Main Floor: 1,280 sq. ft.
Upper Floor: 355 sq. ft.
Total Living: 1,635 sq. ft.
Main Ceiling: 8 ft.
Upper Ceiling: 8 ft.
Bedrooms: 3
Baths: 2 1/2
Foundation: Crawl, Slab,
Optional Basement,
Optional Daylight Basement
Plan Options: page 282

Price Tier: B

Main Floor

Upper Floor

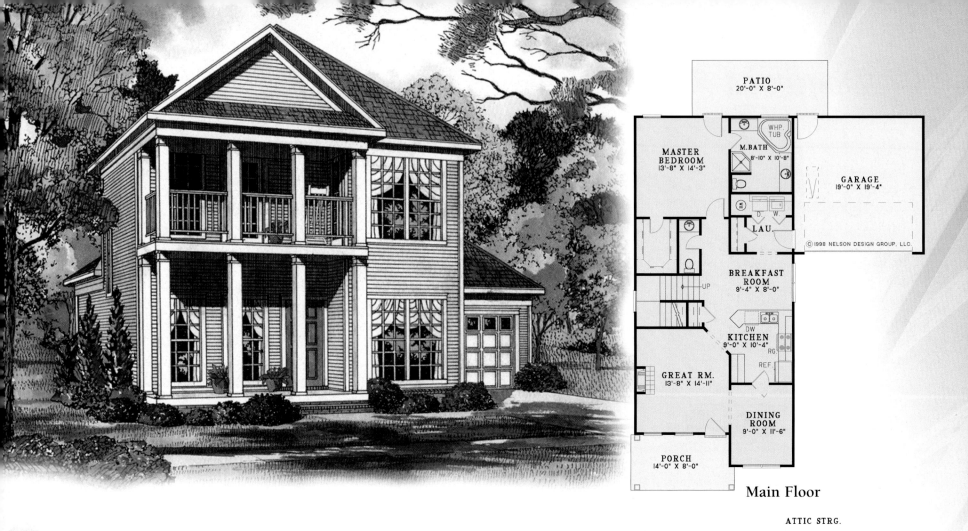

PATIO
20'-0" X 8'-0"

MASTER BEDROOM
13'-8" X 14'-3"

M.BATH
8'-10" X 10'-8"

WHP. TUB

GARAGE
19'-0" X 19'-4"

© 1998 NELSON DESIGN GROUP, LLC.

LAU.

UP

BREAKFAST ROOM
9'-4" X 8'-0"

KITCHEN
9'-0" X 10'-4"

DW

RG.

REF.

GREAT RM.
13'-8" X 14'-11"

DINING ROOM
9'-0" X 11'-6"

PORCH
14'-0" X 8'-0"

Main Floor

ATTIC STRG.

HVAC

DN.

BATH

BED RM. 2
12'-0" X 12'-7"

BED RM. 3
10'-8" X 17'-4"

PORCH
14'-0" X 8'-0"

Upper Floor

512 Maple Drive

Width: 42' 8"
Depth: 54' 0"
Main Floor: 1,133 sq. ft.
Upper Floor: 518 sq. ft.
Total Living: 1,651 sq. ft.

Main Ceiling: 9 ft.
Upper Ceiling: 8 ft.
Bedrooms: 3
Baths: 2 1/2
Foundation: Crawl, Slab,
Optional Basement,
Optional Daylight Basement
Plan Options: page 282

Price Tier: B

BUILDING SYSTEM
NGI
Next Generation Industries
COMPATABLE

To Order Call 1.800.590.2423   Similar plans can be viewed and ordered at www.nelsondesigngroup.com

BEST SELLER
Designers
Choice
NELSON DESIGN GROUP

GRILLING PORCH
26'-6" X 10'-0"

MASTER
SUITE
13'-6" X 12'-0"
9' BOXED CEILING

M.BATH
8'-0" X 7'-10"

DINING RM.
10'-6" X 11'-8"

CLOSET
8'-0" X 6'-0"

GREAT RM.
15'-0" X 23'-4"
9' BOXED CEILING

BEDROOM 2
10'-0" X 9'-0"

BATH

RG.

DW

REF.

KITCHEN
10'-6" X 10'-4"

HVAC

LIN

FOYER
5'-0" X
7'-4"
10' CLNG

LAU
5'-6" X
7'-0"

BREAKFAST
ROOM
10'-6" X 10'-0"

BEDROOM 3
10'-0" X 10'-0"

WH

BEDROOM 4/
OFFICE
9'-6" X 10'-6"

PRCH

GARAGE
19'-0" X 20'-0"

© 1992 NELSON DESIGN GROUP, LLC.

609 Willow Lane

Width: 48' 8"
Depth: 61' 8"
Total Living: 1,658 sq. ft.

Price Tier: **B**

Main Ceiling: 8 ft.
Bedrooms: 4
Baths: 2
Foundation: Crawl, Slab
Plan Options: page 282

BUILDING SYSTEM
NGI
Next Generation Industries
COMPATABLE

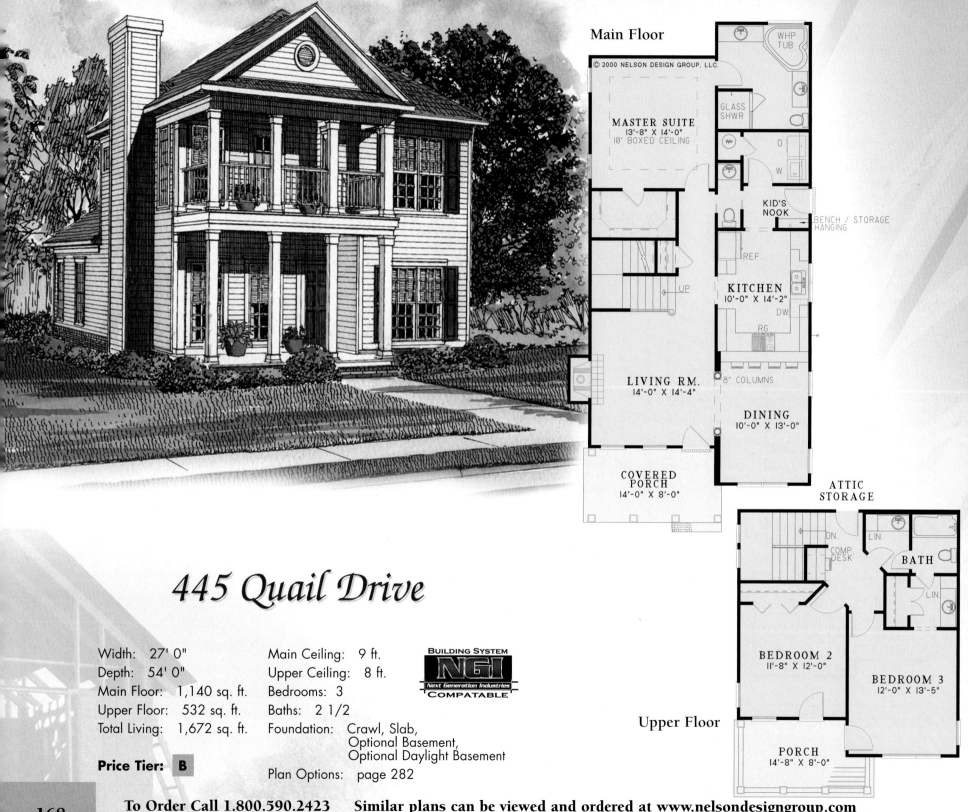

Main Floor

© 2000 NELSON DESIGN GROUP, LLC.

WHP TUB

MASTER SUITE
13'-8" X 14'-0"
10' BOXED CEILING

GLASS SHWR

WH

D

W

KID'S NOOK

BENCH / STORAGE HANGING

REF

UP

KITCHEN
10'-0" X 14'-2"

DW

RG

LIVING RM.
14'-0" X 14'-4"

8" COLUMNS

DINING
10'-0" X 13'-0"

COVERED PORCH
14'-0" X 8'-0"

ATTIC STORAGE

DN

LIN

COMP. DESK

BATH

LIN

BEDROOM 2
11'-8" X 12'-0"

BEDROOM 3
12'-0" X 13'-5"

Upper Floor

PORCH
14'-8" X 8'-0"

445 Quail Drive

Width: 27' 0"
Depth: 54' 0"
Main Floor: 1,140 sq. ft.
Upper Floor: 532 sq. ft.
Total Living: 1,672 sq. ft.

Main Ceiling: 9 ft.
Upper Ceiling: 8 ft.
Bedrooms: 3
Baths: 2 1/2
Foundation: Crawl, Slab,
   Optional Basement,
   Optional Daylight Basement
Plan Options: page 282

Price Tier: B

BUILDING SYSTEM
NGI
Next Generation Industries
COMPATABLE

To Order Call 1.800.590.2423   Similar plans can be viewed and ordered at www.nelsondesigngroup.com

Elevation A

379 Spruce Street

Elevation B

MASTER SUITE
9' PAN CEILING
16'-2" X 12'-6"

PORCH
29'-8" X 8'-0"

8" COLUMNS

FRENCH DOOR

FRENCH DOOR

BEDROOM 3
10'-10" X 11'-8"

BREAKFAST ROOM
12'-10" X 9'-0"

GREAT ROOM
9' CEILING
16'-6" X 18'-4"

KITCHEN
12'-10" X 9'-4"

COMP CENTER

M.BATH
12'-4" X 16'-8"

WHP TUB

ISLAND

LAU.
6'-0" X 7'-10"

HVAC

LIN.

RG.

BATH

DW

REF.

W   D

WH   LIN.

8" COLUMN

FOYER
10' CEILING
6'-10" X 6'-6"

BEDROOM 2
13'-6" X 10'-8"

DINING
10' CEILING
11'-8" X 12'-2"

DN

OPTIONAL BASEMENT PLAN

GARAGE
22'-4" X 20'-8"

PORCH
6'-6" X 5'-10"

8" COLUMNS

© 1994 NELSON DESIGN GROUP, LLC.

Designed For:

JBL

RESIDENTIAL SYSTEMS
COMPLETE HOME
ENTERTAINMENT NETWORKS
& DISTRIBUTED AUDIO

JBL
Home Theater

Designed For:

Pioneer
sound.vision.soul
Pioneer Sound System

Width: 58' 0"
Depth: 53' 6"
Total Living: 1,722 sq. ft.
Main Ceiling: 8 ft.
Bedrooms: 3
Baths: 2
Foundation: Crawl, Slab, Basement, Daylight Basement
Plan Options: page 282

BUILDING SYSTEM
NGI
Next Generation Industries
COMPATABLE

Price Tier: B

313 Chestnut Lane

Width: 67' 0"

Depth: 54' 10"

Total Living: 1,746 sq. ft.

Main Ceiling: 9 ft.

Bedrooms: 3

Baths: 2

Foundation: Crawl, Slab,
Optional Basement,
Optional Daylight Basement

Plan Options: page 282

Price Tier: B

BUILDING SYSTEM
NGI
Next Generation Industries
COMPATABLE

Designed For:

JBL

RESIDENTIAL SYSTEMS
COMPLETE HOME
ENTERTAINMENT NETWORKS
& DISTRIBUTED AUDIO

JBL
Home Theater

Designed For:

Pioneer
sound.vision.soul
Pioneer Sound System

BEST SELLER
Designers Choice
NELSON DESIGN GROUP

Floor Plan Labels

MASTER SUITE
10' BOXED CEILING
12'-8" X 18'-0"

M.BATH
9'-4" X 11'-8"
FRENCH DOORS
LIN
WHP TUB
GLASS BLOCKS

BEDROOM 2
13'-0" X 11'-0"

SCREENED PORCH
17'-0" X 10'-0"

BREAKFAST ROOM
13'-0" X 8'-8"

LAU.
8'-0" X 5'-6"

STORAGE
9'-4" X 5'-6"

ISLAND
PAN
DW
KITCHEN
13'-0" X 10'-10"
REF

GREAT ROOM
11' BOXED CEILING
17'-0" X 16'-4"
10' CEILING

GARAGE
22'-4" X 22'-0"

OPTIONAL SIDE LOAD GARAGE

BEDROOM 3
13'-0" X 11'-0"

DINING ROOM
10' BOXED CEILING
13'-0" X 11'-6"

FOYER
10' CEILING
17'-0" X 4'-0"

COVERED PORCH
44'-10" X 8'-0"

MASTER SUITE
15'-4" X 14'-0"
9' BOX CEILING

GRILLING PORCH
10'-10" X 6'-6"

BRKFST. RM.
10'-10" X 10'-6"

M.BATH
9'-6" X 12'-5"

GLASS BLOCKS

WHP TUB

LIN

STORAGE
9'-6" X 3'-0"

LAU.
5'-6" X 7'-6"

W D

REF

DESK

DW

KITCHEN
10'-10" X 13'-2"

PAN.

RG

BEDROOM 2
12'-0" X 11'-0"

GREAT RM.
16'-0" X 20'-8"
9' BOXED CEILING

LIN

BATH
8'-2" X 7'-10"

LIN

FOYER
6'-10" X 7'-4"
9' CEILING

DN

OPTIONAL BASEMENT

DINING RM.
12'-6" X 14'-0"
10' CEILING

PORCH
8'-2" X 5'-0"

BEDROOM 3
12'-0" X 11'-9"

VAULTED CEILING

GARAGE
20'-10" X 21'-0"

© 1990 NELSON DESIGN GROUP, LLC.

610 Cherry Street

Width: 55' 10"
Depth: 52' 0"
Total Living: 1,763 sq. ft.

Main Ceiling: 8 ft.
Bedrooms: 3
Baths: 2
Foundation: Crawl, Slab, Optional Basement, Optional Daylight Basement
Plan Options: page 282

Price Tier: B

BUILDING SYSTEM
NGI
Next Generation Industries
COMPATABLE

548 Tyler Street

Width: 50' 8"
Depth: 62' 4"
Total Living: 1,832 sq. ft.

Price Tier: B

Main Ceiling: 8 ft.
Bedrooms: 4
Baths: 2
Foundation: Crawl, Slab,
Optional Basement,
Optional Daylight Basement
Plan Options: page 282

BUILDING SYSTEM
NGI
Next Generation Industries
COMPATABLE

Floor Plan Labels

WHP TUB

M.BATH
16'-4" X 11'-9"

MASTER SUITE
16'-4" X 11'-2"
9' BOXED CEILING

BOOK SHELVS

DW. RG

KITCHEN
15'-6" X 11'-3"

REF. PAN.

WH

LAU.
9'-0" X 6'-0"

W. D.

STORAGE
6'-2" X 6'-2"

GARAGE
20'-0" X 20'-0"

GRILLING PORCH
16'-4" X 6'-0"

GREAT RM.
16'-4" X 20'-6"
9' BOXED CEILING

DINING
11'-4" X 12'-0"
9' CEILING

FOYER
7'-0" X 9'-4"

PORCH

BEDROOM 4
10'-8" X 11'-0"

BATH

BEDROOM 3
9'-2" X 10'-0"

LIN

BEDROOM 2
11'-0" X 10'-0"

© 1998 NELSON DESIGN GROUP, LLC.

To Order Call 1.800.590.2423   Similar plans can be viewed and ordered at www.nelsondesigngroup.com

Elevation A

GARAGE
23'-0" X 19'-8"

© 2001 NELSON DESIGN GROUP, LLC.

W.I.C.   WHP TUB   W.I.C.

M.B.
15'-8" X 11'-6"

K.S.

GRILLING PORCH
19'-6" X 5'-8"

OPT. FIREPLACE

BEDROOM 4
12'-0" X 12'-6"

LAU.
9'-6" X 6'-2"

GREAT RM.
16'-10" X 16'-6"

BATH

MASTER SUITE
10' BOXED CLG.
15'-8" X 14'-6"

8" RND. COLUMNS

BEDROOM 3
11'-0" X 10'-0"

REF

KIT.
10'-8" X 9'-10"

FOYER

DINING RM.
10'-2" X 12'-2"

BEDROOM 2
10'-10" X 10'-6"

BRKFAST RM.
10'-8" X 8'-2"

P.

Elevation B

516 Belmont Avenue

Width: 58' 8"	Main Ceiling: 9 ft.
Depth: 56' 6"	Bedrooms: 4
Total Living: 1,841 sq. ft.	Baths: 2
	Foundation: Crawl, Slab
Price Tier: B	Plan Options: page 282

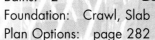
BUILDING SYSTEM
NGI
Next Generation Industries
COMPATABLE

483 Spruce Street

Width: 57' 0"
Depth: 61' 4"
Total Living: 1,880 sq. ft.

Price Tier: B

Main Ceiling: 9 ft.
Bedrooms: 4
Baths: 2
Foundation: Crawl, Slab, Basement, Daylight Basement
Plan Options: page 282

BUILDING SYSTEM NGI Next Generation Industries COMPATABLE

Floor Plan Labels

GRILLING PORCH 27'-0" X 10'-0"

BREAKFAST ROOM 9'-11" X 9'-7"

MASTER SUITE 13'-7" X 15'-0" 10' BOXED CEILING

GREAT ROOM 16'-0" X 17'-8" 10' BOXED CEILING

BEDROOM 2 11'-2" X 10'-6"

BEDROOM 3 10'-0" X 10'-4"

RG. DW KITCHEN 9'-11" X 14'-9"

8" COLUMNS

KNEE SPACE M.BATH 13'-7" X 11'-8"

REF. PAN.

LIN

FOYER 8'-0" X 10'-4" 10' CEILING

BATH

WHP TUB W D LAU.

DINING ROOM 12'-6" X 12'-4" 10' CEILING

LIN

STORAGE

BEDROOM 4 13'-6" X 12'-4"

DESK

OPTIONAL SIDE LOAD

7' COVERED PORCH 10' CEILING

GARAGE 19'-4" X 19'-6"

© 2000 NELSON DESIGN GROUP, LLC.

Main Floor

© 2001 NELSON DESIGN GROUP, LLC.

GARAGE
19'-10" X 20'-6"

STOR.

BEDROOM 3
12'-8" X 9'-4"

LAU.
7'-2" X 5'-10"

GRILLING PORCH
5'-4" X 5'-10"

BATH

W D

DINING
12'-2" X 12'-0"

REF. OVEN
C.T.

KITCHEN
12'-6" X 12'-6"

DW

42" HIGH BAR

OPTIONAL BASEMENT STAIRS

GREAT ROOM
20'-10" X 17'-0"
OPEN TO ABOVE

UP

8' COVERED PORCH

WHP TUB

GLASS SHWR

M. BATH
15'-8" X 11'-4"

BEDROOM 2
11'-6" X 12'-0"

LIN.

BATH

MASTER SUITE
20'-2" X 13'-8"
9' BOXED CEILING

LOFT

BUILT-IN SHELVES

DN

OPEN TO BELOW

Upper Floor

8' UPPER PORCH

622 Maple Drive

Width: 37' 10"
Depth: 65' 6"
Main Floor: 1,104 sq. ft.
Upper Floor: 793 sq. ft.
Total Living: 1,897 sq. ft.

Main Ceiling: 9 ft.
Upper Ceiling: 8 ft.
Bedrooms: 3
Baths: 3
Foundation: Crawl, Slab,
Optional Basement,
Optional Daylight Basement
Plan Options: page 282

Price Tier: B

BUILDING SYSTEM
NGI
Next Generation Industries
COMPATABLE

702 Cherry Street

Width: 69' 6"
Depth: 44' 4"
Total Living: 1,913 sq. ft.
Main Ceiling: 8 ft.
Bedrooms: 4
Baths: 2
Foundation: Crawl, Slab
Plan Options: page 282

Price Tier: B

Best Seller Designers Choice — Nelson Design Group

GRILLING PORCH
29'-0" X 10'-0"

10" COLUMNS

LIN
VAULTED CEILING

M. BATH
8'-8" X 13'-8"

WHP TUB

K.S.

MASTER SUITE
14'-10" X 13'-8"
9' BOXED CEILING

BREAKFAST ROOM
10'-0" X 9'-6"
9' CEILING

GREAT ROOM
18'-0" X 18'-4"
10' BOXED CEILING

BEDROOM 4
11'-4" X 11'-0"

LIN

BATH
7' 10" X 8'-0"

LIN

BENCH W/ HANGING

LAU.
5'-6" X 9'-0"

REF

DW

KITCHEN
12'-0" X 11'-10"
9' CEILING

RG

PAN

9' CEILING

HVAC

GARAGE
20'-8" X 21'-0"

FOYER
6'-8" X 8'-10"
9' CEILING

WH

STRG.
5'-6" X 8'-2"

DINING RM.
12'-0" X 12'-0"
9' CEILING

4' PORCH

BEDROOM 2
11'-0" X 11'-0"
9' CEILING

BEDROOM 3
11'-4" X 11'-2"

© 1992 NELSON DESIGN GROUP, LLC.

To Order Call 1.800.590.2423   Similar plans can be viewed and ordered at www.nelsondesigngroup.com

178 Olive Street

Width: 84' 0"
Depth: 55' 6"
Total Living: 1,921 sq. ft.*
*Optional Bonus: 812 sq. ft.
Main Ceiling: 8 ft.
Bonus Ceiling: 8 ft.
Bedrooms: 3
Baths: 3
Foundation: Crawl, Slab, Basement, Daylight Basement
Plan Options: page 282

Price Tier: B

BUILDING SYSTEM
NGI
Next Generation Industries
COMPATABLE

Designed For:

JBL
RESIDENTIAL SYSTEMS
COMPLETE HOME
ENTERTAINMENT NETWORKS
& DISTRIBUTED AUDIO

JBL
Home Theater

Designed For:

Pioneer
sound.vision.soul
Pioneer Sound System

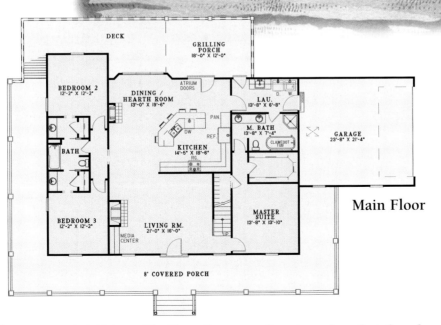

Main Floor

DECK

GRILLING PORCH
18'-0" X 12'-0"

BEDROOM 2
12'-2" X 12'-2"

DINING / HEARTH ROOM
13'-0" X 19'-6"

ATRIUM DOORS

LAU.
13'-8" X 6'-8"

BATH

KITCHEN
14'-5" X 18'-6"

M. BATH
13'-8" X 7'-4"

CLAWFOOT TUB

GARAGE
23'-8" X 21'-4"

BEDROOM 3
12'-2" X 12'-2"

LIVING RM.
21'-0" X 16'-0"

MASTER SUITE
13'-8" X 13'-10"

MEDIA CENTER

8' COVERED PORCH

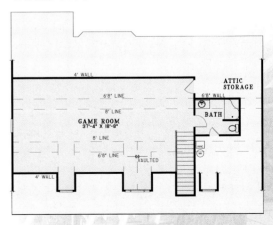

Bonus Floor

4' WALL

6'8" LINE

8' LINE

GAME ROOM
37'-4" X 18'-8"

8' LINE

6'8" LINE

VAULTED

4' WALL

ATTIC STORAGE

6'8" WALL

BATH

670 Olive Street

Width: 64' 0"
Depth: 52' 10"
Total Living: 1,922 sq. ft.

Price Tier: B

Main Ceiling: 8 ft.
Bedrooms: 3
Baths: 2
Foundation: Crawl, Slab
Plan Options: page 282

BUILDING SYSTEM
NGI
Next Generation Industries
COMPATABLE

Floor Plan Labels

WHP TUB

VAULTED CEILING

M.BATH
15'-4" X 14'-0"

GRILLING PORCH
30'-4" X 8'-0"

BRKFAST ROOM
9'-4" X 10'-4"

LAU./HOBBY
9'-0" X 8'-0"

STORAGE
7'-8" X 8'-0"

MASTER SUITE
15'-4" X 15'-0"
9' BOXED CEILING

GREAT RM.
16'-10" X 20'-0"
9' BOXED CEILING

KITCHEN
9'-4" X 12'-0"

REF

DW

RG.

PAN

GARAGE
20'-10" X 21'-0"

ATTIC ACCESS

BATH
11'-6" X 5'-0"

LIN

HVAC

LIN

FOYER
5'-0" X 9'-0"
9' CEILING

DINING RM.
11'-8" X 12'-0"

VAULTED CEILING

© 1991 NELSON DESIGN GROUP, LLC.

BEDROOM 2
11'-6" X 13'-2"

VAULTED CEILING

BEDROOM 3
13'-2" X 11'-8"
9' CEILING

ENTRY

BEDROOM 2
11'-0" X 12'-0"

COVERED GRILLING
PORCH
17'-4" X 6'-0"

WHP
TUB

M.BATH
20'-10" X 12'-0"

LIN

BATH

BUILT-INS

MASTER SUITE
20'-10" X 13'-4"
10' BOXED CEILING

GREAT RM.
17'-4" X 21'-8"
10' TRAY CEILING

BEDROOM 1
11'-0" X 12'-0"

BUILT-INS

LAU.
8'-10" X 6'-6"

D

WH

STORAGE

W

RG

REF PAN.

KITCHEN
11'-0" X 12'-0"

FOYER
10' CEILING

DINING
11'-0" X 12'-0"
10' CEILING

DW

BRKFAST RM.
11'-0" X 10'-0"

PORCH
6'-0" X 7'-6"

GARAGE
20'-10" X 21'-0"

© 1994 NELSON DESIGN GROUP, LLC.

244 Spruce Street

Width: 50' 0"	Main Ceiling: 9 ft.
Depth: 60' 6"	Bedrooms: 3
Total Living: 1,928 sq. ft.	Baths: 2

Price Tier: **B**

Foundation: Crawl, Slab,
Optional Basement,
Optional Daylight Basement

Plan Options: page 282

BUILDING SYSTEM
NGI
Next Generation Industries
COMPATABLE

Designed For:

JBL
RESIDENTIAL SYSTEMS
COMPLETE HOME
ENTERTAINMENT NETWORKS
& DISTRIBUTED AUDIO

JBL
Home Theater

Designed For:

Pioneer
sound.vision.soul
Pioneer Sound System

205 Mockingbird Lane

Width: 58' 0"
Depth: 54' 10"
Total Living: 1,940 sq. ft.

Price Tier: B

Main Ceiling: 8 ft.
Bedrooms: 4
Baths: 2
Foundation: Crawl, Slab, Basement,
Daylight Basement
Plan Options: page 282

BUILDING SYSTEM
NGI
Next Generation Industries
COMPATABLE

Floor Plan Labels

COVERED PORCH 18'-5" X 4'-0"

BREAKFAST ROOM 9'-4" X 10'-11"

MASTER SUITE 15'-0" X 15'-0" 9' PAN CEILING

GREAT ROOM 9' BOX CEILING 15'-0" X 19'-6"

BEDROOM 4 13'-6" X 14'-6"

KITCHEN 9'-11" X 12'-7"

BATH

M.BATH 15'-0" X 11'-8"

KNEE SPACE

GLASS BLOCKS

WHP TUB

FOYER 7'-0" X 7'-0"

DINING ROOM 11'-6" X 9'-8"

BEDROOM 3 10'-0" X 10'-4"

BEDROOM 2 12'-4" X 10'-6"

LAU.

STORAGE

4' PORCH

GARAGE 20'-10" X 20'-0"

347 Maple Street

Width: 66' 0"

Depth: 55' 0"

Total Living: 1,957 sq. ft.*

*Optional Bonus: 479 sq. ft.

Main Ceiling: 9 ft.

Bonus Ceiling: 8 ft.

Bedrooms: 3

Baths: 3

Foundation: Crawl, Slab, Basement, Daylight Basement

Plan Options: page 282

Price Tier: B

BEST SELLER
Designers Choice
NELSON DESIGN GROUP

BUILDING SYSTEM
NGI
Next Generation Industries
COMPATABLE

Designed For:

JBL

RESIDENTIAL SYSTEMS
COMPLETE HOME
ENTERTAINMENT NETWORKS
& DISTRIBUTED AUDIO

JBL
Home Theater

Designed For:

Pioneer
sound.vision.soul
Pioneer Sound System

Main Floor

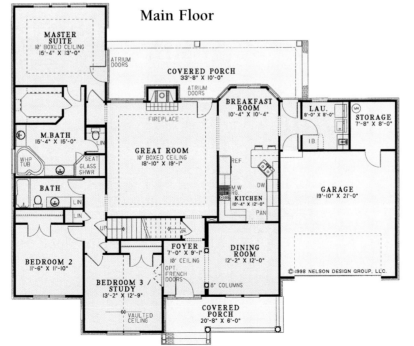

MASTER SUITE
10' BOXED CEILING
15'-4" X 13'-0"

ATRIUM DOORS

COVERED PORCH
33'-8" X 10'-0"

ATRIUM DOORS

M.BATH
15'-4" X 15'-0"

WHP TUB

SEAT
GLASS SHWR

BATH

LIN
LIN

FIREPLACE

GREAT ROOM
10' BOXED CEILING
18'-10" X 19'-1"

BREAKFAST ROOM
10'-4" X 10'-4"

LAU.
8'-0" X 8'-0"

STORAGE
7'-8" X 8'-0"

REF.

KITCHEN
10'-4" X 12'-0"

M.W. FRG.

DW

PAN

GARAGE
19'-10" X 21'-0"

BEDROOM 2
11'-6" X 11'-10"

UP

FOYER
7'-0" X 9'-1"
10' CEILING

OPT. FRENCH DOORS

DINING ROOM
12'-2" X 12'-0"

© 1998 NELSON DESIGN GROUP, LLC.

BEDROOM 3 / STUDY
13'-2" X 12'-9"

VAULTED CEILING

8" COLUMNS

COVERED PORCH
20'-8" X 6'-0"

Bonus Floor

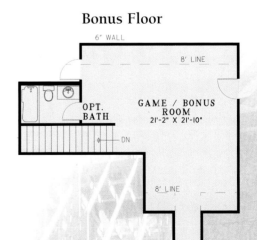

6" WALL

8' LINE

OPT. BATH

GAME / BONUS ROOM
21'-2" X 21'-10"

DN

8' LINE

Elevation A

Elevation B

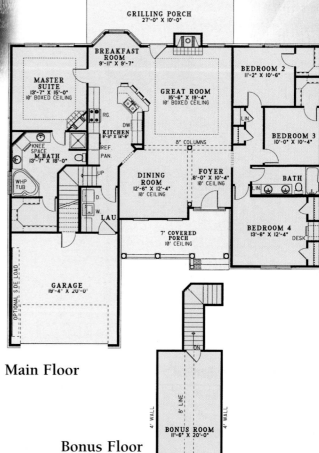

GRILLING PORCH
27'-0" X 10'-0"

BREAKFAST ROOM
9'-11" X 9'-7"

MASTER SUITE
13'-7" X 15'-0"
10' BOXED CEILING

GREAT ROOM
15'-6" X 19'-4"
10' BOXED CEILING

BEDROOM 2
11'-2" X 10'-6"

KITCHEN
9'-11" X 14'-8"

KNEE SPACE

M. BATH
13'-7" X 16'-0"

8" COLUMNS

BEDROOM 3
10'-0" X 10'-4"

WHP TUB

DINING ROOM
12'-6" X 12'-4"
10' CEILING

FOYER
8'-0" X 10'-4"
10' CEILING

BATH

LAU

BEDROOM 4
13'-6" X 12'-4"

DESK

7' COVERED PORCH
10' CEILING

GARAGE
19'-4" X 20'-0"

OPTIONAL S.DE LOAD

Main Floor

BONUS ROOM
11'-6" X 20'-0"

8' LINE

4' WALL

Bonus Floor

Designed For:

Pioneer

sound.vision.soul

Pioneer Sound System

Designed For:

JBL

RESIDENTIAL SYSTEMS
COMPLETE HOME
ENTERTAINMENT NETWORKS
& DISTRIBUTED AUDIO

JBL
Home Theater

544 Glendale Avenue

Width: 57' 0"

Depth: 64' 4"

Total Living: 1,965 sq. ft.*

*Optional Bonus: 251 sq. ft.

Price Tier: B

Main Ceiling: 9 ft.

Bonus Ceiling: 8 ft.

Bedrooms: 4

Baths: 2

Foundation: Crawl, Slab,
Optional Basement,
Optional Daylight Basement

Plan Options: page 282

BUILDING SYSTEM
NGI
Next Generation Industries
COMPATABLE

Elevation A

Elevation B

378 Dogwood Avenue

BATH

BREAKFAST ROOM
12'-4" X 9'-6"

PORCH

KNEE SPACE

WHP TUB

MASTER SUITE
TRAY CEILING
13'-4" X 15'-8"

GUEST ROOM/ BEDROOM 4
12'-8" X 11'-6"

BAR

DW.

RG.

GREAT ROOM
12' CEILING
15'-0" X 18'-4"

M.BATH
8'-10" X 21'-0"

KITCHEN
12'-4" X 13'-6"

REF.

BATH

LIN.

LAU.
5'-6" X 5'-10"

D W

PAN

HVAC

LIN.

8" BOX COL.

FOYER
12' CEILING
7'-4" X 7'-10"

DINING ROOM
10' BOX CEILING
12'-2" X 13'-4"

BEDROOM 3
11'-0" X 10'-4"

BEDROOM 2
11'-2" X 11'-6"

PORCH
7'-0" X 5'-6"

VAULTED CEILING

GARAGE
20'-10" X 25'-0"

© 1999 NELSON DESIGN GROUP, LLC.

Width: 64' 2"
Depth: 49' 0"
Total Living: 1,989 sq. ft.

Main Ceiling: 9 ft.
Bedrooms: 4
Baths: 3
Foundation: Crawl, Slab, Basement, Daylight Basement
Plan Options: page 282

Price Tier: B

BUILDING SYSTEM
NGI
Next Generation Industries
COMPATABLE

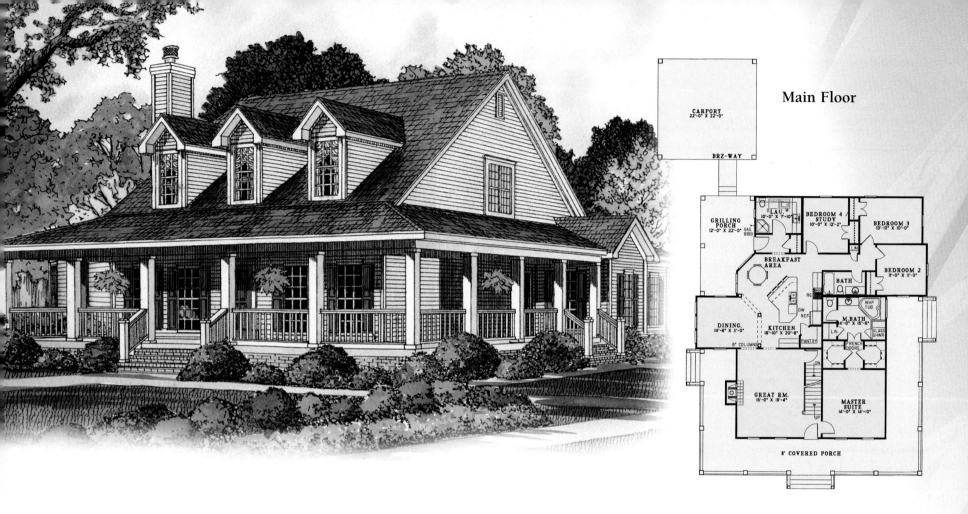

Main Floor

CARPORT
22'-0" X 22'-0"

BRZ-WAY

GRILLING PORCH
12'-0" X 22'-0"

LAU. W
10'-0" X 7'-10"

BEDROOM 4
STUDY
10'-0" X 12'-2"

BEDROOM 3
13'-10" X 10'-0"

BREAKFAST AREA

BATH

BEDROOM 2
11'-0" X 11'-0"

DINING
14'-8" X 11'-0"

KITCHEN
18'-10" X 20'-8"

M. BATH
14'-0" X 16'-8"

WHP TUB

GLASS SHWR

8' COLUMNS

PANTRY

FRENCH DOORS

GREAT RM.
15'-0" X 19'-4"

MASTER SUITE
14'-0" X 14'-10"

UP

8' COVERED PORCH

320 Olive Street

Width: 60' 6"
Depth: 91' 4"
Total Living: 2,039 sq. ft.*
*Optional Bonus: 1,155 sq. ft.

Price Tier: C

Main Ceiling: 9 ft.
Bonus Ceiling: 8 ft.
Bedrooms: 4
Baths: 3
Foundation: Crawl, Slab,
Optional Basement,
Optional Daylight Basement
Plan Options: page 282

BUILDING SYSTEM
NGI
Next Generation Industries
COMPATABLE

Designed For:

JBL
RESIDENTIAL SYSTEMS
COMPLETE HOME
ENTERTAINMENT NETWORKS
& DISTRIBUTED AUDIO

JBL
Home Theater

Designed For:

Pioneer
sound.vision.soul
Pioneer Sound System

Upper Floor

5' WALL

PROPOSED GAME ROOM.
33'-2" X 33'-7"

DN

5' WALL

Main Floor

GRILLING PORCH
16'-0" X 8'-0"

BREAKFAST ROOM
9'-10" X 9'-4"

GREAT RM.
14'-2" X 12'-6"

DW

RG

KITCHEN
12'-8" X 12'-6"

DINING RM.
10'-4" X 12'-6"

PAN   REF

© 1992 NELSON DESIGN GROUP, LLC.

OPT. BASEMENT STAIRS

MEDIA RM./ STUDY
12'-4" X 14'-2"

GARAGE
20'-10" X 21'-2"

COMPUTER CENTER
6'-4"X 6'-6"

FOYER
OPEN ABOVE

COVERED PORCH
13'-6" X 7'-0"

8" COLUMNS

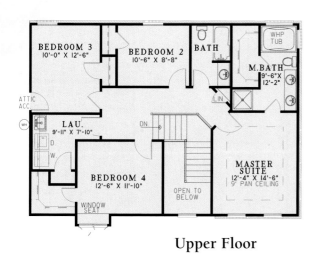

Upper Floor

BEDROOM 3
10'-0" X 12'-6"

BEDROOM 2
10'-6" X 8'-8"

BATH

WHP TUB

M.BATH
9'-6"X 12'-2"

ATTIC ACC.

LIN

LAU.
9'-11" X 7'-10"

DN

WH

D

W

BEDROOM 4
12'-6" X 11'-10"

OPEN TO BELOW

MASTER SUITE
12'-4" X 14'-6"
9' PAN CEILING

WINDOW SEAT

689 Cottonwood Drive

Width: 50' 4"

Depth: 42' 8"

Main Floor: 1,039 sq. ft.

Upper Floor: 1,007 sq. ft.

Total Living: 2,046 sq. ft.

Main Ceiling: 8 ft.

Upper Ceiling: 8 ft.

Bedrooms: 4

Baths: 2 1/2

Foundation: Crawl, Slab,
Optional Basement,
Optional Daylight Basement

Plan Options: page 282

Price Tier: C

BUILDING SYSTEM
NGI
Next Generation Industries
COMPATABLE

BEST SELLER
Designers Choice
NELSON DESIGN GROUP

GRILLING PORCH
27'-2" X 9'-4"
9' CEILING

MASTER SUITE
15'-4" X 14'-0"
10' BOX CEILING

BEDROOM 2
11'-2" X 12'-6"

BRKFST. RM.
10'-10" X 10'-6"
10' CEILING

M.BATH
9'-6" X 12'-5"

GLASS BLOCKS

WHP TUB

LIN.

GREAT RM.
16'-0" X 20'-8"
11' BOXED CEILING

BEDROOM 3
10'-0" X 12'-4"

DESK

DW.

REF RG

KITCHEN
10'-10" X 13'-2"
10' CEILING

LAU.
5'-6" X 7'-6"

W D

PAN.

BATH

STORAGE
9'-6" X 3'-0"

WH

FOYER
6'-10" X 7'-4"
10' CEILING

DN.

OPTIONAL BASEMENT

GARAGE
20'-10" X 21'-0"

DINING RM.
12'-6" X 14'-0"
10' CEILING

PORCH
8'-2" X 5'-0"

BEDROOM 4
13'-6" X 12'-4"

DESK

© 2003 NELSON DESIGN GROUP, LLC.

788 Spruce Street

Width: 59' 8"
Depth: 52' 0"
Total Living: 2,050 sq. ft.

Price Tier: **C**

Main Ceiling: 9 ft.
Bedrooms: 4
Baths: 2
Foundation: Crawl, Slab, Optional Basement, Optional Daylight Basement
Plan Options: page 282

BUILDING SYSTEM
NGI
Next Generation Industries
COMPATABLE

Elevation A

Designed For:

JBL
RESIDENTIAL SYSTEMS
COMPLETE HOME
ENTERTAINMENT NETWORKS
& DISTRIBUTED AUDIO

JBL
Home Theater

Designed For:

Pioneer
sound.vision.soul
Pioneer Sound System

© 1998 NELSON DESIGN GROUP, LLC.

WORK SHOP /
GARAGE
23'-0" X 20'-0"

COVERED GRILLING
PORCH
30'-6" X 12'-6"

GAS
BIBB

STRG.

GARAGE
23'-0" X 22'-4"

WHP
TUB

M.BATH
15'-2" X 18'-0"

LIN

BRKFAST
RM.
12'-4" X 9'-6"

GREAT RM.
17'-0" X 22'-8"
9' BOXED CEILING

REF

W.

D.

LAU

I.B.

BEDROOM 3
11'-8" X 14'-8"

DW

CT

OPT
ISLAND

PAN.

OVEN

KITCHEN
12'-4" X 12'-0"

GALLERY

BOOK
SHELVES

BOOK
SHELVES

FOYER
9' CEILING

MASTER
SUITE
15'-2" X 16'-0"
9' BOXED CEILING

COVERED PORCH
17'-0" X 5'-0"
9' CEILING

DINING RM.
12'-4" X 12'-0"
9' BOXED CEILING

LIN.

BEDROOM 2
13'-4" X 10'-8"

Elevation B

255 Cherry Street

Width:	69' 2"	Main Ceiling:	8 ft.
Depth:	74' 10"	Bedrooms:	3
Total Living:	2,096 sq. ft.	Baths:	2 1/2

Price Tier: **C**

Foundation: Crawl, Slab, Basement, Daylight Basement

Plan Options: page 282

BUILDING SYSTEM
NGI
Next Generation Industries
COMPATABLE

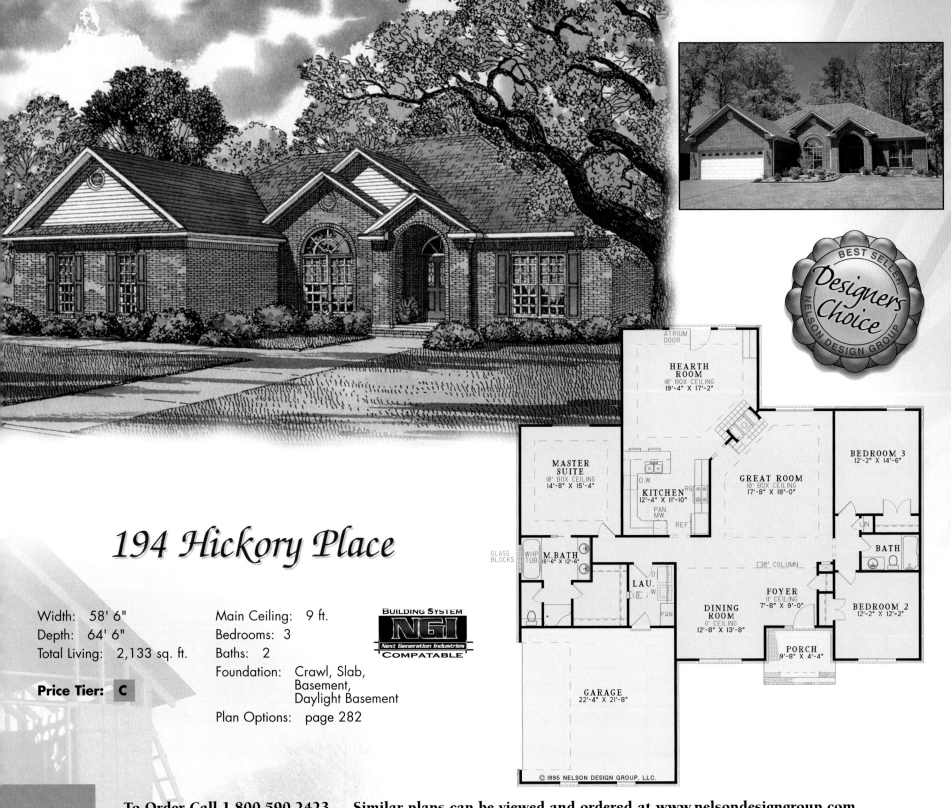

194 Hickory Place

Width: 58' 6"
Depth: 64' 6"
Total Living: 2,133 sq. ft.

Price Tier: C

Main Ceiling: 9 ft.
Bedrooms: 3
Baths: 2
Foundation: Crawl, Slab, Basement, Daylight Basement
Plan Options: page 282

BUILDING SYSTEM
NGI
Next Generation Industries
COMPATABLE

Floor Plan Labels

ATRIUM DOOR

HEARTH ROOM
10' BOX CEILING
19'-4" X 17'-2"

MASTER SUITE
10' BOX CEILING
14'-8" X 15'-4"

KITCHEN
12'-4" X 11'-10"
D.W.
RGE
PAN.
MW
REF

GREAT ROOM
10' BOX CEILING
17'-8" X 18'-0"

BEDROOM 3
12'-2" X 14'-6"

LIN

BATH

GLASS BLOCKS

WHP TUB

M. BATH
15'-6" X 12'-6"

LAU.
D
W
PAN

8" COLUMN

FOYER
11' CEILING
7'-8" X 9'-0"

BEDROOM 2
12'-2" X 12'-2"

DINING ROOM
11' CEILING
12'-8" X 13'-8"

PORCH
9'-8" X 4'-4"

GARAGE
22'-4" X 21'-8"

© 1995 NELSON DESIGN GROUP, LLC.

BEST SELLER
Designers Choice
NELSON DESIGN GROUP

To Order Call 1.800.590.2423   Similar plans can be viewed and ordered at www.nelsondesigngroup.com

Elevation A

Designed For:

JBL

RESIDENTIAL SYSTEMS
COMPLETE HOME
ENTERTAINMENT NETWORKS
& DISTRIBUTED AUDIO

JBL
Home Theater

Designed For:

Pioneer
sound.vision.soul
Pioneer Sound System

PATIO

COVERED PORCH
31'-8" X 9'-0"

WHP TUB

M. BATH
16'-8" X 11'-0"

MASTER BEDROOM
16'-8" X 14'-0"
9' BOXED CEILING

BED RM. 4
14'-4" X 11'-0"

BRKFST. RM.
12'-6" X 9'-6"

KITCHEN
12'-6" X 10'-0"

LAUNDRY
7'-6" X 8'-8"

GREAT RM.
19'-6" X 17'-0"
10' CEILING

BATH

REF.

PAN

1/2 B.

W. D.

I.B.

BUILT-INS
(OPT. TO STUDY)

DW

OVEN

CT.

BED RM. 3
10'-6" X 12'-0"

FOYER
10' CEILING

DN

BED RM. 2 / STUDY
11'-0" X 12'-0"

OPT. DOOR

DINING RM.
11'-0" X 12'-0"
9' BOXED CEILING
8' CEILING

GARAGE
20'-4" X 22'-10"

OPTIONAL SIDE GARAGE

PORCH

PLANTER

© 1998 NELSON DESIGN GROUP, LLC.

Elevation B

190-1 Cherry Street

Width: 64' 8"	Main Ceiling: 8 ft.
Depth: 62' 1"	Bedrooms: 4
Total Living: 2,158 sq. ft.	Baths: 2 1/2

Price Tier: C

Foundation: Crawl, Slab, Basement, Daylight Basement

Plan Options: page 282

BUILDING SYSTEM
NGi
Next Generation Industries
COMPATABLE

To Order Call 1.800.590.2423   Similar plans can be viewed and ordered at www.nelsondesigngroup.com

189

562 Thomas Road

Width: 69' 10"
Depth: 55' 6"
Total Living: 2,169 sq. ft.*
*Optional Bonus: 319 sq. ft.
Main Ceiling: 9 ft.
Bonus Ceiling: 8 ft.
Bedrooms: 4
Baths: 2
Foundation: Crawl, Slab
Plan Options: page 282

Price Tier: C

BUILDING SYSTEM
NGI
Next Generation Industries
COMPATABLE

BEST SELLER
Designers Choice
NELSON DESIGN GROUP

Main Floor

LIN.
GLASS SHWR
MASTER SUITE 13'-0" X 14'-0"
M.BATH 9'-2" X 14'-0"
WHP TUB
LAU. 9'-2" X 5'-10"
D W
UP
GARAGE 21'-4" X 20'-0"
GRILLING PORCH 40'-2" X 8'-0"
BREAKFAST ROOM 13'-0" X 9'-0"
VAULTED CEILING
PANTRY
DW
REF.
KITCHEN 13'-0" X 13'-0"
GREAT ROOM 17'-2" X 19'-4"
COMPUTER ROOM
DINING ROOM 11'-8" X 11'-8"
FOYER 7'-8" X 11'-8"
8' COVERED PORCH
BEDROOM 4 / STUDY 11'-6" X 11'-8"
BEDROOM 4 11'-4" X 11'-4"
BEDROOM 3 11'-10" X 13'-2"
BATH
LIN
© 2001 NELSON DESIGN GROUP, LLC.

Bonus Floor

4' WALL
8' LINE
ATTIC STORAGE / FUTURE SPACE
DN
8' LINE
BONUS ROOM 21'-8" X 19'-4"
4' WALL

To Order Call 1.800.590.2423   Similar plans can be viewed and ordered at www.nelsondesigngroup.com

Main Floor

CARPORT
22'-0" X 22'-0"

10X10 BOXED COLUMNS

COVERED WALK

PORCH
12'-0" X 22'-0"

GLASS SHWR

LAU.
10'-2" X 7'-10"

BEDROOM 4
STUDY
10'-0" X 12'-2"

BEDROOM 3
13'-10" X 10'-0"

BEDROOM 2
13'-4" X 11'-0"

BREAKFAST AREA
18'-10" X 9'-2"

BATH

DINING ROOM
14'-0" X 11'-0"

ISLAND

KITCHEN
13'-6" X 16'-6"

PANTRY

M.BATH
17'-10" X 14'-4"

WHP TUB

GLASS BLOCKS

SEAT

FRENCH DOORS

GREAT ROOM
15'-0" X 19'-4"

BUILT-INS

MASTER SUITE
14'-8" X 14'-10"

FOYER

UP

PORCH
38'-8" X 8'-0"

© 1998 NELSON DESIGN GROUP, LLC.

10X10 BOXED COLUMNS

Bonus Floor

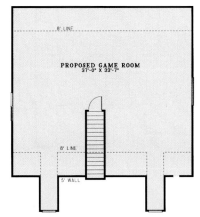

8' LINE

PROPOSED GAME ROOM
37'-0" X 33'-7"

8' LINE

5' WALL

Designed For:

RESIDENTIAL SYSTEMS
COMPLETE HOME
ENTERTAINMENT NETWORKS
& DISTRIBUTED AUDIO

JBL
Home Theater

Designed For:

sound.vision.soul
Pioneer Sound System

340 Olive Street

Width: 62' 10"	Main Ceiling: 9 ft.
Depth: 91' 4"	Bonus Ceiling: 8 ft.
Total Living: 2,186 sq. ft.*	Bedrooms: 4
*Optional Bonus: 1,283 sq. ft.	Baths: 3

BUILDING SYSTEM
NGI
Next Generation Industries
COMPATABLE

Price Tier: C

Foundation: Crawl, Slab, Basement, Daylight Basement

Plan Options: page 282

Designed For:

JBL

RESIDENTIAL SYSTEMS
COMPLETE HOME
ENTERTAINMENT NETWORKS
& DISTRIBUTED AUDIO

JBL
Home Theater

Designed For:

Pioneer
sound.vision.soul
Pioneer Sound System

467 Kensington Cove

Width: 65' 2"

Depth: 63' 8"

Total Living: 2,147 sq. ft.

Price Tier: C

Main Ceiling: 8 ft.

Bedrooms: 4

Baths: 2 1/2

Foundation: Crawl, Slab,
Optional Basement,
Optional Daylight Basement

Plan Options: page 282

BUILDING SYSTEM
NGI
Next Generation Industries
COMPATABLE

Floor Plan Labels

- WHP TUB — 12" STEP
- M. BATH 16'-8" X 11'-0"
- MASTER SUITE 16'-8" X 13'-10" 8' CEILING 10' BOX 9' BOX
- PATIO 32'-6" X 8'-0"
- COVERED PORCH 32'-6" X 9'-0"
- BEDROOM 4 14'-4" X 11'-0"
- BRKFST. RM. 13'-0" X 9'-2"
- BATH
- STORAGE 9'-6" X 5'-4"
- ISLAND PAN. REF.
- KITCHEN 13'-0" X 10'-2"
- GREAT RM. 19'-6" X 17'-0" 10' CEILING
- BUILT-INS
- BEDROOM 2 10'-6" X 12'-0"
- FOYER 10' CEILING
- GARAGE 22'-8" X 22'-8"
- DINING RM. 10' CEILING 11'-0" X 12'-0"
- BEDROOM 3 11'-0" X 12'-0"
- PORCH

© 1991 NELSON DESIGN GROUP, LLC.

To Order Call 1.800.590.2423   Similar plans can be viewed and ordered at www.nelsondesigngroup.com

651 Olive Street

BEST SELLER
Designers Choice
NELSON DESIGN GROUP

BEDROOM 2
11'-4" X 12'-0"

FRENCH FXD   FRENCH DOOR

BREAKFAST ROOM
11'-4" X 13'-4"

WHP TUB

M. BATH
18'-2" X 12'-0"

GREAT ROOM
20'-6" X 21'-0"

BAR
T.C.
D.W.

KITCHEN
11'-4" X 12'-6"

REF
RG
PAN

MASTER SUITE
10' BOXED CEILING
18'-2" X 13'-6"

11' BOX
10' BOX

BATH
LIN
HVAC

LAU.
10'-0" X 5'-10"
W D

STOR.

10" COLUMNS

BEDROOM 4
9'-10" X 10'-6"

FOYER
7'-2" X 10'-4"

DINING ROOM
10' CEILING
11'-0" X 11'-3"

BEDROOM 3
11'-4" X 11'-10"

GARAGE
22'-0" X 21'-8"

PORCH
20'-4" X 8'-6"

10" COLUMNS

© 2002 NELSON DESIGN GROUP, LLC.

Width: 63' 0"
Depth: 54' 10"
Total Living: 2,214 sq. ft.

Price Tier: C

Main Ceiling: 9 ft.
Bedrooms: 4
Baths: 2
Foundation: Crawl, Slab, Optional Basement, Optional Daylight Basement

Plan Options: page 282

BUILDING SYSTEM
NGi
Next Generation Industries
COMPATABLE

108 Olive Street

Width: 67' 8"
Depth: 58' 0"
Total Living: 2,216 sq. ft.

Price Tier: C

Main Ceiling: 9 ft.
Bedrooms: 3
Baths: 2 1/2
Foundation: Crawl, Slab
Plan Options: page 282

BUILDING SYSTEM
NGI
Next Generation Industries
COMPATABLE

Floor plan labels:

DECK OR PATIO

HEARTH ROOM
10'-8" X 13'-4"

GRILLING PORCH
9'-0" X 6'-0"

WHP TUB

M. BATH
9'-8" X 22'-2"

MASTER SUITE
15'-0" X 17'-0"
10' BOXED CEILING

GREAT RM.
17'-2" X 22'-2"
10' BOXED CEILING

BREAKFAST ROOM
12'-8" X 12'-4"

BOOK SHELVES

PAN.

REF.

ISLAND

KITCHEN
12'-8" X 11'-4"
DW

LIN

LIN

GALLERY
9' CEILING

RG

L/S

PAN

BEDROOM 2
11'-0" X 11'-2"

LIN

FOYER
7'-10" X 9'-10"
10' CEILING

10" COLUMNS

DINING RM.
11'-4" X 13'-10"
10' CEILING W/
11' BOXED CEILING

LAUNDRY
9'-0" X 5'-8"

STORAGE
8'-0" X 5'-8"

W   D

WH

BEDROOM 3
11'-4" X 14'-2"
10' CEILING

GARAGE
22'-0" X 21'-4"

PORCH
7'-0" X 9'-10"

© 1991 NELSON DESIGN GROUP, LLC.

700 Linden Avenue

BEST SELLER
Designers Choice
NELSON DESIGN GROUP

GLASS BLOCKS

M. BATH
15'-9" X 14'-4"

BREAKFAST ROOM
11'-4" X 12'-4"

GRILLING PORCH
17'-6" X 8'-0"

BEDROOM 4
14'-10" X 12'-6"

MASTER SUITE
15'-8" X 14'-0"
10' BOXED CEILING

KITCHEN
11'-4" X 12'-6"

GREAT ROOM
17'-6" X 20'-8"
10' CEILING

LIN.

BEDROOM 3
11'-0" X 10'-8"

10' CEILING

STORAGE
12'-0" X 5'-6"

LAU.
8'-5" X 5'-6"

8" COLUMNS

FOYER
6'-4" X 7'-8"
10' CEILING

BEDROOM 2
11'-0" X 13'-6"

OPTIONAL BASEMENT PLAN

DINING ROOM
11'-4" X 14'-10"
10' CEILING

ENTRY

BATH

GARAGE
20'-10" X 20'-0"

© 1993 NELSON DESIGN GROUP, LLC.

Width: 61' 2"	Main Ceiling: 9 ft.
Depth: 55' 6"	Bedrooms: 4
Total Living: 2,217 sq. ft.	Baths: 2
	Foundation: Crawl, Slab, Optional Basement, Optional Daylight Basement
Price Tier: C	Plan Options: page 282

BUILDING SYSTEM NGi Next Generation Industries **COMPATABLE**

652 Tyler Street

Width: 63' 0"
Depth: 55' 8"
Total Living: 2,239 sq. ft.

Price Tier: C

Main Ceiling: 9 ft.
Bedrooms: 4
Baths: 2
Foundation: Crawl, Slab,
Optional Basement,
Optional Daylight Basement

Plan Options: page 282

BUILDING SYSTEM
NGI
Next Generation Industries
COMPATABLE

GRILLING PORCH
20'-10" X 9'-0"

BREAKFAST ROOM
11'-4" X 14'-2"

MASTER SUITE
18'-2" X 12'-0"
10' BOXED CEILING

BEDROOM 2
11'-4" X 12'-0"

GREAT ROOM
20'-6" X 21'-0"
10' BOXED CEILING

KITCHEN
11'-4" X 12'-6"

BAR
T.C.
D.W.
REF.
RG
PAN

M.BATH
14'-4" X 14'-4"
8' COLUMNS

KNEE SPACE

WHP TUB

LAU.
9'-10" X 5'-10"

STOR.

BATH
LIN
HVAC

BEDROOM 3
11'-4" X 11'-10"

BEDROOM 4
9'-10" X 10'-6"

FOYER
7'-2" X 10'-4"

10' COLUMNS

DINING ROOM
11'-0" X 11'-3"
10' CEILING

GARAGE
22'-0" X 21'-8"

PORCH
20'-4" X 8'-6"
10' COLUMNS

© 2002 NELSON DESIGN GROUP, LLC.

To Order Call 1.800.590.2423   Similar plans can be viewed and ordered at www.nelsondesigngroup.com

Main Floor

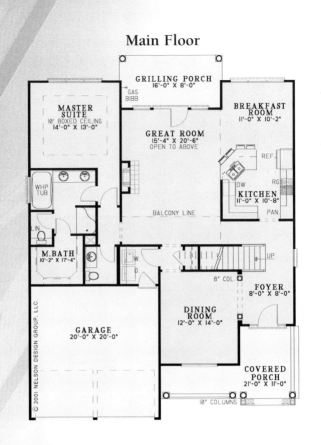

GRILLING PORCH
16'-0" X 8'-0"

GAS BIBB

MASTER SUITE
10' BOXED CEILING
14'-0" X 13'-0"

BREAKFAST ROOM
11'-0" X 10'-2"

GREAT ROOM
15'-4" X 20'-6"
OPEN TO ABOVE

REF.

WHP TUB

DW
RG

KITCHEN
11'-0" X 10'-8"

PAN

BALCONY LINE

M.BATH
10'-2" X 17'-4"

LIN

W
D

UP

8' COL.

FOYER
8'-0" X 8'-0"

GARAGE
20'-0" X 20'-0"

DINING ROOM
12'-0" X 14'-0"

COVERED PORCH
21'-0" X 11'-0"

© 2001 NELSON DESIGN GROUP, LLC.

10" COLUMNS

Upper Floor

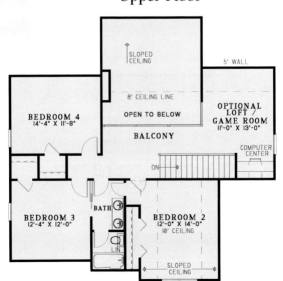

SLOPED CEILING

5' WALL

8' CEILING LINE
OPEN TO BELOW

OPTIONAL LOFT / GAME ROOM
11'-0" X 13'-0"

BEDROOM 4
14'-4" X 11'-8"

BALCONY

COMPUTER CENTER

DN

BEDROOM 3
12'-4" X 12'-0"

BATH

LIN

BEDROOM 2
12'-0" X 14'-0"
10' CEILING

SLOPED CEILING

Designed For:

JBL

RESIDENTIAL SYSTEMS
COMPLETE HOME
ENTERTAINMENT NETWORKS
& DISTRIBUTED AUDIO

JBL
Home Theater

Designed For:

Pioneer
sound.vision.soul
Pioneer Sound System

604 Cypress Drive

Width: 41' 8"
Depth: 55' 6"
Main Floor: 1,449 sq. ft.
Upper Floor: 795 sq. ft.
Total Living: 2,244 sq. ft.*
*Optional Bonus: 181 sq. ft.

Price Tier: C

Main Ceiling: 9 ft.
Bonus Ceiling: 8 ft.
Bedrooms: 4
Baths: 2 1/2
Foundation: Crawl, Slab,
Optional Basement,
Optional Daylight Basement
Plan Options: page 282

BUILDING SYSTEM
NGi
Next Generation Industries
COMPATABLE

275 Olive Street

Width: 69' 6"
Depth: 31' 0"
Main Floor: 1,154 sq. ft.
Upper Floor: 1,093 sq. ft.
Total Living: 2,247 sq. ft.
Main Ceiling: 9 ft.
Bonus Ceiling: 9 ft.
Bedrooms: 3
Baths: 2 1/2
Foundation: Crawl, Slab, Basement, Daylight Basement
Plan Options: page 282

Price Tier: C

BUILDING SYSTEM
NGI
Next Generation Industries
COMPATABLE

Designed For:

Pioneer
sound.vision.soul
Pioneer Sound System

Designed For:

JBL
RESIDENTIAL SYSTEMS
COMPLETE HOME
ENTERTAINMENT NETWORKS
& DISTRIBUTED AUDIO

JBL
Home Theater

Main Floor

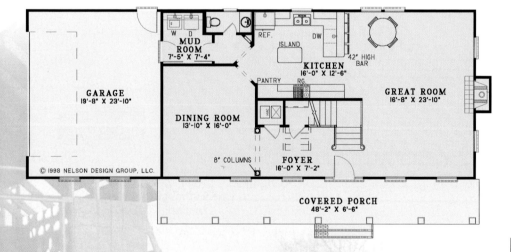

Upper Floor

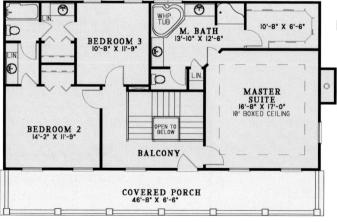

To Order Call 1.800.590.2423   **Similar plans can be viewed and ordered at www.nelsondesigngroup.com**

175 Richmond Drive

Width: 68' 6"
Depth: 65' 0"
Total Living: 2,250 sq. ft.

Price Tier: C

Main Ceiling: 9 ft.
Bedrooms: 4
Baths: 2
Foundation: Crawl, Slab, Optional Basement, Optional Daylight Basement
Plan Options: page 282

Floor plan labels

- MAKE-UP
- W.I.C.
- M. BATH 17'-4" X 14'-6"
- BUILT-IN DRAWERS
- WHP TUB
- LIN
- SHWR
- MASTER SUITE 17'-6" X 14'-0" 10' BOXED CEILING
- COMPUTER CENTER
- DESK
- GRILLING PORCH 20'-4" X 10'-0"
- BREAKFAST 15'-2" X 11'-2"
- BEDROOM 4 11'-4" X 12'-2"
- STOR. 6'-0" X 6'-2"
- LAU. 7'-4" X 6'-2"
- W D LIN
- KID'S NOOK
- BENCH W/ HANGING
- PAN
- VAULTED CEILING
- D.W
- GREAT ROOM 19'-4" X 17'-2" 10' CEILING
- LIN
- OVEN/ MW
- KITCHEN 11'-4" X 13'-8" 10' BOX CEILING
- C.T.
- LIN
- BATH
- GARAGE 21'-4" X 21'-4"
- REF
- R.A.
- © 1995 NELSON DESIGN GROUP, LLC.
- DINING ROOM 11'-6" X 12'-8"
- FOYER 6'-4" X 16'-2"
- BEDROOM 2 11'-6" X 12'-8"
- BEDROOM 3 11'-4" X 11'-0"
- PORCH 31'-8" X 6'-0"

BUILDING SYSTEM NGI Next Generation Industries COMPATABLE

Elevation B

Bonus Floor

4' WALL

8' LINE

BONUS ROOM
21'-10" X 13'-2"

FUTURE SPACE

DN

BATH

ATTIC STORAGE

Elevation A

Designed For:

Pioneer
sound.vision.soul
Pioneer Sound System

Designed For:

JBL

RESIDENTIAL SYSTEMS
COMPLETE HOME
ENTERTAINMENT NETWORKS
& DISTRIBUTED AUDIO

JBL
Home Theater

526 Olive Street

Width: 66' 0"
Depth: 65' 2"
Total Living: 2,261 sq. ft.*
*Optional Bonus: 367 sq. ft.

Main Ceiling: 9 ft.
Bonus Ceiling: 8 ft.
Bedrooms: 4
Baths: 3 1/2
Foundation: Crawl, Slab, Basement, Daylight Basement
Plan Options: page 282

Price Tier: C

BUILDING SYSTEM
NGI
Next Generation Industries
COMPATABLE

Main Floor

WHP TUB

M. BATH
16'-8" X 11'-6"

8' CEILING

PATIO

COVERED GRILLING PORCH
31'-8" X 9'-0"

MASTER SUITE
16'-8" X 14'-0"
9' BOXED CEILING

BEDROOM 4
14'-4" X 11'-0"

BRKFST. RM.
12'-6" X 9'-6"

LIN

KITCHEN
12'-6" X 10'-0"

LAUNDRY
7'-6" X 8'-8"

GREAT RM.
19'-6" X 17'-0"
10' CEILING

REF.

PAN

BATH

LIN

1/2 B.

BUILT-INS
(OPT. TO STUDY)

OVEN

CT

DW

UP OR DN

OPT

BEDROOM 3
10'-6" X 12'-0"

OPT DOOR

FOYER
10' CEILING

DINING RM.
11'-0" X 14'-4"
11' BOXED CEILING

GARAGE
20'-4" X 23'-7"

BEDROOM 2 / STUDY
11'-0" X 12'-0"
10' CEILING

COVERED PORCH
30'-4" X 8'-0"

OPTIONAL FRONT GARAGE

© 2001 NELSON DESIGN GROUP, LLC.

HEARTH RM./
MEDIA ROOM
13'-10" X 12'-0"

BRKFAST RM.
13'-10" X 10'-4"

GRILLING
PORCH
16'-8" X 10'-0"

PORCH
14'-4" X 6'-0"

GLASS
SHWR

WHP
TUB

M.BATH
12'-6" X 17'-8"

K.S.

LIN.

9' CEILING

DW.

ISLAND

CT.

MW
OVEN

REF.

KITCHEN
13'-10" X 15'-0"

PAN.

W.

D.

LAU.
9'-4" X 7'-6"

STORAGE
14'-0" X 3'-2"

KID'S
NOOK

BENCH W/
HANGING

CURB

GARAGE
20'-8" X 24'-0"

© 1993 NELSON DESIGN GROUP, LLC.

GREAT RM.
16'-8" X 16'-0"
10' BOXED CEILING

MASTER SUITE
14'-0" X 16'-0"
9' BOXED CEILING

BEDROOM 4
12'-6" X 11'-0"

BATH

8" COLUMN

FOYER
12' CEILING
7'-4" X
6'-4"

LIN.

DINING RM.
10'-8" X 13'-8"
9' CEILING

PORCH
11' CEILING

BEDROOM 2
13'-0" X 11'-0"

BEDROOM 3
12'-0" X 12'-0"

773 Cherry Street

Width: 70' 0"
Depth: 73' 8"
Total Living: 2,285 sq. ft.

Price Tier: C

Main Ceiling: 8 ft.
Bedrooms: 4
Baths: 2
Foundation: Crawl, Slab,
Optional Basement,
Optional Daylight Basement
Plan Options: page 282

BUILDING SYSTEM
NGi
Next Generation Industries
COMPATABLE

180 Olive Street

Width: 69' 2"
Depth: 39' 4"
Main Floor: 1,591 sq. ft.
Upper Floor: 729 sq. ft.
Total Living: 2,320 sq. ft.*
*Optional Bonus: 510 sq. ft.
Main Ceiling: 9 ft.
Upper Ceiling: 8 ft.
Bedrooms: 3
Baths: 2 1/2
Foundation: Crawl, Slab,
Optional Basement,
Optional Daylight Basement
Plan Options: page 282

Price Tier: C

Designed For:

sound.vision.soul
Pioneer Sound System

BUILDING SYSTEM
NGI
Next Generation Industries
COMPATABLE

Designed For:

JBL
RESIDENTIAL SYSTEMS
COMPLETE HOME
ENTERTAINMENT NETWORKS
& DISTRIBUTED AUDIO

JBL
Home Theater

Main Floor

GRILLING PORCH 22'-8" X 7'-0"
LAUNDRY CHUTE
STORAGE 13'-6" X 9'-4"
LAU.
BREAKFAST/ MORNING ROOM 17'-8" X 13'-4"
KITCHEN 13'-0" X 13'-4"
DW
K.S.
RG.
REF.
M. BATH 14'-10" X 8'-10"
WHP TUB
LIN.
W.I.C.
W.I.C.
OPTIONAL BASEMENT STAIR LOCATION
PANTRY
COMPUTER CENTER
UP TO ABOVE
GARAGE 22'-4" X 22'-0"
GREAT ROOM 17'-8" X 18'-0"
MASTER SUITE 14'-10" X 16'-2"
FOYER 5'-4" X 18'-0"
UP
COVERED PORCH 27'-4" X 5'-10"
© 1990 NELSON DESIGN GROUP, LLC.

Upper Floor

LAU. CHUTE
OPTIONAL COMPUTER CENTER
LOFT / TV AREA 14'-6" X 10'-0"
DN
BEDROOM 3 18'-4" X 10'-7"
PROPOSED BONUS ROOM 22'-4" X 26'-6"
BEDROOM 2 12'-4" X 22'-10"
BATH
OPEN TO BELOW
8' LINE
8' LINE
6' WALL
LEDGE
4' WALL
ATTIC STORAGE
ATTIC STORAGE

To Order Call 1.800.590.2423   Similar plans can be viewed and ordered at www.nelsondesigngroup.com

ATTIC STORAGE

BATH

BONUS / MEDIA ROOM
20'-8" X 20'-10"

5'7" WALL

8' LINE

DINING BELOW
10' CEILING

DN

Bonus Floor

GRILLING PORCH

10' COVERED PORCH

GAS BIBB

HEARTH. ROOM
19'-8" X 11'-4"

BEDROOM 2
11'-2" X 9'-10"

BEDROOM 3
11'-8" X 11'-6"

MASTER SUITE
13'-0" X 16'-10"
10' BOXED CEILING

GREAT ROOM
16'-0" X 22'-8"
10' CEILING

KITCHEN
13'-4" X 11'-8"

DW   RG

REF.   PAN.

GLASS SHWR

BATH

LIN

BUTLER'S PANTRY

M.BATH
8'-2" X 15'-2"

WHP TUB

BEDROOM 4 / GAME ROOM
15'-6" X 11'-0"

FOYER
9'-0" X 8'-4"
10' CEILING

DINING
11'-10" X 13'-0"
10' CEILING

8" COLUMNS

D.

W.

LAU.
6'-4" X 11'-4"

UP

STORAGE

COVERED PORCH
38'-0" X 6'-0"

GARAGE
20'-10" X 24'-6"

© 2000 NELSON DESIGN GROUP, LLC.

Main Floor

Designed For:

Pioneer
sound.vision.soul
Pioneer Sound System

Designed For:

JBL
RESIDENTIAL SYSTEMS
COMPLETE HOME
ENTERTAINMENT NETWORKS
& DISTRIBUTED AUDIO

JBL
Home Theater

620 Emery Lane

Width: 61' 0"
Depth: 71' 8"
Total Living: 2,338 sq. ft.*
*Optional Bonus: 553 sq. ft.

Price Tier: C

Main Ceiling: 9 ft.
Bonus Ceiling: 8 ft.
Bedrooms: 4
Baths: 3
Foundation: Crawl, Slab,
Optional Basement,
Optional Daylight Basement
Plan Options: page 282

BUILDING SYSTEM
NGI
Next Generation Industries
COMPATABLE

To Order Call 1.800.590.2423   Similar plans can be viewed and ordered at www.nelsondesigngroup.com

203

646 Quail Drive

Width: 76' 10"

Depth: 53' 4"

Total Living: 2,373 sq. ft.*

*Optional Bonus 1: 776 sq. ft.

*Optional Bonus 2: 896 sq. ft.

Main Ceiling: 9 ft.

Bonus Ceiling: 8 ft.

Bedrooms: 4

Baths: 3

Foundation: Crawl, Slab,
Optional Basement,
Optional Daylight Basement

Plan Options: page 282

Price Tier: C

BUILDING SYSTEM
NGI
Next Generation Industries
COMPATABLE

Designed For:

JBL
RESIDENTIAL SYSTEMS
COMPLETE HOME
ENTERTAINMENT NETWORKS
& DISTRIBUTED AUDIO

JBL
Home Theater

Designed For:

PIONEER
sound.vision.soul
Pioneer Sound System

BEST SELLER
Designers Choice
NELSON DESIGN GROUP

Main Floor

MASTER SUITE 17'-9" X 16'-4"

M.BATH

WHP TUB

SEAT

LIN

K.S.

TV CAB

LAUNDRY 8'-10" X 6'-4"

W   D

BENCH W/ HANGING

HANGING

GRILLING PORCH 35'-10" X 10'-0"

BREAKFAST ROOM 12'-0" X 8'-0"

PAN.

REF

KITCHEN 12'-0" X 12'-8"

OVEN
MW

DW

CT

8' COLUMNS

GREAT ROOM 19'-4" X 17'-8"

MEDIA CENTER

BEDROOM 4 12'-6" X 11'-0"

BATH

BEDROOM 3 11'-0" X 11'-0"

LIN

BATH

R.A.

OPTIONAL BASEMENT STAIRS

GARAGE 21'-0" X 22'-0"

UP

STORAGE 7'-8" X 4'-4"

DINING 11'-10" X 12'-0"

FOYER 7'-0" X 11'-10"

BEDROOM 2/ STUDY 12'-0" X 12'-0"

OPTIONAL FRENCH DOORS

COVERED PORCH 33'-0" X 8'-0"

© 2002 NELSON DESIGN GROUP, LLC.

Upper Floor

BONUS ROOM 13'-4" X 17'-5"

4' WALL

8' LINE

STORAGE

4' WALL

8' LINE

BONUS ROOM 1 21'-4" X 19'-6"

DN

8' LINE

BONUS ROOM 2 31'-8" X 25'-7"

ATTIC STORAGE

4' WALL

8' LINE

To Order Call 1.800.590.2423   **Similar plans can be viewed and ordered at www.nelsondesigngroup.com**

© 1999 NELSON DESIGN GROUP, LLC.

GARAGE
21'-0" X 21'-0"

STOR.

LAU.
10'-10" X 6'-0"

1/2 BATH

BEDROOM 2
10'-10" X 12'-0"

BATH

BEDROOM 3
12'-4" X 12'-0"

DINING ROOM
13'-0" X 13'-0"

KITCHEN
13'-0" X 15'-0"

ATRIUM DOOR

BREAKFAST ROOM
13'-0" X 9'-0"

ISLAND

PORCH
31'-4" X 16'-0"

14" COLUMNS

ATRIUM DOOR

MEDIA CENTER

GREAT ROOM
10' CEILING
20'-4" X 19'-6"

GAS FIREPLACE

FOYER
7'-0" X 13'-0"

BEDROOM 4
13'-0" X 10'-8"

WHP TUB

SEAT

GLASS SHWR.

M. BATH
14'-8" X 18'-4"

KNEE SPACE

LIN

MASTER SUITE
14'-8" X 15'-0"

PORCH
35'-4" X 6'-0"

14" COLUMNS

368 Olive Street

Width: 68' 0"	Bedrooms: 4
Depth: 74' 0"	Baths: 2 1/2
Total Living: 2,388 sq. ft.	Foundation: Crawl, Slab,
Main Ceiling: 9 ft.	Optional Basement,
	Optional Daylight Basement
Price Tier: C	Plan Options: page 282

BUILDING SYSTEM
NGI
Next Generation Industries
COMPATABLE

Bonus Floor

563 Country Club Drive

Width: 66' 4"

Depth: 67' 2"

Total Living: 2,405 sq. ft.*

*Optional Bonus: 358 sq. ft.

Price Tier: C

Main Ceiling: 9 ft.

Bonus Ceiling: 8 ft.

Bedrooms: 4

Baths: 3

Foundation: Crawl, Slab, Optional Basement, Optional Daylight Basement

Plan Options: page 282

Designed For:

JBL

RESIDENTIAL SYSTEMS

COMPLETE HOME
ENTERTAINMENT NETWORKS
& DISTRIBUTED AUDIO

JBL
Home Theater

Designed For:

Pioneer
sound.vision.soul
Pioneer Sound System

Main Floor

To Order Call 1.800.590.2423   Similar plans can be viewed and ordered at www.nelsondesigngroup.com

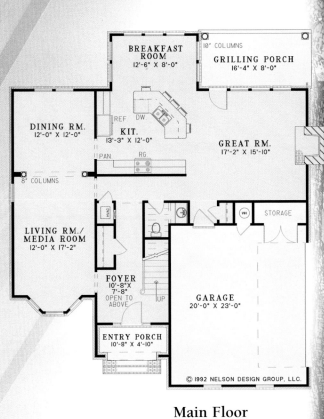

Main Floor

BREAKFAST ROOM
12'-6" X 8'-0"

GRILLING PORCH
16'-4" X 8'-0"

10" COLUMNS

DINING RM.
12'-0" X 12'-0"

REF. DW.

KIT.
13'-3" X 12'-0"

PAN RG

GREAT RM.
17'-2" X 15'-10"

8" COLUMNS

LIVING RM./
MEDIA ROOM
12'-0" X 17'-2"

HVAC

STORAGE

FOYER
10'-8"X
7'-8"
OPEN TO
ABOVE

UP

GARAGE
20'-0" X 23'-0"

ENTRY PORCH
10'-8" X 4'-10"

© 1992 NELSON DESIGN GROUP, LLC.

Upper Floor

WHP TUB

D.
W

M. BATH
16'-8" X 12'-0"

LAU.

K.S.

BEDROOM 2
16'-2" X 12'-0"

LIN

LIN

MASTER SUITE
14'-10" X 17'-2"
9' BOXED CEILING

DN

BEDROOM 3
16'-2" X 10'-0"

OPEN TO FOYER

BONUS ROOM

8' LINE

4' WALL

706 Dogwood Avenue

Width: 46' 5"
Depth: 51' 2"
Main Floor: 1,245 sq. ft.
Upper Floor: 1,190 sq. ft.
Total Living: 2,435 sq. ft.*
*Optional Bonus: 184 sq. ft.

Main Ceiling: 9 ft.
Upper Ceiling: 8 ft.
Bedrooms: 3
Baths: 2 1/2
Foundation: Crawl, Slab,
Optional Basement,
Optional Daylight Basement
Plan Options: page 282

Price Tier: C

BUILDING SYSTEM
NGI
Next Generation Industries
COMPATABLE

Designed For:

JBL
RESIDENTIAL SYSTEMS
COMPLETE HOME
ENTERTAINMENT NETWORKS
& DISTRIBUTED AUDIO

JBL
Home Theater

Designed For:

Pioneer
sound.vision.soul
Pioneer Sound System

204 Richmond Drive

Width: 65' 8"
Depth: 61' 7"
Total Living: 2,439 sq. ft.

Price Tier: C

Main Ceiling: 9 ft.
Bedrooms: 4
Baths: 3
Foundation: Crawl, Slab, Basement,
Daylight Basement
Plan Options: page 282

BUILDING SYSTEM
NGI
Next Generation Industries
COMPATABLE

Floor plan labels:

GLASS SHWR
WHP TUB
M.BATH 16'-0" X 11'-0"
COVERED PORCH 14'-10" X 5'-8"
BREAKFAST ROOM 13'-0" X 12'-0"
COMP DESK
REF
BEDROOM 2 14'-10" X 11'-6"
MASTER SUITE 16'-0" X 13'-0" 10' PAN CEILING
FAMILY ROOM 17'-10" X 16'-0"
PASS-THRU FIREPLACE
KITCHEN 13'-0" X 12'-0"
DW
PAN
RG
LIN
BATH
BATH
GALLERY
LIN
BEDROOM 3 13'-0" X 11'-6"
8" BOXED COLUMNS
FRENCH DOORS
FOYER 10' CEILING
LAU. 7'-4" X 7'-0"
D
W
BEDROOM 4 11'-0" X 10'-8"
STUDY 11'-6" X 15'-0"
DINING ROOM 11'-0" X 13'-6" 11' BOXED CEILING
PORCH
GARAGE 23'-0" X 22'-0"

377 Olive Street

Width: 82' 10"
Depth: 51' 6"
Main Floor: 1,674 sq. ft.
Upper Floor: 802 sq. ft.
Total Living: 2,476 sq. ft.*
*Optional Bonus: 460 sq. ft.
Main Ceiling: 9 ft.
Upper Ceiling: 8 ft.
Bedrooms: 4
Baths: 3 1/2
Foundation: Crawl, Slab,
   Optional Basement,
   Optional Daylight Basement

Plan Options: page 282

Price Tier: C

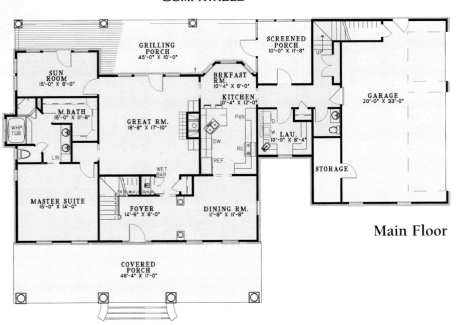

Main Floor

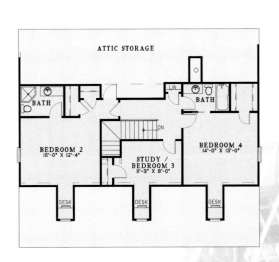

Upper Floor

Bonus Floor

479 Willow Lane

Width: 64' 0"
Depth: 49' 4"
Main Floor: 2,249 sq. ft.
Lower Floor: 246 sq. ft.
Total Living: 2,495 sq. ft.*
*Optional Bonus: 776 sq. ft.
Main Ceiling: 9 ft.
Lower Ceiling: 8 ft.
Bedrooms: 4
Baths: 2 1/2
Foundation: Daylight Basement
Plan Options: page 282

Price Tier: C

BUILDING SYSTEM
NGI Next Generation Industries
COMPATABLE

Designed For:

JBL
RESIDENTIAL SYSTEMS
COMPLETE HOME
ENTERTAINMENT NETWORKS
& DISTRIBUTED AUDIO

JBL
Home Theater

Designed For:

Pioneer
sound.vision.soul
Pioneer Sound System

Main Floor

10" COLUMNS

GRILLING PORCH 24'-0" X 10'-0"

BRKFAST ROOM 12'-0" X 11'-1"

BEDROOM 4 10'-0" X 11'-6"

GREAT ROOM 17'-0" X 19'-0"

KITCHEN 12'-0" X 13'-6"

WHP TUB

M.BATH 16'-8" X 12'-0"

BEDROOM 3 11'-5" X 11'-7"

WINDOW SEAT

MASTER SUITE 16'-8" X 16'-5" 10' BOX CEILING

WHP TUB

BATH 11'-5" X 9'-4"

PLANTER

FOYER

DINING ROOM 11'-6" X 13'-8"

8" COLUMNS

BEDROOM 2 / STUDY 10'-11" X 12'-8"

COVERED PORCH 8'-8" X 7'-0"

Upper Floor

© 2000 NELSON DESIGN GROUP, LLC.

STORAGE 11'-4" X 6'-8"

HANGING

LAU / HOBBY 6'-0" X 13'-11"

GARAGE 30'-7" X 28'-8"

FUTURE BONUS / GAME ROOM 25'-2" X 41'-0"

PLANTER

To Order Call 1.800.590.2423   Similar plans can be viewed and ordered at www.nelsondesigngroup.com

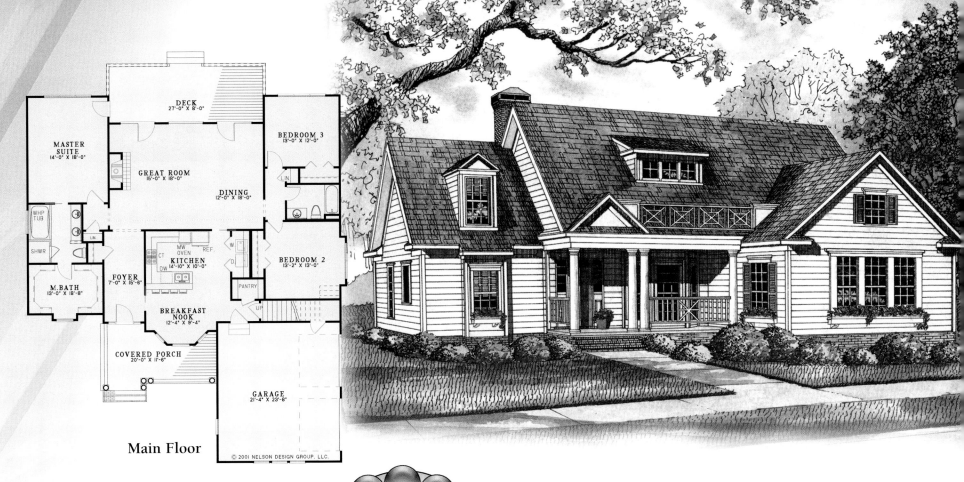

Main Floor

DECK
27'-0" X 8'-0"

MASTER
SUITE
14'-0" X 18'-0"

GREAT ROOM
15'-0" X 18'-0"

BEDROOM 3
13'-0" X 12'-0"

DINING
12'-0" X 18'-0"

WHP TUB

SHWR

LIN

KITCHEN
14'-10" X 10'-0"
MW OVEN
CT
REF.
DW

W
D

M.BATH
13'-0" X 18'-8"

FOYER
7'-0" X 15'-6"

BEDROOM 2
13'-2" X 13'-0"

PANTRY

BREAKFAST
NOOK
12'-4" X 9'-4"

UP

COVERED PORCH
20'-0" X 11'-6"

GARAGE
21'-4" X 23'-8"

© 2001 NELSON DESIGN GROUP, LLC.

Upper Floor

OFFICE/GAME ROOM/
BEDROOM 4
23'-4" X 20'-0"

OPTIONAL BATH

DN

8" WALL   7'4" WALL

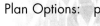
BEST SELLER
Designers' Choice
NELSON DESIGN GROUP

585 Laurel Street

Width: 56' 4"	Main Ceiling: 9 ft.
Depth: 68' 6"	Bonus Ceiling: 8 ft.
Main Floor: 2,071 sq. ft.	Bedrooms: 4
Upper Floor: 443 sq. ft.	Baths: 3
Total Living: 2,514 sq. ft.	Foundation: Crawl, Slab
	Plan Options: page 282

Price Tier: D

BUILDING SYSTEM
NGI
Next Generation Industries
COMPATABLE

Designed For:

JBL
RESIDENTIAL SYSTEMS
COMPLETE HOME
ENTERTAINMENT NETWORKS
& DISTRIBUTED AUDIO

JBL
Home Theater

Designed For:

Pioneer
sound.vision.soul
Pioneer Sound System

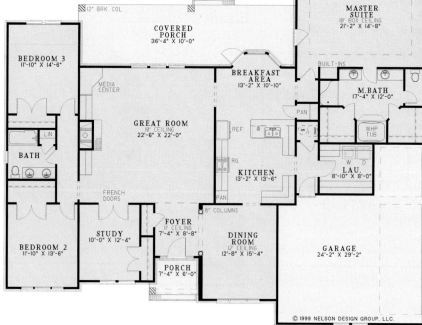

371 Dogwood Avenue

Width: 70' 4"

Depth: 57' 2"

Total Living: 2,534 sq. ft.

Price Tier: D

Main Ceiling: 9 ft.

Bedrooms: 3

Baths: 2

Foundation: Crawl, Slab,
Optional Basement,
Optional Daylight Basement

Plan Options: page 282

BUILDING SYSTEM
NGI
Next Generation Industries
COMPATABLE

© 1999 NELSON DESIGN GROUP, LLC.

To Order Call 1.800.590.2423   **Similar plans can be viewed and ordered at www.nelsondesigngroup.com**

Main Floor

Floor plan labels:
- M. BATH 13'-0" X 13'-8"
- WHP TUB
- LIN
- BRKFAST ROOM 13'-0" X 11'-4"
- GRILLING PORCH 16'-8" X 8'-0" + GAS BIBB
- BEDROOM 3 12'-10" X 13'-4"
- MASTER SUITE 13'-0" X 18'-0" 10' BOXED CEILING
- DW.
- REF
- ISLAND
- K.T.
- KITCHEN 13'-0" X 16'-0" OVEN PANTRY
- GREAT RM. 16'-8" X 21'-10" 10' CEILING
- BATH
- OPTIONAL MEDIA CENTER
- BEDROOM 2 12'-10" X 11'-2"
- UP
- LAUNDRY 7'-6" X 5'-10"
- LINEN
- W D
- BUTLER'S PANTRY
- 8" COLUMN
- FOYER 9'-0" X 13'-6"
- BATH
- GARAGE 21'-8" X 21'-2"
- DINING RM. 12'-0" X 13'-6" 12' CEILING
- VAULTED CEILING
- GUEST RM. / STUDY 15'-2" X 11'-4"
- VAULTED CEILING
- PORCH 9'-0" X 7'-0"
- © 2002 NELSON DESIGN GROUP, LLC.

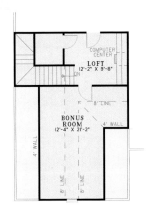

Bonus Floor

Bonus floor labels:
- COMPUTER CENTER
- LOFT 12'-2" X 9'-8"
- 8" LINE
- BONUS ROOM 12'-4" X 21'-2"
- 4' WALL
- 4" WALL
- 8" LINE

Designed For:

JBL
RESIDENTIAL SYSTEMS
COMPLETE HOME ENTERTAINMENT NETWORKS & DISTRIBUTED AUDIO

JBL
Home Theater

Designed For:

Pioneer
sound.vision.soul
Pioneer Sound System

664 Dogwood Lane

Width: 59' 6"
Depth: 64' 2"
Total Living: 2,542 sq. ft.*
*Optional Bonus: 473 sq. ft.

Price Tier: D

Main Ceiling: 9 ft.
Bonus Ceiling: 8 ft.
Bedrooms: 4
Baths: 3
Foundation: Crawl, Slab, Optional Basement, Optional Daylight Basement
Plan Options: page 282

BUILDING SYSTEM
NGi
Next Generation Industries
COMPATABLE

539 *Madison Drive*

Width: 74' 7"

Depth: 70' 6"

Total Living: 2,556 sq. ft.

Price Tier: D

Main Ceiling: 9 ft.

Bedrooms: 4

Baths: 3

Foundation: Crawl, Slab

Plan Options: page 282

BUILDING SYSTEM
NGI
Next Generation Industries
COMPATABLE

© 2001 NELSON DESIGN GROUP, LLC.

GARAGE 25'-4" X 32'-2"

ATTIC STORAGE

UP

BRKFST. ROOM 10' CEILING 14'-5" X 10'-2"

42" HIGH BAR

GRILLING PORCH 10' CEILING 18'-2" X 6'-8"

MASTER SUITE 10' BOXED CEILING 15'-0" X 13'-0"

3' GAS FIRE PLACE

STORAGE BINS

BENCH KID'S NOOK

STOR.

WH HVAC

KITCHEN 10' CEILING 14'-5" X 16'-0"

DW

CT

OVEN MW

REF

GREAT ROOM 11' BOXED CEILING 18'-2" X 19'-6"

BUILT-INS

M.BATH 10'-8" X 10'-4"

WHP TUB

SEAT

SHWR

LIN

W.I.C 12'-6" X 6'-0"

BEDROOM 2 13'-2" X 12'-0"

PANTRY

BATH

LAU. 6'-5" X 9'-6"

DINING ROOM 10' CEILING 12'-2" X 12'-2"

FOYER 11' CEILING 7'-8" X 11'-10"

FRENCH DOORS

OFFICE / GUEST ROOM 10' CEILING 11'-10" X 12'-0"

LIN

HANGING

BEDROOM 3 10' CEILING 14'-0" X 12'-8"

14" COLUMNS

COVERED PORCH 14' CEILING 33'-6" X 8'-0"

To Order Call 1.800.590.2423 **Similar plans can be viewed and ordered at www.nelsondesigngroup.com**

597 Hampton Circle

Width: 70' 2"

Depth: 53' 4"

Main Floor: 1,813 sq. ft.

Upper Floor: 790 sq. ft.

Total Living: 2,603 sq. ft.*

*Optional Bonus: 410 sq. ft.

Main Ceiling: 9 ft.

Upper Ceiling: 9 ft.

Bedrooms: 4

Baths: 2 1/2

Foundation: Crawl, Slab,
Optional Basement,
Optional Daylight Basement

Plan Options: page 282

Price Tier: D

BUILDING SYSTEM
NGI
Next Generation Industries
COMPATABLE

Designed For:

JBL

RESIDENTIAL SYSTEMS
COMPLETE HOME
ENTERTAINMENT NETWORKS
& DISTRIBUTED AUDIO

JBL
Home Theater

Designed For:

Pioneer

sound.vision.soul
Pioneer Sound System

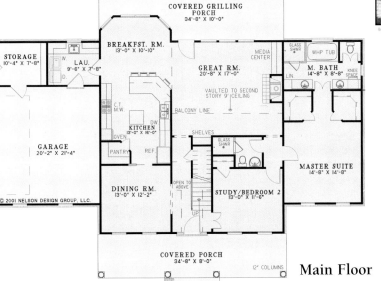

Main Floor

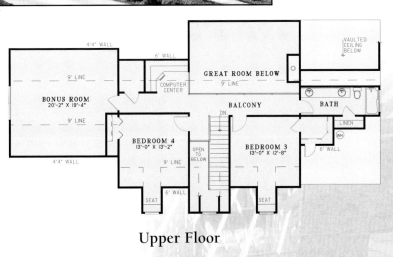

Upper Floor

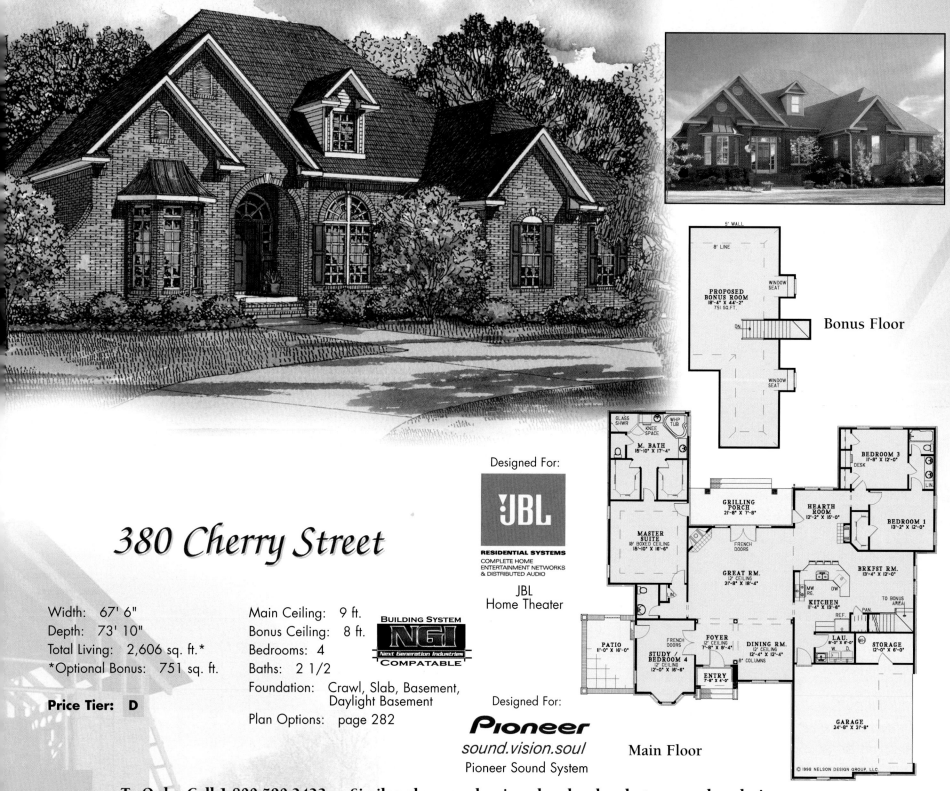

380 Cherry Street

Width: 67' 6"
Depth: 73' 10"
Total Living: 2,606 sq. ft.*
*Optional Bonus: 751 sq. ft.

Price Tier: D

Main Ceiling: 9 ft.
Bonus Ceiling: 8 ft.
Bedrooms: 4
Baths: 2 1/2
Foundation: Crawl, Slab, Basement, Daylight Basement
Plan Options: page 282

Designed For:

JBL
RESIDENTIAL SYSTEMS
COMPLETE HOME
ENTERTAINMENT NETWORKS
& DISTRIBUTED AUDIO

JBL
Home Theater

Designed For:

Pioneer
sound.vision.soul
Pioneer Sound System

BUILDING SYSTEM
NGI
Next Generation Industries
COMPATABLE

Bonus Floor

Main Floor

© 1998 NELSON DESIGN GROUP, LLC.

To Order Call 1.800.590.2423   **Similar plans can be viewed and ordered at www.nelsondesigngroup.com**

502 Willow Lane

Width: 66' 4"
Depth: 64' 0"
Total Living: 2,624 sq. ft.*
*Optional Bonus: 561 sq. ft.
Main Ceiling: 9 ft.
Bonus Ceiling: 8 ft.
Bedrooms: 4
Baths: 3
Foundation: Crawl, Slab,
Optional Basement,
Optional Daylight Basement
Plan Options: page 282

Price Tier: D

BUILDING SYSTEM
NGI
Next Generation Industries
COMPATABLE

Designed For:

JBL

RESIDENTIAL SYSTEMS
COMPLETE HOME
ENTERTAINMENT NETWORKS
& DISTRIBUTED AUDIO

JBL
Home Theater

Designed For:

Pioneer
sound.vision.soul
Pioneer Sound System

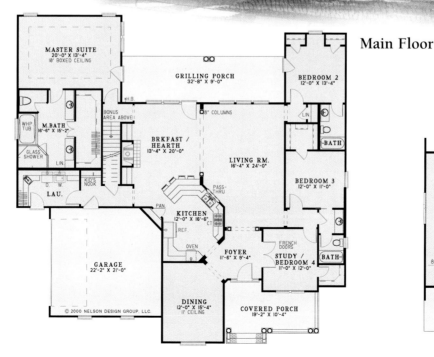

Main Floor

MASTER SUITE
20'-0" X 13'-4"
10' BOXED CEILING

GRILLING PORCH
32'-8" X 9'-0"

BEDROOM 2
12'-0" X 13'-4"

BONUS AREA ABOVE

8" COLUMNS

M.BATH
16'-6" X 15'-2"

WHP TUB

GLASS SHOWER

BRKFAST / HEARTH
13'-4" X 20'-0"

LIVING RM.
16'-4" X 24'-0"

LIN

BATH

LIN

KID'S NOOK

D.W.

LAU.

PASS-THRU

BEDROOM 3
12'-0" X 11'-0"

PAN

KITCHEN
12'-0" X 16'-6"

CT

REF.

OVEN

FOYER
11'-6" X 9'-0"

FRENCH DOORS

STUDY / BEDROOM 4
11'-0" X 12'-0"

BATH

GARAGE
22'-2" X 21'-0"

© 2000 NELSON DESIGN GROUP, LLC.

DINING
12'-0" X 15'-4"
11' CEILING

COVERED PORCH
19'-2" X 10'-4"

Bonus Floor

ATTIC STORAGE

BONUS ROOM
27'-3" X 22'-2"

SLOPED CEILING

8' LINE

8' LINE

5' WALL

Elevation A

Upper Floor

GAME ROOM
15'-8" X 17'-4"

Elevation B

Main Floor

GOLF CART / BOAT STORAGE
20'-0" X 10'-0"

SCREENED PORCH
18'-0" X 14'-0"

COVERED PORCH
15'-4" X 14'-0"

MASTER SUITE
17'-4" X 13'-8"

LAU.

GARAGE
20'-0" X 21'-0"

M.BATH
17'-4" X 12'-10"

GREAT RM.
19'-8" X 17'-8"

GALLERY

BEDROOM 2
13'-6" X 11'-6"

KITCHEN
12'-0" X 16'-0"

DINING
10'-0" X 12'-0"

FOYER

BEDROOM 1 / STUDY
12'-4" X 14'-10"

BRKFAST RM.
12'-0" X 11'-0"

COVERED PORCH
14'-0" X 6'-0"

135 Olive Street

Width: 72' 0"
Depth: 59' 10"
Main Floor: 2,266 sq. ft.
Upper Floor: 370 sq. ft.
Total Living: 2,636 sq. ft.

Price Tier: D

Main Ceiling: 10 ft.
Upper Ceiling: 8 ft.
Bedrooms: 3
Baths: 2 1/2
Foundation: Crawl, Slab,
Optional Basement,
Optional Daylight Basement
Plan Options: page 282

BUILDING SYSTEM
NGI
Next Generation Industries
COMPATABLE

Designed For:

Pioneer
sound.vision.soul
Pioneer Sound System

Designed For:

JBL
RESIDENTIAL SYSTEMS
COMPLETE HOME ENTERTAINMENT NETWORKS & DISTRIBUTED AUDIO

JBL
Home Theater

698 Spruce Street

Width: 73' 6"

Depth: 58' 8"

Total Living: 2,671 sq. ft.

Main Ceiling: 9 ft.

Bedrooms: 4

Baths: 2 1/2

Foundation: Crawl, Slab

Plan Options: page 282

Price Tier: D

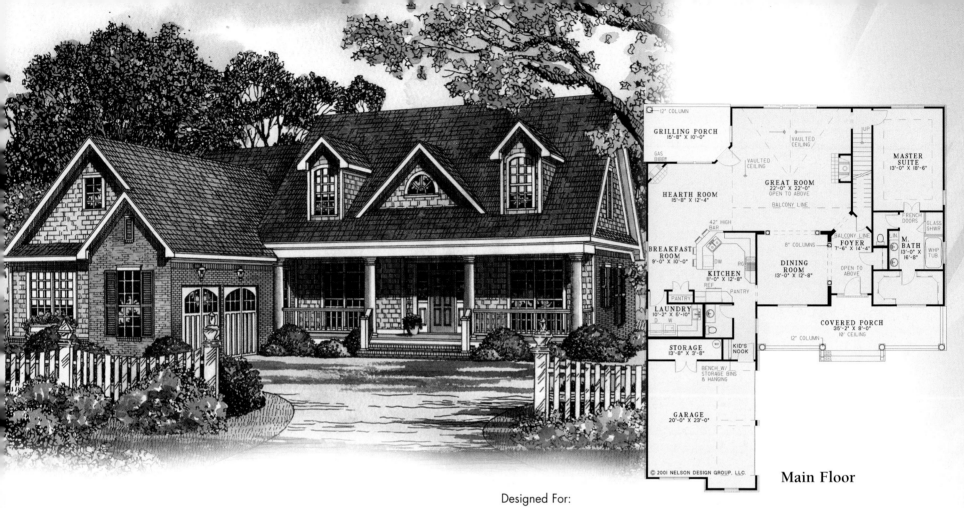

Main Floor

GRILLING PORCH
15'-8" X 10'-0"

GAS BIBB

12" COLUMN

VAULTED CEILING

VAULTED CEILING

GREAT ROOM
22'-0" X 22'-0"
OPEN TO ABOVE

UP

MASTER SUITE
13'-0" X 18'-6"

HEARTH ROOM
15'-8" X 12'-4"

BALCONY LINE

FRENCH DOORS

GLASS SHWR

42" HIGH BAR

BREAKFAST ROOM
9'-0" X 10'-0"

DW

KITCHEN
11'-0" X 12'-8"

RG

REF

PANTRY

BALCONY LINE

8" COLUMNS

FOYER
7'-6" X 14'-4"

LIN.

M. BATH
13'-0" X 16'-8"

WHP TUB

DINING ROOM
13'-0" X 12'-8"

OPEN TO ABOVE

LAUNDRY
10'-2" X 5'-10"

D W

PANTRY

STORAGE
13'-8" X 3'-8"

KID'S NOOK

BENCH W/ STORAGE BINS 8 HANGING

12" COLUMN

COVERED PORCH
35'-2" X 8'-0"
10' CEILING

GARAGE
20'-0" X 23'-0"

12" COLUMN

© 2001 NELSON DESIGN GROUP, LLC.

Designed For:

Pioneer
sound.vision.soul
Pioneer Sound System

547 Autumn Drive

Width: 55' 6"
Depth: 69' 6"
Main Floor: 1,990 sq. ft.
Upper Floor: 695 sq. ft.
Total Living: 2,685 sq. ft.*
*Optional Bonus: 301 sq. ft.

Price Tier: D

Main Ceiling: 9 ft.
Upper Ceiling: 8 ft.
Bedrooms: 4
Baths: 2 1/2
Foundation: Crawl, Slab,
Optional Basement,
Optional Daylight Basement
Plan Options: page 282

BUILDING SYSTEM
NGI
Next Generation Industries
COMPATABLE

Designed For:

JBL
RESIDENTIAL SYSTEMS
COMPLETE HOME
ENTERTAINMENT NETWORKS
& DISTRIBUTED AUDIO

JBL
Home Theater

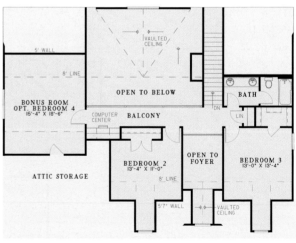

5' WALL

8' LINE

VAULTED CEILING

OPEN TO BELOW

DN

BATH

LIN

BONUS ROOM
OPT. BEDROOM 4
15'-4" X 18'-6"

COMPUTER CENTER

BALCONY

ATTIC STORAGE

BEDROOM 2
13'-4" X 11'-0"

OPEN TO FOYER

BEDROOM 3
13'-0" X 13'-4"

8' LINE

5'7" WALL

VAULTED CEILING

Upper Floor

To Order Call 1.800.590.2423   Similar plans can be viewed and ordered at www.nelsondesigngroup.com

Upper Bonus Floor B

OPTIONAL BEDROOM 5
14'-0" X 20'-10"

BATH

5' WALL
8' LINE
8' LINE
5' WALL

Upper Bonus Floor A

BONUS ROOM
20'-2" X 20'-10"

5' WALL
8' LINE
8' LINE
5' WALL

DN

Main Floor

SITTING AREA

MASTER SUITE
17'-2" X 17'-8"
10' BOXED CEILING

WHP TUB

GLASS SHWR

MASTER BATH
12'-2" X 19'-4"

LIN

BRKFAST ROOM
12'-4" X 12'-0"

COVERED GRILLING DECK
17'-0" X 8'-0"

BEDROOM 3
15'-8" X 12'-0"

BATH

PANTRY

REF

DW

KITCHEN
12'-4" X 13'-0"

MW OVEN

GREAT ROOM
17'-0" X 21'-4"
10' BOXED CEILING

LINEN

BEDROOM 2
10'-2" X 21'-4"

BATH

WINDOW SEAT

OPTIONAL BASEMENT

8' COLUMNS

DINING ROOM
14'-10" X 12'-8"
10' CEILING

FOYER
8'-0" X 12'-8"
12' CEILING

GUEST ROOM / STUDY
12'-8" X 13'-0"
10' CEILING

FRENCH DOORS

D W

LAU.
8'-2" X 6'-0"

UP

COVERED PORCH
35'-0" X 10'-0"

GARAGE
24'-0" X 22'-0"

© 2002 NELSON DESIGN GROUP, LLC.

Designed For:

JBL
RESIDENTIAL SYSTEMS
COMPLETE HOME
ENTERTAINMENT NETWORKS
& DISTRIBUTED AUDIO

JBL
Home Theater

Designed For:

Pioneer
sound.vision.soul
Pioneer Sound System

663 Thomas Road

Width: 63' 10"
Depth: 73' 0"
Total Living: 2,716 sq. ft.*
*Optional Bonus A: 421 sq. ft.
*Optional Bonus B: 438 sq. ft.

Main Ceiling: 9 ft.
Upper Ceiling: 8 ft.
Bedrooms: 4
Baths: 3
Foundation: Crawl, Slab,
Optional Basement,
Optional Daylight Basement

Price Tier: D

Plan Options: page 282

BUILDING SYSTEM
NGI
Next Generation Industries
COMPATABLE

327 Willow Lane

Width: 84' 6"
Depth: 58' 6"
Total Living: 2,742 sq. ft.*
*Optional Bonus: 916 sq. ft.
Main Ceiling: 9 ft.
Bonus Ceiling: 8 ft.
Bedrooms: 4
Baths: 2 1/2
Foundation: Crawl, Slab, Basement, Daylight Basement
Plan Options: page 282

Price Tier: D

Main Floor

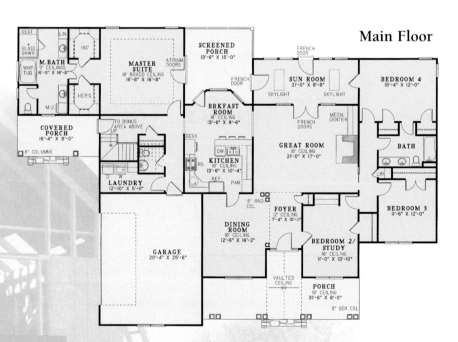

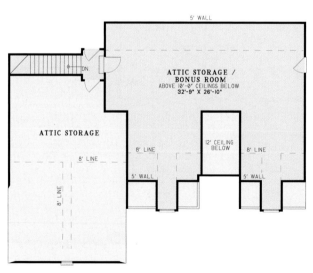

Bonus Floor

Designed For:

Pioneer
sound.vision.soul
Pioneer Sound System

Designed For:

RESIDENTIAL SYSTEMS
COMPLETE HOME
ENTERTAINMENT NETWORKS
& DISTRIBUTED AUDIO

JBL
Home Theater

209 Olive Street

Width: 69' 0"

Depth: 69' 10"

Main Floor: 2,406 sq. ft.

Upper Floor: 349 sq. ft.

Total Living: 2,755 sq. ft.

Main Ceiling: 9 ft.

Upper Ceiling: 8 ft.

Bedrooms: 3

Baths: 4 1/2

Foundation: Crawl, Slab, Basement,
   Daylight Basement

Plan Options: page 282

Price Tier: D

BUILDING SYSTEM
NGI
Next Generation Industries
COMPATABLE

Designed For:

JBL
RESIDENTIAL SYSTEMS
COMPLETE HOME
ENTERTAINMENT NETWORKS
& DISTRIBUTED AUDIO

JBL
Home Theater

Designed For:

Pioneer
sound.vision.soul
Pioneer Sound System

Main Floor

© 1998 NELSON DESIGN GROUP, LLC.

Upper Floor

Upper Floor

BEDROOM 3
12'-0" X 17'-2"

ATTIC STORAGE

DN

W.I.C.

LIN.

BATH

Main Floor

LIVING ROOM
20'-0" X 15'-0"
10' BOXED CEILING

PORCH
33'-4" X 5'-0"

W.I.C.

UP

KITCHEN
16'-2" X 15'-2"

GREAT ROOM
18'-4" X 18'-0"
OPTIONAL 10' CEILING

GAS
FIREPLACE

MASTER SUITE
15'-4" X 21'-4"
10' BOXED CEILING

GLASS
SHWR

M.BATH
9'-8" X
16'-0"

WHP
TUB

LIN.

BREAKFAST
NOOK
8'-0" X 9'-10"

PAN.

REF.

OVEN

8' COLUMNS

LIN.

W.I.C.

PAN.

LAU.
10'-8" X 8'-0"

5' GALLERY

SHWR

DINING ROOM
11'-0" X 12'-0"
12' CEILING

FOYER
7'-0" X 9'-9"

LIN.

BATH

PORCH
7'-8" X 7'-0"

BEDROOM 2
15'-4" X 12'-0"
11'6" CEILING

GARAGE
20'-0" X 23'-0"

VAULT

VAULT

VAULT

© 1991 NELSON DESIGN GROUP, LLC.

665 Cherry Street

Width: 65' 0"

Depth: 64' 10"

Main Floor: 2,406 sq. ft.

Upper Floor: 354 sq. ft.

Total Living: 2,760 sq. ft.

Main Ceiling: 9 ft.

Upper Ceiling: 8 ft.

Bedrooms: 3

Baths: 3 1/2

Foundation: Crawl, Slab,
Optional Basement,
Optional Daylight Basement

Plan Options: page 282

BUILDING SYSTEM
NGI
Next Generation Industries
COMPATABLE

Price Tier: D

Main Floor

Floor plan labels:
- GLASS BLOCKS
- WHP TUB
- SEAT
- GLASS SHWR.
- M.BATH 11'-8" X 16'-6"
- MASTER SUITE 16'-0" X 18'-10"
- 12" COLUMNS
- GRILLING PORCH 26'-0" X 7'-6"
- ATRIUM DOORS
- BREAKFAST AREA 10' CEILING 12'-0" X 10'-0"
- UP
- LAUNDRY 11'-2" X 8'-2"
- W D
- MEDIA CENTER
- GREAT ROOM 10' CEILING 20'-10" X 18'-10"
- PAN.
- REF.
- DW
- STRG. 7'-2" X 9'-2"
- HWC
- BUILT-INS
- KITCHEN 10' CEILING 12'-0" X 13'-10"
- RG
- 8" COLUMNS
- FOYER 8'-6" X 7'-4"
- DINING ROOM 10' CEILING 11'-4" X 12'-0"
- GARAGE 20'-0" X 35'-8"
- FORMAL LIVING 10' CEILING 12'-0" X 14'-0"
- PORCH 8'-6" X 5'-8"
- ARCH OPENING

© 1993 NELSON DESIGN GROUP, LLC.

Upper Floor

- BEDROOM 3 12'-0" X 12'-2"
- LIN
- BATH
- BEDROOM 2 10'-4" X 14'-0"
- LIN.
- DN
- ATTIC STORAGE
- BEDROOM 4 12'-0" X 13'-0"

Designed For:

JBL

RESIDENTIAL SYSTEMS
COMPLETE HOME
ENTERTAINMENT NETWORKS
& DISTRIBUTED AUDIO

JBL
Home Theater

Designed For:

Pioneer
sound.vision.soul
Pioneer Sound System

348 Willow Lane

Width: 54' 2"	Main Ceiling: 9 ft.
Depth: 73' 6"	Bonus Ceiling: 8 ft.
Main Floor: 1,895 sq. ft.	Bedrooms: 4
Upper Floor: 889 sq. ft.	Baths: 2 1/2
Total Living: 2,784 sq. ft.	Foundation: Crawl, Slab, Basement, Daylight Basement
Price Tier: D	Plan Options: page 282

BUILDING SYSTEM
NGI
Next Generation Industries
COMPATABLE

129-3 Olive Street

Width: 72' 4"
Depth: 48' 4"
Main Floor: 1,977 sq. ft.
Upper Floor: 812 sq. ft.
Total Living: 2,789 sq. ft.*
*Optional Bonus: 306 sq. ft.
Main Ceiling: 9 ft.
Upper Ceiling: 8 ft.
Bedrooms: 4
Baths: 3
Foundation: Crawl, Slab, Basement, Daylight Basement
Plan Options: page 282

Price Tier: D

BUILDING SYSTEM
NGI
Next Generation Industries
COMPATABLE

Main Floor

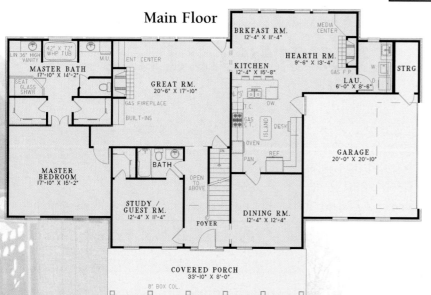

- MASTER BATH
- LIN 36" HIGH VANITY
- 42" X 72" WHP TUB
- M.U.
- ENT CENTER
- SEAT GLASS SHWR
- GREAT RM. 20'-6" X 17'-10"
- GAS FIREPLACE
- BUILT-INS
- MASTER BEDROOM 17'-10" X 15'-2"
- BATH
- STUDY / GUEST RM. 12'-4" X 11'-4"
- OPEN TO ABOVE
- FOYER
- DINING RM. 12'-4" X 12'-4"
- BRKFAST RM. 12'-4" X 11'-4"
- MEDIA CENTER
- KITCHEN 12'-4" X 15'-8"
- HEARTH RM. 9'-6" X 13'-4"
- GAS F.P.
- ISLAND
- DESK
- OVEN
- REF
- PAN
- LAU. 6'-0" X 8'-6"
- W
- STRG
- GARAGE 20'-0" X 20'-10"
- COVERED PORCH 33'-10" X 8'-0"
- 8" BOX COL.

Upper Floor

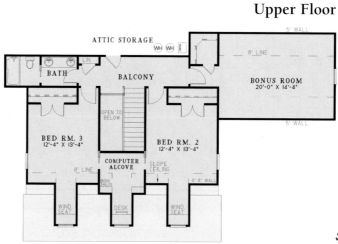

- ATTIC STORAGE
- WH WH
- BATH
- BALCONY
- 5' WALL
- 8' LINE
- BONUS ROOM 20'-0" X 14'-4"
- OPEN TO BELOW
- BED RM. 3 12'-4" X 13'-4"
- BED RM. 2 12'-4" X 13'-4"
- COMPUTER ALCOVE
- SLOPE CEILING
- 8' LINE
- BOOK SHLVS
- DESK
- WIND SEAT
- WIND SEAT
- 5' WALL
- 6' 8" WALL

Designed For:

JBL
RESIDENTIAL SYSTEMS
COMPLETE HOME
ENTERTAINMENT NETWORKS
& DISTRIBUTED AUDIO

JBL
Home Theater

Designed For:

Pioneer
sound.vision.soul
Pioneer Sound System

125 Cherry Street

Width: 60' 4"

Depth: 55' 2"

Main Floor: 1,834 sq. ft.

Upper Floor: 968 sq. ft.

Total Living: 2,802 sq. ft.

Main Ceiling: 9 ft.

Upper Ceiling: 9 ft.

Bedrooms: 4

Baths: 3 1/2

Foundation: Crawl, Slab,
Optional Basement,
Optional Daylight Basement

Plan Options: page 282

Price Tier: D

Designed For:

JBL
RESIDENTIAL SYSTEMS
COMPLETE HOME
ENTERTAINMENT NETWORKS
& DISTRIBUTED AUDIO

JBL
Home Theater

Designed For:

Pioneer
sound.vision.soul
Pioneer Sound System

Main Floor

© 1991 NELSON DESIGN GROUP, LLC.

GOLF/GARAGE 20'-0" X 12'-0"

GRILLING PORCH 8'-10" X 8'-4"

GREAT RM. 15'-10" X 20'-0"

MASTER SUITE 14'-0" X 17'-10"

STORAGE

W. D.

LAU.

1/2 BATH

BRKFAST RM. 10'-0" X 11'-0"

PAN.

REF.

KITCHEN 12'-0" X 13'-0"

DW

RG

WHP TUB

M.BATH 16'-10" X 13'-8"

GARAGE 22'-0" X 21'-0"

FOYER

BOOK SHELVES

DINING RM. 12'-0" X 13'-10"

FRENCH DOORS

FORMAL LIVING/STUDY 14'-0" X 14'-0"

UP

ENTRY

Upper Floor

ATTIC STORAGE

BATH

LIN

LOFT 10'-8" X 16'-0"

BATH

BEDROOM 4 11'-2" X 12'-2"

LIN

COMPUTER CENTER

HVAC

DN

BEDROOM 2 12'-0" X 13'-0"

FOYER OPEN TO BELOW

BEDROOM 3 14'-0" X 11'-2"

© 2001 NELSON DESIGN GROUP, LLC.

GRILLING PORCH
24'-0" X 8'-0"

STOR.

KITCHEN
11'-0" X 11'-9"

NOOK
8'-0" X 11'-8"

GARAGE
19'-8" X 19'-4"

LAU.
5'-6" X 6'-4"

DW

REF

C.T.

GREAT ROOM
15'-0" X 19'-4"

HIGH BAR

PANTRY

8' COLUMNS

GRAND FOYER
10'-0" X 11'-8"

UP

GLASS SHWR

WHP TUB

LIN

M.BATH
10'-10" X 11'-8"

DINING
11'-8" X 11'-8"

W.I.C.

8' COVERED PORCH

10" COLUMNS

MASTER SUITE
18'-6" X 15'-4"

Main Floor

592 Olive Street

BEST SELLER
Designers Choice
NELSON DESIGN GROUP

COMPUTER CENTER

BEDROOM 4
18'-6" X 19'-2"

BEDROOM 3
10'-10" X 13'-0"

8' LINE

BATH

DN

4' WALL

WINDOW SEAT

LIN

BEDROOM 2/ GAME ROOM
18'-6" X 14'-10"

Upper Floor

Width: 61' 4"
Depth: 62' 0"
Main Floor: 1,610 sq. ft.
Upper Floor: 1,200 sq. ft.
Total Living: 2,810 sq. ft.

Price Tier: D

Main Ceiling: 9 ft.
Upper Ceiling: 8 ft.
Bedrooms: 4
Baths: 2 1/2
Foundation: Crawl, Slab,
  Optional Basement,
  Optional Daylight Basement
Plan Options: page 282

BUILDING SYSTEM
NGI
Next Generation Industries
COMPATABLE

612 Cherry Street

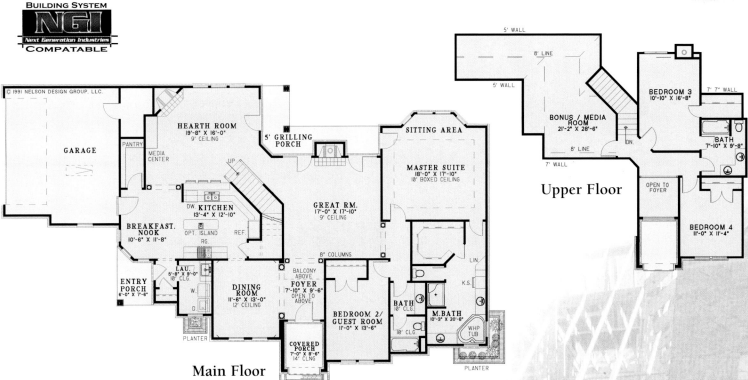

Width: 84' 4"

Depth: 48' 4"

Main Floor: 2,279 sq. ft.

Upper Floor: 545 sq. ft.

Total Living: 2,824 sq. ft.*

*Optional Bonus: 410 sq. ft.

Main Ceiling: 9 ft.

Upper Ceiling: 8 ft.

Bedrooms: 4

Baths: 3

Foundation: Crawl, Slab,
Optional Basement,
Optional Daylight Basement

Plan Options: page 282

Price Tier: **D**

BUILDING SYSTEM
NGI
Next Generation Industries
COMPATABLE

Designed For:

JBL
RESIDENTIAL SYSTEMS
COMPLETE HOME
ENTERTAINMENT NETWORKS
& DISTRIBUTED AUDIO

JBL
Home Theater

Designed For:

Pioneer
sound.vision.soul
Pioneer Sound System

Main Floor

Upper Floor

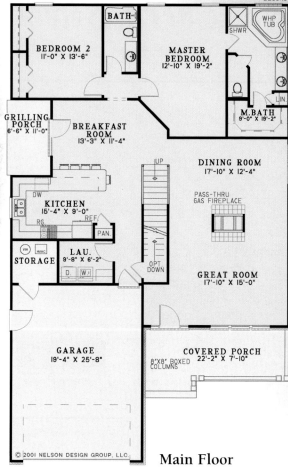

Main Floor

576 Spruce Street

Width: 42' 0"
Depth: 67' 4"
Main Floor: 1,828 sq. ft.
Upper Floor: 1,029 sq. ft.
Total Living: 2,857 sq. ft.

Price Tier: D

Main Ceiling: 8 ft.
Upper Ceiling: 8 ft.
Bedrooms: 4
Baths: 3
Foundation: Crawl, Slab,
   Optional Basement,
   Optional Daylight Basement
Plan Options: page 282

BUILDING SYSTEM
NGI
Next Generation Industries
COMPATABLE

Designed For:

JBL

RESIDENTIAL SYSTEMS
COMPLETE HOME
ENTERTAINMENT NETWORKS
& DISTRIBUTED AUDIO

JBL
Home Theater

Designed For:

Pioneer
sound.vision.soul
Pioneer Sound System

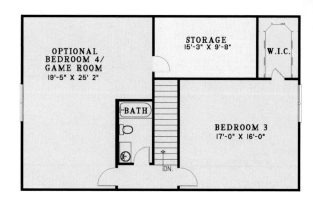

Upper Floor

Main Floor

GRILLING PORCH
22'-4" X 7'-0"

BUILT-INS

HEARTH ROOM
17'-6" X 14'-0"

GREAT ROOM
18'-0" X 14'-10"

MASTER BATH
14'-0" X 19'-4"

WHP. TUB

SEAT
GLASS SHWR

UP

RAISED BAR

BOOK SHLVS BELOW

DW

CT

DINING ROOM
11'-0" X 11'-8"

FOYER
6'-8" X 11'-4"

BUTLER'S PANTRY

BREAKFAST ROOM
9'-4" X 11'-0"

KITCHEN
10'-0" X 15'-3"

PAN

REF

MW OVEN

COVERED PORCH
18'-4" X 7'-0"

MASTER SUITE
14'-0" X 17'-10"

W

D

LAU.
6'-4" X 10'-8"

BENCH W/ STORAGE BINS

GARAGE
21'-4" X 22'-0"

© 2001 NELSON DESIGN GROUP, LLC.

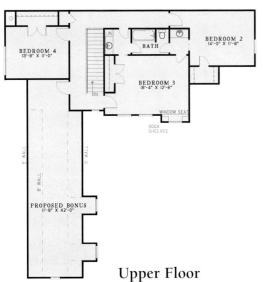

Upper Floor

BEDROOM 4
13'-8" X 11'-0"

BATH

BEDROOM 2
14'-0" X 11'-8"

BEDROOM 3
18'-4" X 12'-6"

WINDOW SEAT

BOOK SHELVES

5' WALL

5' WALL

8' WALL

PROPOSED BONUS
11'-8" X 42'-0"

Designed For:

JBL

RESIDENTIAL SYSTEMS
COMPLETE HOME
ENTERTAINMENT NETWORKS
& DISTRIBUTED AUDIO

JBL
Home Theater

Designed For:

Pioneer
sound.vision.soul
Pioneer Sound System

Price Tier: D

572 Brittany Lane

Width: 57' 0"		Main Ceiling: 9 ft.	
Depth: 71' 8"		Upper Ceiling: 8 ft.	
Main Floor: 1,921 sq. ft.		Bedrooms: 4	
Upper Floor: 965 sq. ft.		Baths: 2 1/2	
Total Living: 2,886 sq. ft.*		Foundation: Crawl, Slab	
*Optional Bonus: 528 sq. ft.		Plan Options: page 282	

BUILDING SYSTEM
NGI
Next Generation Industries
COMPATABLE

To Order Call 1.800.590.2423   **Similar plans can be viewed and ordered at www.nelsondesigngroup.com**

616 Cherry Street

Width: 72' 0"

Depth: 51' 0"

Total Living: 2,930 sq. ft.

Main Ceiling: 8 ft.

Bedrooms: 3

Baths: 2 1/2

Foundation: Crawl, Slab, Optional Basement, Optional Daylight Basement

Plan Options: page 282

Price Tier: D

BUILDING SYSTEM
NGI
Next Generation Industries
COMPATABLE

Designed For:

JBL
RESIDENTIAL SYSTEMS
COMPLETE HOME
ENTERTAINMENT NETWORKS
& DISTRIBUTED AUDIO

JBL
Home Theater

Designed For:

Pioneer
sound.vision.soul
Pioneer Sound System

BEST SELLER
Designers Choice
NELSON DESIGN GROUP

BATH
11'-0" X 7'-6"

BEDROOM 2/
IN-LAWS SUITE
16'-4" X 13'-10"

OPTIONAL
FRENCH
DOOR

OPTIONAL SUN RM.
31'-4" X 8'-10"

MASTER
SUITE
15'-0" X 20'-0"
9' BOX CEILING

BREAKFAST ROOM
17'-2" X 11'-2"
10' CEILING

BEDROOM 3
14'-2" X 10'-6"

LAU.
6'-6" X 10'-0"

FREZ

REF

GREAT ROOM
15'-0" X 20'-0"
11' BOXED CEILING

KITCHEN
16'-10" X 11'-8"

PAN

OVEN
W/MW

C.T.

BUTLER'S
PANTRY

M.
BATH
11'-3" X
22'-0"

GARAGE
20'-0" X 21'-0"

DINING ROOM
14'-0" X 14'-0"
12' CEILING

FOYER
10'-4" X 7'-6"
10' CEILING

STUDY/ MEDIA
ROOM
14'-0" X 14'-0"
12' CEILING

BARREL
VAULT

WHP
TUB

OPTIONAL
MEDIA
CENTER

8" COLUMNS

VAULTED
CEILING

PORCH

© 1991 NELSON DESIGN GROUP, LLC.

To Order Call 1.800.590.2423 **Similar plans can be viewed and ordered at www.nelsondesigngroup.com**

Main Floor

GRILLING PORCH
31'-6" X 10'-0"

FIXED FRENCH DOORS
FRENCH DOORS

GREAT RM.
18'-2" X 14'-0"

BREAKFAST ROOM
11'-6" X 14'-0"

D.W.

C.T.

DINING RM.
11'-6" X 13'-0"

COMPUTER DESK

KITCHEN
12'-6" X 14'-0"

PANTRY

REF.

8" COLUMNS

UP

BATH

FORMAL LIVING
11'-6" X 16'-10"

GARAGE
22'-4" X 25'-0"

FOYER
8'-10" X 18'-8"
OPEN ABOVE

GUEST RM.
11'-0" X 11'-2"

PORCH

© 1994 NELSON DESIGN GROUP, LLC.

Upper Floor

WHP TUB

BATH

MASTER SUITE
18'-0" X 14'-0"
9' BOXED CEILING

FRENCH DOORS

M. BATH
19'-2" X 10'-2"

BEDROOM 4
11'-6" X 10'-2"

K.S.

DN.

LAU.
D   W

DN.

BONUS RM.
17'-0" X 25'-0"

BEDROOM 3
11'-6" X 13'-8"

OPEN TO BELOW

BATH

BEDROOM 2
11'-0" X 13'-0"
11' CEILING

4'7" WALL   8' LINE   8' LINE   4'7" WALL

SLOPE   SLOPE

164 Brittany Lane

Width: 55' 4"
Depth: 53' 10"
Main Floor: 1,547 sq. ft.
Upper Floor: 1,395 sq. ft.
Total Living: 2,942 sq. ft.*
*Optional Bonus: 366 sq. ft.

Main Ceiling: 9 ft.
Upper Ceiling: 8 ft.
Bedrooms: 5
Baths: 4
Foundation: Crawl, Slab,
Optional Basement,
Optional Daylight Basement
Plan Options: page 282

BUILDING SYSTEM
NGI
Next Generation Industries
COMPATABLE

Price Tier: D

To Order Call 1.800.590.2423   **Similar plans can be viewed and ordered at www.nelsondesigngroup.com**

233

Main Floor

615 Thomas Road

Width: 59' 6"
Depth: 70' 10"
Main Floor: 2,530 sq. ft.
Upper Floor: 445 sq. ft.
Total Living: 2,975 sq. ft.*
*Optional Bonus: 425 sq. ft.

Price Tier: D

Main Ceiling: 9 ft.
Upper Ceiling: 8 ft.
Bedrooms: 5
Baths: 4
Foundation: Crawl, Slab,
Optional Basement,
Optional Daylight Basement
Plan Options: page 282

BUILDING SYSTEM
NGI
Next Generation Industries
COMPATABLE

Designed For:

RESIDENTIAL SYSTEMS
COMPLETE HOME
ENTERTAINMENT NETWORKS
& DISTRIBUTED AUDIO

JBL
Home Theater

Designed For:

Pioneer
sound.vision.soul
Pioneer Sound System

Upper Floor

To Order Call 1.800.590.2423   Similar plans can be viewed and ordered at www.nelsondesigngroup.com

Main Floor

GRILLING PATIO
13'-4" X 12'-0"

GAS BIBB

SCREENED PORCH
29'-8" X 12'-0"

M.BATH
15'-0" X 17'-4"

MASTER SUITE
13'-0" X 17'-2"

GREAT RM.
18'-0" X 22'-0"

DINING
13'-8" X 13'-8"

SKYLIGHTS

VAULTED CEILING

BATH

OPTIONAL BASEMENT

COMPUTER CENTER

KITCHEN
12'-10" X 10'-6"

RANGE W/ M.W.

REF

DW

FRENCH DOORS

FOYER
7'-7" X 11'-10"

STORM SHELTER
8'-2" X 6'-8"

PANTRY

W LAU.
8'-7" X 7'-8"

D.

KID'S NOOK BENCH / HANGING

WINDOW SEAT

BEDROOM 2
16'-8" X 12'-6"

BEDROOM 3 / DEN
15'-4" X 14'-2"

COVERED PORCH
36'-8" X 8'-0"

GARAGE
21'-0" X 27'-4"

© 2002 NELSON DESIGN GROUP, LLC.

Upper Floor

SLOPED CEILING
ATTIC STORAGE
7'2" WALL

8' LINE

BATH

BEDROOM 4
12'-0" X 19'-0"

COMPUTER CENTER

DN.

SKYLIGHTS   SKYLIGHTS

VAULTED CEILING

OPEN TO BELOW

LOFT
20'-4" X 13'-8"

RAIL

8' LINE

5' WALL

BEST SELLER
Designers Choice
NELSON DESIGN GROUP

650 Olive Street

Designed For:

JBL
RESIDENTIAL SYSTEMS
COMPLETE HOME
ENTERTAINMENT NETWORKS
& DISTRIBUTED AUDIO

JBL
Home Theater

Designed For:

Pioneer
sound.vision.soul
Pioneer Sound System

Width: 67' 8"
Depth: 72' 6"
Main Floor: 2,277 sq. ft.
Upper Floor: 728 sq. ft.
Total Living: 3,005 sq. ft.

Price Tier: E

Main Ceiling: 9 ft.
Bonus Ceiling: 8 ft.
Bedrooms: 4
Baths: 3 1/2
Foundation: Crawl, Slab,
Optional Basement,
Optional Daylight Basement
Plan Options: page 282

BUILDING SYSTEM
NGi
Next Generation Industries
COMPATABLE

Designed For:

JBL
RESIDENTIAL SYSTEMS
COMPLETE HOME
ENTERTAINMENT NETWORKS
& DISTRIBUTED AUDIO

JBL
Home Theater

Designed For:

Pioneer
sound.vision.soul
Pioneer Sound System

DECK
28'-0" X 12'-0"

BEDROOM 3
11'-4" X 12'-4"

GREAT ROOM
21'-0" X 15'-4"

MASTER SUITE
21'-4" X 15'-4"

LIN

FOYER 12' CLG.

PAN.

KITCHEN
13'-4" X 10'-0"

MASTER BATH
13'-2" X 9'-8"

BEDROOM 2
13'-8" X 12'-4"

DINING ROOM
11'-4" X 13'-8"

ENTRY

RG

REF

DW

WHP
TUB

GLASS
BLOCKS

BREAKFAST ROOM
13'-4" X 9'-8"

VAULTED CEILING

DN

Main Floor

Elevation B

388 Madison Drive

BEDROOM 4
13'-4" X 14'-4"

GAME ROOM
26'-4" X 19'-10"

GARAGE
21'-2" X 24'-10"

UP

BATH

LAU.
7'-4" X 8'-10"

W   D

Lower Floor

Width: 70' 6"
Depth: 48' 0"
Main Floor: 2,005 sq. ft.
Lower Floor: 1,047 sq. ft.
Total Living: 3,052 sq. ft.

Main Ceiling: 9 ft.
Lower Ceiling: 8 ft.
Bedrooms: 4
Baths: 3
Foundation: Daylight Basement
Plan Options: page 282

BUILDING SYSTEM
NGI
Next Generation Industries
COMPATABLE

Price Tier: E

To Order Call 1.800.590.2423   Similar plans can be viewed and ordered at www.nelsondesigngroup.com

Main Floor

Upper Floor

Lower Floor

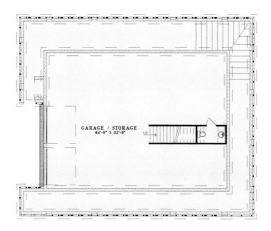

369 Waterfront Cove

Width: 58' 0"
Depth: 48' 0"
Main Floor: 1,564 sq. ft.
Upper Floor: 1,496 sq. ft.
Total Living: 3,060 sq. ft.

Price Tier: E

Main Ceiling: 10 ft.
Upper Ceiling: 9 ft.
Bedrooms: 3
Baths: 3, 2-1/2
Foundation: Crawl, Slab, Basement, Daylight Basement
Plan Options: page 282

BUILDING SYSTEM
NGi
Next Generation Industries
COMPATABLE

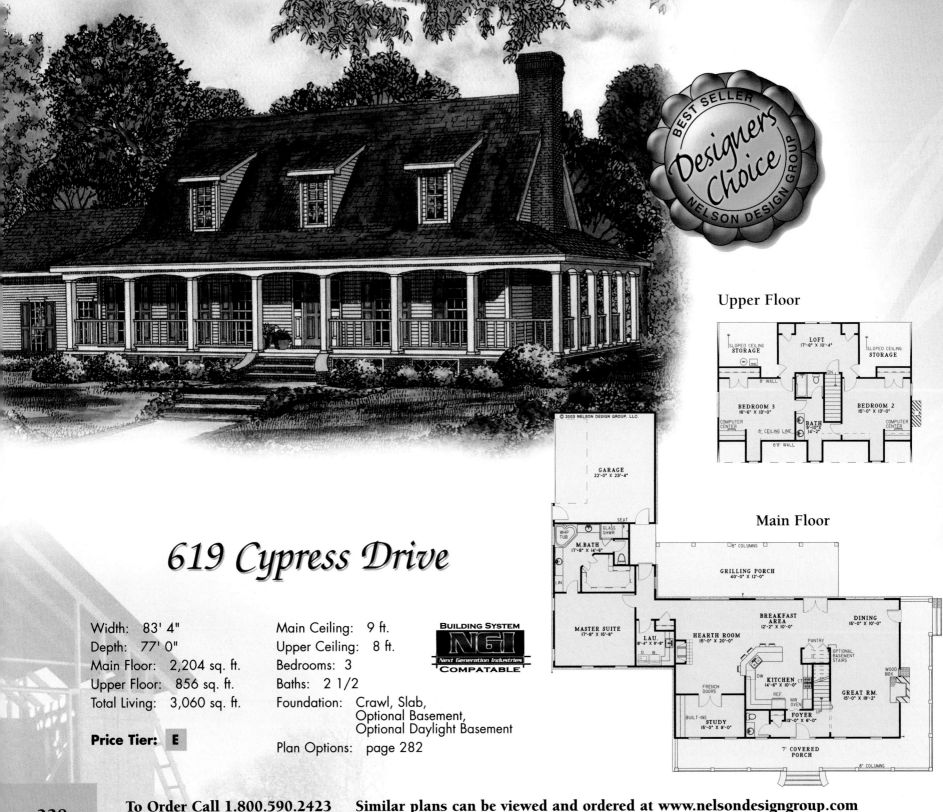

Upper Floor

LOFT 17'-6" X 10'-4"
SLOPED CEILING STORAGE
SLOPED CEILING STORAGE

8' WALL

BEDROOM 3 16'-6" X 13'-0"
COMPUTER CENTER

8' CEILING LINE

BATH 9'-10" 14'-2"

BEDROOM 2 15'-0" X 13'-0"
COMPUTER CENTER

6'-8" WALL

Main Floor

© 2003 NELSON DESIGN GROUP, LLC.

GARAGE 22'-0" X 23'-4"

SEAT
GLASS SHWR
WHP TUB
M.BATH 17'-8" X 11'-6"
LIN

GRILLING PORCH 40'-0" X 12'-0"
8" COLUMNS

MASTER SUITE 17'-8" X 15'-6"

LAU. 8'-4" X 9'-8"
D W

BREAKFAST AREA 12'-2" X 10'-0"

DINING 15'-0" X 10'-0"

HEARTH ROOM 15'-0" X 20'-0"

PANTRY

OPTIONAL BASEMENT STAIRS

WOOD BOX

FRENCH DOORS

KITCHEN 14'-6" X 10'-0"
DW
REF
MW OVEN

CT

GREAT RM. 15'-0" X 19'-2"

BUILT-INS
STUDY 15'-0" X 9'-0"

FOYER 20'-0" X 6'-0"
UP

7' COVERED PORCH

8" COLUMNS

619 Cypress Drive

Width: 83' 4"
Depth: 77' 0"
Main Floor: 2,204 sq. ft.
Upper Floor: 856 sq. ft.
Total Living: 3,060 sq. ft.

Price Tier: E

Main Ceiling: 9 ft.
Upper Ceiling: 8 ft.
Bedrooms: 3
Baths: 2 1/2
Foundation: Crawl, Slab, Optional Basement, Optional Daylight Basement
Plan Options: page 282

BUILDING SYSTEM
NGI
Next Generation Industries
COMPATABLE

To Order Call 1.800.590.2423   Similar plans can be viewed and ordered at www.nelsondesigngroup.com

Main Floor

WHP TUB
GLASS SHWR
M. BATH 14'-2" X 24'-4"
SITTING RM. 11'-10" X 9'-4"
GRILLING PORCH 37'-10" X 11'-0"
8' BOXED COLUMNS
LIN
FRENCH DOORS
W.I.C.
DRAWERS
MASTER SUITE 16'-2" X 15'-0"
GREAT RM. 20'-2" X 18'-2"
BRKFAST RM. 13'-2" X 10'-8"
UP
DESK
BOOK SHELVES
REF
SEASONAL CLOSET
BUILT-INS
PAN.
GAS CKT.
BEDROOM 2 14'-0" X 12'-0"
8' BOXED COLUMNS
GALLERY
KITCHEN 13'-2" X 14'-0"
OVEN
D.W.
LIN
FOYER 7'-10" X 10'-0" 11' CEILING
BATH 14'-0" X 10'-4"
GUEST ROOM/ BEDROOM 4 12'-2" X 10'-0"
BEDROOM 3/ STUDY 12'-0" X 16'-4"
DINING RM. 11'-10" X 13'-10" 9' CEILING
PORCH 8'-4" X 6'-4"
LAUNDRY 12'-2" X 9'-0"
BATH
PORCH
GARAGE 1 21'-4" X 21'-0"
GARAGE 2 21'-4" X 11'-0"
© 1996 NELSON DESIGN GROUP, LLC.

Upper Floor

ATTIC STORAGE
PROPOSED GAME ROOM 20'-2" X 22'-0"
BATH
PROPOSED BEDROOM 5 12'-8" X 12'-8"
DN
OFFICE 9'-0" X 11'-0"

Designed For:

JBL
RESIDENTIAL SYSTEMS
COMPLETE HOME
ENTERTAINMENT NETWORKS
& DISTRIBUTED AUDIO
JBL
Home Theater

Designed For:

Pioneer
sound.vision.soul
Pioneer Sound System

179 Olive Street

Width: 69' 2"
Depth: 88' 10"
Main Floor: 2,889 sq. ft.
Upper Floor: 188 sq. ft.
Total Living: 3,077 sq. ft.*
*Optional Bonus: 648 sq. ft.

Price Tier: E

Main Ceiling: 9 ft.
Bonus Ceiling: 9 ft.
Bedrooms: 5
Baths: 4
Foundation: Crawl, Slab,
Optional Basement,
Optional Daylight Basement
Plan Options: page 282

BUILDING SYSTEM
NGi
Next Generation Industries
COMPATABLE

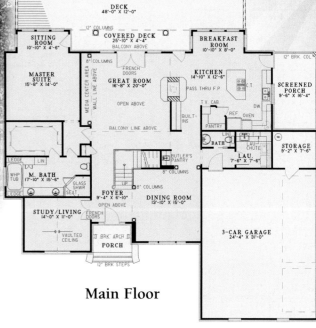

Main Floor

362 Cherry Street

Width: 66' 8"
Depth: 60' 4"
Main Floor: 2,107 sq. ft.
Upper Floor: 1,001 sq. ft.
Total Living: 3,108 sq. ft.*
*Optional Bonus: 485 sq. ft.

Price Tier: E

Main Ceiling: 9 ft.
Upper Ceiling: 8 ft.
Bedrooms: 3
Baths: 2 1/2
Foundation: Crawl, Slab,
Optional Basement,
Optional Daylight Basement
Plan Options: page 282

BUILDING SYSTEM
NGI
Next Generation Industries
COMPATABLE

Designed For:

JBL
RESIDENTIAL SYSTEMS
COMPLETE HOME
ENTERTAINMENT NETWORKS
& DISTRIBUTED AUDIO
JBL
Home Theater

Designed For:

Pioneer
sound.vision.soul
Pioneer Sound System

Upper Floor

606 Dogwood Avenue

Width: 60' 2"
Depth: 60' 2"
Main Floor: 1,600 sq. ft.
Upper Floor: 1,530 sq. ft.
Total Living: 3,130 sq. ft.*
*Upper Bonus Floor: 1,744 sq. ft.

Main Ceiling: 9 ft.
Upper Ceiling: 9 ft.
Bedrooms: 3
Baths: 3 1/2
Foundation: Crawl, Slab
Plan Options: page 282

BUILDING SYSTEM
NGI
Next Generation Industries
COMPATABLE

Price Tier: E

Main Floor

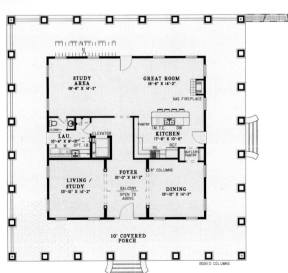

Upper Floor

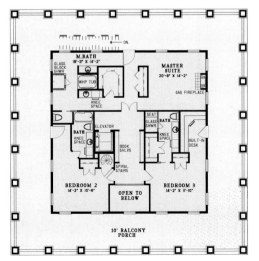

Upper Bonus

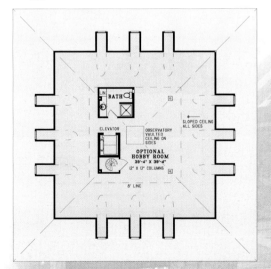

600 Brittany Lane

Width: 75' 0"
Depth: 54' 6"
Main Floor: 2,025 sq. ft.
Upper Floor: 1,130 sq. ft.
Total Living: 3,155 sq. ft.*
*Optional Bonus: 572 sq. ft.
Main Ceiling: 9 ft.
Upper Ceiling: 8 ft.
Bedrooms: 5
Baths: 4 1/2
Foundation: Crawl, Slab,
      Optional Basement,
      Optional Daylight Basement
Plan Options: page 282

Price Tier: E

BUILDING SYSTEM
NGI
Next Generation Industries
COMPATABLE

Designed For:

Pioneer
sound.vision.soul
Pioneer Sound System

Designed For:

JBL
RESIDENTIAL SYSTEMS
COMPLETE HOME
ENTERTAINMENT NETWORKS
& DISTRIBUTED AUDIO

JBL
Home Theater

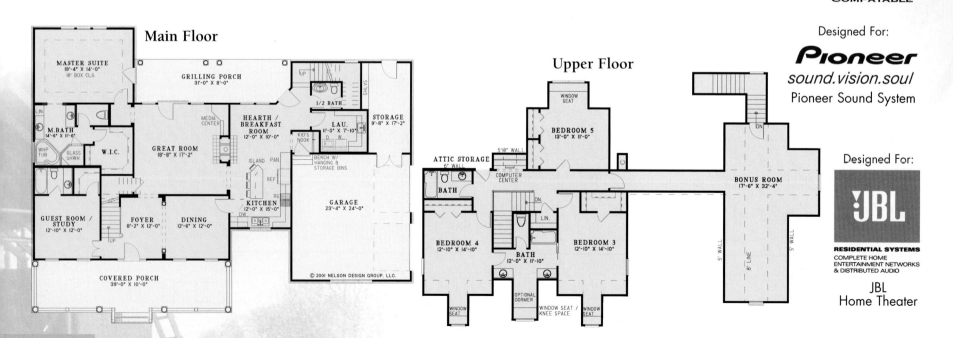

Main Floor

Upper Floor

© 2001 NELSON DESIGN GROUP, LLC.

To Order Call 1.800.590.2423   Similar plans can be viewed and ordered at www.nelsondesigngroup.com

336 Birchwood Lane

Designed For:

JBL
RESIDENTIAL SYSTEMS
COMPLETE HOME
ENTERTAINMENT NETWORKS
& DISTRIBUTED AUDIO

JBL
Home Theater

Designed For:

Pioneer
sound.vision.soul
Pioneer Sound System

Width: 82' 4"
Depth: 81' 6"
Total Living: 3,183 sq. ft.

Price Tier: E

Main Ceiling: 9 ft.
Bedrooms: 4
Baths: 2 1/2
Foundation: Crawl, Slab
Plan Options: page 282

BUILDING SYSTEM
NGI
Next Generation Industries
COMPATABLE

Floor Plan Labels

- WHP TUB
- M.BATH 18'-0" X 18'-2"
- STORAGE 23'-6" X 8'-2"
- HER'S
- HIS
- KNEE SPACE
- GLASS SHWR.
- LIN.
- VAULTED CEILING
- 12" BRK. COL.
- GRILLING PORCH 20'-4" X 12'-0"
- MASTER SUITE 18'-0" X 22'-0" 10' BOXED CEILING
- ATRIUM DOORS
- 3 CAR GARAGE 23'-6" X 32'-0"
- ATRIUM DOORS
- BUILT-INS
- MEDIA CENTER
- © 1994 NELSON DESIGN GROUP, LLC.
- BEDROOM 4 16'-4" X 11'-7"
- DESK
- LIVING ROOM 10' BOX CEILING W/ VAULTED CEILING 20'-0" X 23'-7"
- LIN
- 1/2 B.
- LAU. 7'-4" X 8'-10"
- BATH
- LIN
- KNEE SPACE
- LIN
- KITCHEN 13'-8" X 15'-6"
- TC. DW. REF
- C.T.
- ISLAND
- OVEN W/ CABINET
- BREAKFAST ROOM 14'-4" X 11'-8"
- PAN.
- DESK
- 8" COLUMNS
- BEDROOM 3 11'-0" X 12'-0"
- FOYER 10'-6" X 10'-4" VAULTED CEILING FRENCH DOORS
- DINING ROOM 16'-4" X 12'-0" VAULTED CEILING
- HEARTH ROOM 12'-0" X 14'-4"
- BEDROOM 2 14'-4" X 13'-0"
- PORCH 10'-2" X 8'-10" VAULTED CEILING
- 8" COLUMNS

376 Brandon Circle

Width: 86' 0"
Depth: 46' 0"
Main Floor: 2,036 sq. ft.
Upper Floor: 1,181 sq. ft.
Total Living: 3,217 sq. ft.
Main Ceiling: 9 ft.
Upper Ceiling: 8 ft.
Bedrooms: 4
Baths: 4
Foundation: Crawl, Slab,
Optional Basement,
Optional Daylight Basement
Plan Options: page 282

Price Tier: E

Elevation B

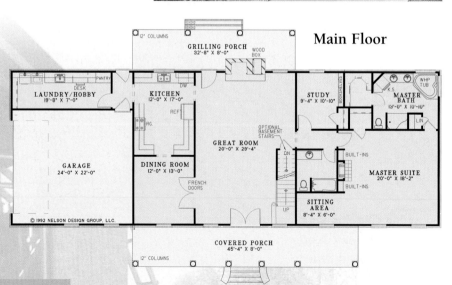

Main Floor

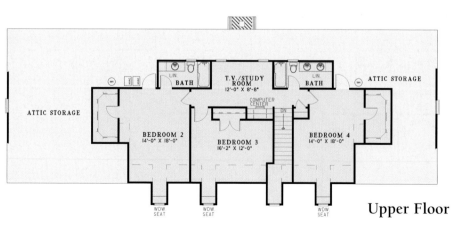

Upper Floor

To Order Call 1.800.590.2423   Similar plans can be viewed and ordered at www.nelsondesigngroup.com

Main Floor

MASTER BATH
WHP TUB
GLASS SHWR
11" BOXED CEILING
15'-0" X 18'-10" LIN

MASTER SUITE
11" BOXED CEILING
15'-0" X 16'-0"

FRENCH DOORS

STUDY / MEDIA
11'-8" X 12'-6"

FOYER

OPEN TO ABOVE

UP

COVERED ENTRY

FIXED ATRIUM DOORS

ATRIUM DOORS

HEARTH ROOM
15'-4" X 13'-0"

GREAT RM.
22'-4" X 18'-0"

OPTIONAL MEDIA CENTER

8" COLUMNS

BRKFAST RM.
15'-4" X 10'-0"

OPTIONAL STAIRS TO BASEMENT

BUTLER'S PANTRY

T.C.
D.W.

KITCHEN
15'-4" X 14'-2"

REF.

M.W. OVEN

PANTRY

C.T.

DINING RM.
12'-8" X 12'-6"

SIDE ENTRY

COMPUTER DESK

KID'S NOOK

BENCH W/ STRG.

D. W.

LAU.

STORAGE

COURT YARD GARAGE ENTRY

3-CAR GARAGE
21'-4" X 33'-2"

ATTIC STORAGE

BED RM. 2
12'-8" X 11'-0"

BED RM. 3
15'-8" X 12'-2"

DN

LIN

OPEN TO BELOW

BED RM. 4
12'-8" X 12'-6"

LIN

PLANT LEDGE

Upper Floor

Designed For:

259 Cherry Street

Width: 60' 0"
Depth: 96' 6"
Main Floor: 2,328 sq. ft.
Upper Floor: 875 sq. ft.
Total Living: 3,203 sq. ft.

Price Tier: E

Main Ceiling: 10 ft.
Upper Ceiling: 9 ft.
Bedrooms: 4
Baths: 3 1/2
Foundation: Crawl, Slab,
Optional Basement,
Optional Daylight Basement
Plan Options: page 282

BUILDING SYSTEM
NGI
Next Generation Industries
COMPATABLE

534 Autumn Drive

Width: 58' 6"

Depth: 60' 6"

Main Floor: 2,021 sq. ft.

Upper Floor: 1,227 sq. ft.

Total Living: 3,248 sq. ft.

Main Ceiling: 9 ft.

Upper Ceiling: 9 ft.

Bedrooms: 5

Baths: 3

Foundation: Crawl, Slab, Optional Basement, Optional Daylight Basement

Plan Options: page 282

Price Tier: E

Main Floor

GRILLING PORCH 16'-4" X 7'-0"

GAS BIBB

HEARTH ROOM 17'-8" X 10'-8"

BUILT-INS

FRENCH DOORS

ARCHED OPENING

8' COLUMNS

GREAT ROOM 16'-0" X 22'-8" 10' BOXED CLG.

PANTRY

KITCHEN 11'-0" X 12'-8"

DW

MW OVEN

REF

CT

BATH

GUEST ROOM / TEENAGE ROOM 11'-10" X 14'-10"

LAU. 10'-2" X 6'-6"

W D

HANGING

STOR.

UP FOYER

COVERED PORCH 24'-6" X 8'-0" 12' COLUMNS

DINING ROOM 11'-0" X 14'-0"

GARAGE 22'-0" X 21'-0"

MASTER SUITE 14'-2" X 16'-4" 10' BOXED CLG.

LIN.

M.BATH 13'-3" X 16'-4"

60X60 WHP TUB

W.I.C.

GLASS SEAT SHWR.

© 2001 NELSON DESIGN GROUP, LLC.

Upper Floor

ADJUSTABLE BOOK SHELVES

WINDOW SEAT

T.V. AREA 8'-0" X 10'-0"

DN

LOFT

OPEN TO BELOW

BEDROOM 3 11'-0" X 14'-0"

BEDROOM 4 11'-0" X 11'-0"

LIN.

BATH

LIN.

BEDROOM 2 13'-7" X 13'-10"

WINDOW SEAT

GAME ROOM 12'-8" X 19'-6"

8' WALL

8' WALL

5' WALL

5' WALL

564 Brittany Lane

Width: 69' 0"
Depth: 52' 10"
Main Floor: 2,184 sq. ft.
Upper Floor: 1,099 sq. ft.
Total Living: 3,283 sq. ft.*
*Optional Bonus: 494 sq. ft.
Main Ceiling: 9 ft.
Upper Ceiling: 8 ft.
Bedrooms: 5
Baths: 2 1/2
Foundation: Crawl, Slab,
Optional Basement,
Optional Daylight Basement
Plan Options: page 282

Price Tier: E

BUILDING SYSTEM
NGI
Next Generation Industries
COMPATABLE

Designed For:

RESIDENTIAL SYSTEMS
COMPLETE HOME
ENTERTAINMENT NETWORKS
& DISTRIBUTED AUDIO

JBL
Home Theater

Designed For:

sound.vision.soul
Pioneer Sound System

Main Floor

Upper Floor

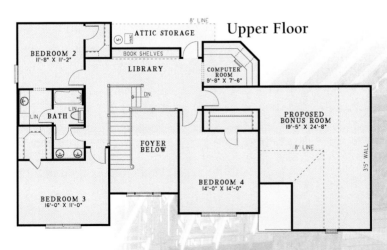

Designed For:

JBL
RESIDENTIAL SYSTEMS
COMPLETE HOME
ENTERTAINMENT NETWORKS
& DISTRIBUTED AUDIO

JBL
Home Theater

Designed For:

Pioneer
sound.vision.soul
Pioneer Sound System

386 Dogwood Avenue

Width: 80' 11"
Depth: 95' 8"
Total Living: 3,554 sq. ft.
Main Ceiling: 10 ft.

Bedrooms: 3
Baths: 3
Foundation: Crawl, Slab, Basement, Daylight Basement
Plan Options: page 282

BUILDING SYSTEM
NGI
Next Generation Industries
COMPATABLE

Price Tier: F

DEN 25'-0" X 22'-0"

13' LANAI

MASTER SUITE 20'-0" X 23'-4"

BREAKFAST AREA 15'-8" X 11'-2"

16" COLUMNS 24" BRICK BASE

ATRIUM DOOR

ATRIUM DOOR

ATRIUM DOORS

BATH

BEDROOM 2 9' CEILING 13'-0" X 12'-8"

KITCHEN 16'-0" X 14'-8"

GREAT ROOM 12' CEILING 27'-8" X 16'-4"

HER'S SHWR

BATH

12' CEILING

BUTLER'S PANTRY

8" RND. COLUMNS

M. BATH 12'-0" X 24'-6"

KNEE SPACE

BEDROOM 3 9' CEILING 13'-0" X 12'-8"

LAU. 9' CEILING 8'-8" X 10'-0"

PANTRY

DINING ROOM 13'-0" X 14'-0"

FOYER 12' CEILING 9'-0" X 12'-8"

LIBRARY 12'-8" X 16'-4"

HIS SHWR

WHP TUB

PORCH

GARAGE 22'-0" X 33'-10"

© 1995 NELSON DESIGN GROUP, LLC.

To Order Call 1.800.590.2423   Similar plans can be viewed and ordered at www.nelsondesigngroup.com

230 Main Street

Width: 68' 2"

Depth: 61' 0"

Main Floor: 1,583 sq. ft.

Upper Floor: 1,973 sq. ft.

Total Living: 3,556 sq. ft.

Main Ceiling: 10 ft.

Upper Ceiling: 9 ft.

Bedrooms: 3

Baths: 3 1/2

Foundation: Crawl, Slab, Basement, Daylight Basement

Plan Options: page 282

Price Tier: F

Designed For:

JBL
RESIDENTIAL SYSTEMS
COMPLETE HOME
ENTERTAINMENT NETWORKS
& DISTRIBUTED AUDIO

JBL
Home Theater

Designed For:

Pioneer
sound.vision.soul
Pioneer Sound System

Main Floor

Upper Floor

240 Linden Avenue

Width: 71' 4"
Depth: 66' 0"
Main Floor: 2,746 sq. ft.
Upper Floor: 820 sq. ft.
Total Living: 3,566 sq. ft.
Main Ceiling: 9 ft.
Upper Ceiling: 8 ft.
Bedrooms: 5
Baths: 3
Foundation: Crawl, Slab,
Optional Basement,
Optional Daylight Basement
Plan Options: page 282

Price Tier: F

BUILDING SYSTEM
NGI
Next Generation Industries
COMPATABLE

Main Floor

GRILLING PORCH
46'-0" X 10'-0"

MASTER SUITE
22'-0" X 14'-0"
10' BOXED CEILING

FRENCH DOORS

HEARTH ROOM
14'-0" X 17'-4"

BREAKFAST ROOM
12'-4" X 9'-8"

HIGH BAR

SEAT
SHWR

LIN

COMPUTER CENTER

KITCHEN
12'-4" X 15'-0"

GREAT ROOM
19'-3" X 18'-8"
10' CEILING

LAUNDRY
9'-0" X 6'-10"

36" HIGH VANITY

WHP TUB

GLASS BLOCKS

M. BATH
12'-8" X 18'-8"

BATH
10'-0" X 7'-10"

DW

CT

BUILT-INS

REF

DBL OVEN

PAN

STORAGE
9'-0" X 4'-0"

STOR.

UP

BEDROOM 2 /
STUDY
12'-4" X 11'-4"

FOYER
10' CEILING

DINING ROOM
11'-8" X 13'-4"

GARAGE
22'-0" X 20'-0"

BEDROOM 3
14'-0" X 12'-0"

OPTIONAL FRENCH DOORS

© 1996 NELSON DESIGN GROUP, LLC.

COVERED PORCH
33'-0" X 8'-0"

Upper Floor

BEDROOM 4
10'-8" X 20'-0"

5' WALL

6'4" WALL

8' CEILING LINE

GAME ROOM
19'-3" X 24'-0"

ATTIC STORAGE

UP

BATH

DN

8' WALL

8' CEILING LINE

Designed For:

JBL
RESIDENTIAL SYSTEMS
COMPLETE HOME ENTERTAINMENT NETWORKS & DISTRIBUTED AUDIO

JBL
Home Theater

Designed For:

PIONEER
sound.vision.soul
Pioneer Sound System

Main Floor

BEDROOM 4 /
IN-LAWS SUITE
11" BOXED CEILING
14'-0" X 17'-0"

WHP
TUB

SITTING
AREA

GRILLING PORCH
22'-8" X 11'-0"

KITCHENETTE
RG.   REF

GLASS
SHWR
SEAT

KS

M.BATH
11'-0" X 24'-6"

WHP
TUB

ATRIUM
DOOR

MASTER
SUITE
14'-6" X 24'-6"

MEDIA
CENTER

FRENCH DOOR

BREAKFAST
ROOM
12'-0" X 9'-0"

GREAT ROOM
10' CEILING
20'-10" X 18'-0"

UP

DESK

FRENCH
DOORS

BUILT-INS

KITCHEN
14'-0" X 16'-0"

DW

BEDROOM 2
12'-0" X 12'-0"

GALLERY

OPTIONAL
BASEMENT

BOOK
SHLVS

OVEN
MW

T.C.

REF

14" COLUMNS

FOYER
14' CEILING
10'-0" X 13'-0"

LAU.
9'-6" X 6'-1"

BATH

LIN

BUILT-INS

DINING
ROOM
14' CEILING
12'-10" X 12'-6"

BEDROOM 3
12' CEILING
11'-8" X 15'-0"

ARCHED OPENING

STORAGE
7'-2" X 4'-4"

9' CEILING LINE

GARAGE
20'-0" X 28'-2"

© 2001 NELSON DESIGN GROUP, LLC.

6' WALL

8' LINE

6' WALL

GAME ROOM /
OFFICE
24'-6" X 14'-2"

BATH

8' LINE

LIN

8' LINE

8' LINE

Upper Floor

Designed For:

JBL

RESIDENTIAL SYSTEMS
COMPLETE HOME
ENTERTAINMENT NETWORKS
& DISTRIBUTED AUDIO

JBL
Home Theater

Designed For:

Pioneer
sound.vision.soul
Pioneer Sound System

573 Linden Avenue

Width: 70' 0"
Depth: 81' 0"
Main Floor: 3,051 sq. ft.
Upper Floor: 517 sq. ft.
Total Living: 3,568 sq. ft.

Price Tier: F

Main Ceiling: 10 ft.
Upper Ceiling: 8 ft.
Bedrooms: 4
Baths: 4 1/2
Foundation: Crawl, Slab,
Optional Basement,
Optional Daylight Basement
Plan Options: page 282

BUILDING SYSTEM
NGI
Next Generation Industries
COMPATABLE

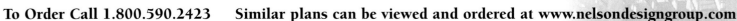

To Order Call 1.800.590.2423   Similar plans can be viewed and ordered at www.nelsondesigngroup.com

251

Main Floor

3-CAR GARAGE
21'-4" X 31'-8"

PATIO

14" BRICK COLUMNS

SEAT GLASS SHWR

WHP TUB

M.BATH
15'-0" X 18'-10"

LIN

COVERED PORCH
22'-4" X 10'-0"

FRENCH DOORS

FRENCH DOORS

FRENCH DOORS

FRENCH DOORS

SEWING CENTER

LAU. HOBBY
8'-8" X 11'-2"

GAS FIREPLACE

GREAT ROOM
22'-4" X 18'-0"

GAS FIREPLACE

MASTER SUITE
15'-0" X 16'-0"

PATIO

KID'S NOOK

BENCH W/ STRG BINS ABOVE

W D

PAN

FRENCH DOORS

FRENCH DOORS

D-OVEN

DW

DROP BAR

BUTLER'S PANTRY

COMP DESK

UP

GAS FIREPLACE

FRENCH DOORS

REF.

CT

DINING ROOM
12'-8" X 12'-6"

FOYER
OPEN TO ABOVE
9'-0" X 11'-6"

STUDY
11' CEILING
12'-0" X 12'-4"

KITCHEN
15'-4" X 14'-2"

BRKFAST AREA

GAS FIREPLACE

HEARTH ROOM
15'-4" X 15'-4"

COMPUTER ROOM
15'-8" X 7'-8"

GAME ROOM
26'-0" X 10'-11"

OPT. STAGE

BEDROOM 2
15'-8" X 12'-2"

LIN

STRG.
9'-0" X 5'-2"

BATH

BEDROOM 3
17'-0" X 12'-6"

OPEN TO BELOW

Upper Floor

260 Dogwood Avenue

Width: 60' 0"
Depth: 73' 8"
Main Floor: 2,391 sq. ft.
Upper Floor: 1,232 sq. ft.
Total Living: 3,623 sq. ft.

Price Tier: F

Main Ceiling: 10 ft.
Upper Ceiling: 8 ft.
Bedrooms: 3
Baths: 3 1/2
Foundation: Crawl, Slab,
Optional Basement,
Optional Daylight Basement
Plan Options: page 282

BUILDING SYSTEM
NGI
Next Generation Industries
COMPATABLE

Designed For:

JBL
RESIDENTIAL SYSTEMS
COMPLETE HOME ENTERTAINMENT NETWORKS & DISTRIBUTED AUDIO

JBL
Home Theater

Designed For:

Pioneer
sound.vision.soul
Pioneer Sound System

To Order Call 1.800.590.2423   **Similar plans can be viewed and ordered at www.nelsondesigngroup.com**

708 Cottonwood Drive

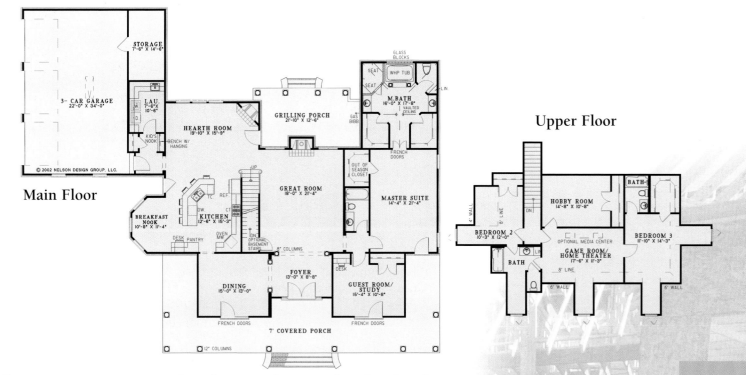

Width: 89' 2"
Depth: 71' 8"
Main Floor: 2,580 sq. ft.
Upper Floor: 1,098 sq. ft.
Total Living: 3,670 sq. ft.
Main Ceiling: 9 ft.
Upper Ceiling: 8 ft.
Bedrooms: 3
Baths: 4
Foundation: Crawl, Slab,
Optional Basement,
Optional Daylight Basement
Plan Options: page 282

Price Tier: F

BUILDING SYSTEM
NGI
Next Generation Industries
COMPATABLE

Designed For:

JBL

RESIDENTIAL SYSTEMS
COMPLETE HOME
ENTERTAINMENT NETWORKS
& DISTRIBUTED AUDIO

JBL
Home Theater

Designed For:

Pioneer
sound.vision.soul
Pioneer Sound System

Main Floor

STORAGE
7'-6" X 14'-6"

3- CAR GARAGE
22'-0" X 34'-0"

LAU.
7'-6" X 10'-6"

KID'S NOOK

HEARTH ROOM
19'-10" X 15'-9"

BENCH W/ HANGING

GRILLING PORCH
21'-10" X 12'-6"

GLASS BLOCKS

SEAT   WHP TUB   SEAT

M.BATH
16'-0" X 17'-8"
VAULTED CEILING

LIN

GAS BIBB

FRENCH DOORS

GREAT ROOM
18'-0" X 21'-4"

OUT OF SEASON CLOSET

BREAKFAST NOOK
10'-8" X 11'-4"

KITCHEN
12'-6" X 15'-3"

REF   TC

DW   CT

OVEN MW

MASTER SUITE
14'-4" X 21'-4"

DESK   PANTRY

OPTIONAL BASEMENT STAIRS

8" COLUMNS

DINING
15'-0" X 13'-0"

FOYER
13'-0" X 8'-6"

DESK

GUEST ROOM/ STUDY
15'-4" X 10'-8"

FRENCH DOORS   FRENCH DOORS

7' COVERED PORCH

12" COLUMNS

© 2002 NELSON DESIGN GROUP, LLC.

Upper Floor

HOBBY ROOM
14'-8" X 10'-8"

BATH

BEDROOM 2
10'-3" X 12'-0"

DN.

OPTIONAL MEDIA CENTER

GAME ROOM/ HOME THEATER
17'-6" X 11'-3"

BEDROOM 3
11'-10" X 14'-3"

BATH

4' WALL   8' LINE   8' LINE   6' WALL   6' WALL

Main Floor

© 2001 NELSON DESIGN GROUP, LLC.

GARAGE
20'-0" X 38'-0"

TIRE CURB

BENCH W/ HANGING

BRKFAST RM.
10'-8" X 11'-10"

SCREENED PORCH
24'-2" X 13'-10"

SKYLIGHTS

VAULTED CEILING

TORNADO RM. / CLOSET
12'-8" X 8'-6"

BATH

SEAT

REF.

KITCHEN
14'-4" X 19'-2"

M. BATH
15'-8" X 13'-8"

WHP TUB
SKY L.

KNEE SPACE

GAS FIREPLACE

GATHERING ROOM
22'-7" X 17'-0"

MEDIA CENTER

GLASS SHELVES

ISLAND

OVEN

PAN.

WET BAR

COMPUTER CENTER

MASTER SUITE
15'-8" X 16'-6"
11' BOXED CEILING

LAUNDRY
7'-8" X 9'-6"

OPEN TO ABOVE

LIN.

BATH

DINING
11'-0" X 16'-8"

LIVING / STUDY
11'-6" X 14'-4"

GRAND FOYER
9'-4" X 19'-10"

GUEST ROOM / NURSERY / OFFICE
13'-4" X 11'-0"

8' CEILING

8' CEILING

ENTRY
9'-4" X 6'-2"

631 Cherry Street

Width: 65' 0"
Depth: 89' 11"
Main Floor: 2,802 sq. ft.
Upper Floor: 890 sq. ft.
Total Living: 3,692 sq. ft.*
*Optional Bonus: 439 sq. ft.

Price Tier: F

Main Ceiling: 10 ft.
Upper Ceiling: 9 ft.
Bedrooms: 5
Baths: 5
Foundation: Crawl, Slab,
Optional Basement,
Optional Daylight Basement
Plan Options: page 282

BUILDING SYSTEM
NGI
Next Generation Industries
COMPATABLE

Designed For:

JBL
RESIDENTIAL SYSTEMS
COMPLETE HOME
ENTERTAINMENT NETWORKS
& DISTRIBUTED AUDIO

JBL
Home Theater

Designed For:

Pioneer
sound.vision.soul
Pioneer Sound System

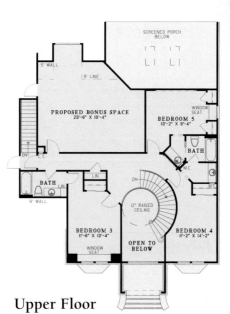

SCREENED PORCH BELOW

5' WALL

9' LINE

PROPOSED BONUS SPACE
23'-6" X 19'-4"

BEDROOM 5
13'-2" X 9'-4"

WINDOW SEAT

BATH

BATH

LIN.

DN

9' WALL

12' RAISED CEILING

BEDROOM 3
11'-6" X 13'-4"

OPEN TO BELOW

BEDROOM 4
11'-2" X 14'-2"

WINDOW SEAT

Upper Floor

Main Floor

STORAGE
24'-0" X 9'-10"

3-CAR GARAGE
24'-0" X 36'-4"

8' COVERED BREEZEWAY

DESK / SEWING

COVERED ENTRY

SUN ROOM / SCREENED PORCH
21'-8" X 12'-6"

SEAT
"GLASS" SHWR.

WHP TUB

M.BATH
14'-2" X 12'-4"

KNEE SPACE

LAUNDRY / HOBBY
9'-8" X 13'-4"

EXER.RM / HOBBY
9'-4" X 9'-2"

UP

1/2 BATH

BATH

LIN

GREAT RM.
21'-8" X 18'-0"

OVEN MW REF

KITCHEN
14'-2" X 12'-4"

DW

CT

OPT. BASEMENT STAIRS

COMPUTER DESK

PANTRY

BREAKFAST ROOM
14'-2" X 9'-2"

8" COLUMNS

MASTER BEDROOM
14'-2" X 18'-0"

WINDOW SEAT

FOYER

DINING RM.
12'-0" X 13'-2"

GUEST BEDROOM / NURSERY
12'-2" X 13'-8"

COVERED PORCH
51'-0" X 9'-0"

© 2002 NELSON DESIGN GROUP, LLC.

OPTIONAL H/C RAMP

Upper Floor

BALCONY
22'-4" X 6'-0"

HOME THEATER / GAME ROOM
21'-8" X 14'-6"

BUILT-IN MEDIA CENTER

REF.

LIN

OFFICE
14'-2" X 11'-0"

DN

LINEN

KID'S LAUNDRY

BEDROOM 3
12'-2" X 14'-0"

BEDROOM 4
12'-2" X 14'-0"

COMPUTER CENTER

WALK-OUT BALCONY

Designed For:

JBL

RESIDENTIAL SYSTEMS

COMPLETE HOME
ENTERTAINMENT NETWORKS
& DISTRIBUTED AUDIO

JBL
Home Theater

Designed For:

Pioneer

sound.vision.soul

Pioneer Sound System

667 Olive Street

Width: 65' 6"

Depth: 108' 6"

Main Floor: 2,484 sq. ft.

Upper Floor: 1,336 sq. ft.

Total Living: 3,820 sq. ft.

Price Tier: F

Main Ceiling: 9 ft.

Upper Ceiling: 9 ft.

Bedrooms: 4

Baths: 3 1/2

Foundation: Crawl, Slab,
Optional Basement,
Optional Daylight Basement

Plan Options: page 282

BUILDING SYSTEM

NGi
Next Generation Industries

COMPATABLE

Main Floor

© 1992 NELSON DESIGN GROUP, LLC.

3-CAR GARAGE
20'-8" X 32'-0"

LAUNDRY
9'-10" X 11'-0"

GRILLING PORCH
14'-0" X 18'-0"

BREAKFAST ROOM
13'-2" X 12'-0"

PORCH
18'-4" X 4'-4"

KITCHEN
14'-4" X 13'-0"

GREAT RM.
17'-0" X 18'-0"
10' CEILING

MASTER SUITE
14'-8" X 20'-0"
10' PAN CEILING

DINING RM.
13'-8" X 11'-4"

M.BATH
14'-8" X 14'-0"

STUDY
17'-8" X 15'-8"
10' CEILING

FOYER
9'-0" X 12'-4"
OPEN TO ABOVE

BATH

CLOSET
12'-10" X 10'-0"

ENTRY PORCH
10'-0" X 6'-8"

DEN/HOME THEATER/ GUEST ROOM
15'-8" X 15'-4"

668 Willow Lane

Width: 59' 4"
Depth: 90' 8"
Main Floor: 2,654 sq. ft.
Upper Floor: 1,169 sq. ft.
Total Living: 3,823 sq. ft.

Price Tier: F

Main Ceiling: 9 ft.
Upper Ceiling: 8 ft.
Bedrooms: 3
Baths: 3 1/2
Foundation: Crawl, Slab,
Optional Basement,
Optional Daylight Basement
Plan Options: page 282

Designed For:

JBL
RESIDENTIAL SYSTEMS
COMPLETE HOME
ENTERTAINMENT NETWORKS
& DISTRIBUTED AUDIO

JBL
Home Theater

Designed For:

Pioneer
sound.vision.soul
Pioneer Sound System

Upper Floor

GAME RM.
15'-6" X 16'-0"

ATTIC STORAGE

BEDROOM 3
15'-8" X 13'-10"

ATTIC STORAGE

LOFT

CLOSET
7'-2" X 5'-0"

BATH

CLOSET
7'-2" X 5'-0"

OPEN TO BELOW

BEDROOM 2
15'-8" X 16'-2"

To Order Call 1.800.590.2423   Similar plans can be viewed and ordered at www.nelsondesigngroup.com

Main Floor

GARAGE 18'-2" X 13'-0"

STORM SAFE ROOM 6'-0" X 7'-8"

HIS

SEATS

GLASS BLOCKS

SHELVES

VAULTED CEILING

8" COLUMNS

WHP TUB

SHELVES HER'S

M.BATH

FRENCH DOORS

PATIO 20'-0" X 20'-0"

© 2000 NELSON DESIGN GROUP, LLC.

GARAGE 24'-6" X 26'-3"

MASTER SUITE 18'-2" X 17'-4" TRAY CEILING

GRILLING PORCH 20'-0" X 12'-0" FRENCH DOORS VAULTED CEILING

STAMPED CONCRETE FLOOR

SUMMER KITCHEN

BATH 15'-8" X 7'-8"

BOOK SHLVS

STORAGE BENCH W/ HANGING

LAU./HOBBY 16'-2" X 8'-10"

KIDS NOOK

BATH

PANTRY

FRENCH DOORS

MEDIA CENTER

BEDROOM 4 14'-10" X 13'-7" 10' BOXED CEILING

WINDOW SEAT

BOOK SHLVS

COVERED PORCH 11'-0" X 15'-4"

BREAKFAST ROOM 11'-6" X 12'-8"

REF

KITCHEN 14'-10" X 15'-2"

GREAT ROOM 17'-10" X 21'-8" 18'-6" CEILING

BUILT-INS

BEDROOM 3 11'-0" X 11'-0"

STONE

COMPUTER DESK

SLOPED CEILING

ARCHED HEADER

ARCHED OPENING

FOYER 10'-2" X 8'-2"

BEDROOM 2 14'-4" X 13'-2"

BATH

DINING RM. 16'-6" X 12'-3" COFFERED CEILING

BOOK SHLVS

WINDOW SEAT

BOOK SHLVS

ARCHED OPENING

COVERED PORCH 12' CEILING 10'-2" X 13'-0"

ARCHED OPENING

COVERED PORCH 14'-4" X 6'-8"

Upper Floor

STORAGE 24'-3" X 24'-0"

8' LINE

BATH

DN

BONUS ROOM 29'-0" X 16'-7"

5' WALL

BUILT-INS BY BLDR.

FRENCH DOORS

BALCONY RAILING

OPEN TO GREAT ROOM

BUILT-INS BY BLDR.

8' LINE

8' LINE

5' WALL

SLOPED

PLANT LEDGE

501 Brittany Lane

Width: 79' 10"
Depth: 86' 8"
Main Floor: 3,354 sq. ft.
Upper Floor: 615 sq. ft.
Total Living: 3,969 sq. ft.

Main Ceiling: 9 ft.
Upper Ceiling: 9 ft.
Bedrooms: 4
Baths: 4
Foundation: Crawl, Slab, Optional Basement, Optional Daylight Basement
Plan Options: page 282

Price Tier: F

BUILDING SYSTEM
NGI
Next Generation Industries
COMPATABLE

258 Cherry Street

Width: 61' 6"
Depth: 78' 6"
Main Floor: 2,405 sq. ft.
Upper Floor: 1,071 sq. ft.
Lower Floor: 546 sq. ft.
Total Living: 4,022 sq. ft.
Main Ceiling: 9 ft.
Upper Ceiling: 9 ft.
Lower Ceiling: 9 ft.
Bedrooms: 5
Baths: 4 1/2
Foundation: Daylight Basement
Plan Options: page 282

Price Tier: G

BUILDING SYSTEM
NGI
Next Generation Industries
COMPATABLE

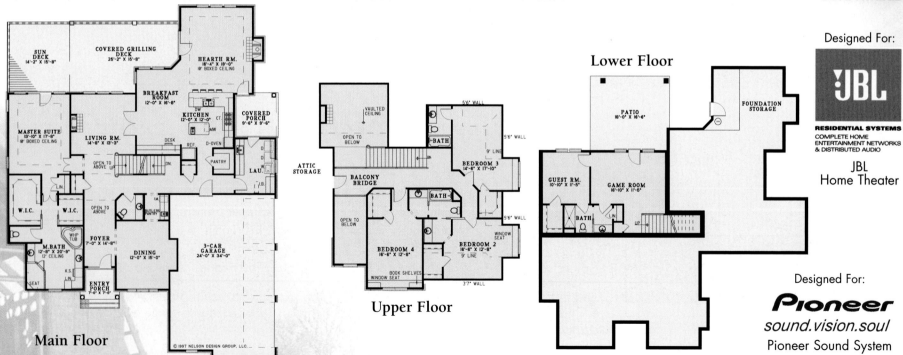

Lower Floor

Upper Floor

Main Floor

Designed For:

JBL

RESIDENTIAL SYSTEMS
COMPLETE HOME
ENTERTAINMENT NETWORKS
& DISTRIBUTED AUDIO

JBL
Home Theater

Designed For:

Pioneer
sound.vision.soul
Pioneer Sound System

© 1997 Nelson Design Group, LLC.

To Order Call 1.800.590.2423   Similar plans can be viewed and ordered at www.nelsondesigngroup.com

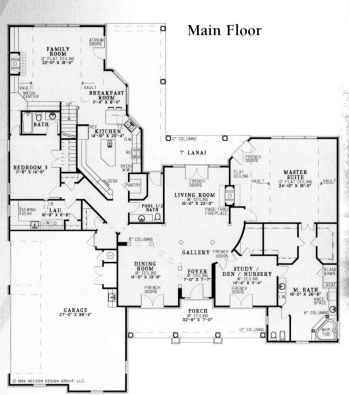

Main Floor

FAMILY ROOM
12' FLAT CEILING
22'-0" X 19'-0"

ATRIUM DOORS

VAULT MEDIA CENTER

VAULT
BREAKFAST ROOM
11'-4" X 8'-11"

BATH

UP

REF.
KITCHEN
14'-10" X 20'-4"
D.W

OVEN M.W

BEDROOM 3
11'-8" X 14'-6"

DESK

PANTRY

12" COLUMNS

7' LANAI

FRENCH DOORS

FLAT CEILING

VAULT

MASTER SUITE
12' FLAT CEILING
24'-10" X 19'-0"

VAULT

FRENCH DOORS

LIVING ROOM
10' CEILING
15'-0" X 22'-0"

PASS-THRU FIREPLACE

POOL 1/2 BATH

SEWING DESK

LAU.
16'-8" X 6'-8"

W.D

8" COLUMNS

GALLERY

FRENCH DOORS

GARAGE
27'-0" X 36'-4"

DINING ROOM
10' CEILING
14'-0" X 13'-8"

FRENCH DOORS

FOYER
10' CEILING
7'-0" X 7'-7"

STUDY / DEN / NURSERY
10' CEILING
14'-4" X 11'-4"

FRENCH DOORS

LIN

M. BATH
16'-0" X 26'-8"

GLASS SHWR

SEAT

KNEE SPACE

PORCH
10' CEILING
32'-8" X 7'-0"

6" COLUMNS

12" COLUMNS

WHP TUB

© 1996 NELSON DESIGN GROUP, LLC.

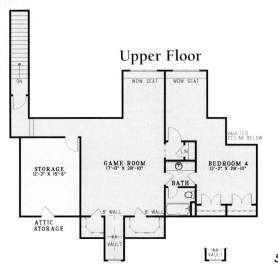

Upper Floor

ON

WDW. SEAT   WDW. SEAT

VAULTED CEILING BELOW

STORAGE
12'-2" X 15'-6"

GAME ROOM
17'-0" X 28'-10"

LIN

BATH

BEDROOM 4
12'-2" X 28'-10"

ATTIC STORAGE

8' WALL   8' WALL

VAULT

VAULT

157 Birchwood Lane

Width: 77' 0"
Depth: 83' 6"
Main Floor: 3,190 sq. ft.
Upper Floor: 1,053 sq. ft.
Total Living: 4,243 sq. ft.

Price Tier: G

Main Ceiling: 9 ft.
Upper Ceiling: 8 ft.
Bedrooms: 4
Baths: 3 1/2
Foundation: Crawl, Slab, Optional Basement, Optional Daylight Basement
Plan Options: page 282

BUILDING SYSTEM
NGI
Next Generation Industries
COMPATABLE

669 Glendale Avenue

Width: 76' 0"
Depth: 67' 10"
Main Floor: 3,275 sq. ft.
Upper Floor: 1,028 sq. ft.
Total Living: 4,303 sq. ft.
Main Ceiling: 8 ft.
Upper Ceiling: 8 ft.
Bedrooms: 5
Baths: 4 1/2
Foundation: Crawl, Slab,
Optional Basement,
Optional Daylight Basement
Plan Options: page 282

Price Tier: G

BUILDING SYSTEM
NGI
Next Generation Industries
COMPATABLE

Main Floor

Upper Floor

Designed For:

JBL

RESIDENTIAL SYSTEMS
COMPLETE HOME
ENTERTAINMENT NETWORKS
& DISTRIBUTED AUDIO

JBL
Home Theater

Designed For:

Pioneer
sound.vision.soul
Pioneer Sound System

To Order Call 1.800.590.2423   Similar plans can be viewed and ordered at www.nelsondesigngroup.com

Main Floor

W.I.C. / SAFE RM. 8'-8" X 12'-8"
M. BATH 13'-6" X 15'-4"
STORM SHELTER
SHOP AREA
42 X 72 WHP TUB
REC. SHWR
K.S.
M.C.
9' CEILING
MASTER SUITE 18'-4" X 18'-4"
18' BOX CEILING
9' CEILING
COFFEE BAR
9' CEILING
T.V. NICHE
4" CURB
GARAGE 21'-8" X 21'-4"
LAU. 7'-8" X 7'-6"
BRKFST. ROOM 12'-0" X 12'-4"
KITCHEN 15'-8" X 17'-3"
FZR.
REF.
GAS C.T.
T.C.
ISLAND
MW OVEN
D.W.
12' COLUMNS
LANAI 25'-10" X 13'-10" VAULTED CEILING
PANTRY
42" BAR
ARCHED OPENING
BAR
GREAT ROOM 23'-2" X 19'-8" VAULTED CEILING
MEDIA CENTER
SPORTS / PLAY MOTOR COURT
PRIVACY WALL
LINE OF BALCONY ABOVE
DINING 13'-4" X 13'-2"
PLANT SHELF
M.C.
BATH
BRICK ARCH
GARAGE 19'-4" X 21'-4"
BRICK ARCH
UP
GRAND FOYER 8'-6" X 8'-10" OPEN TO ABOVE
LIVING 13'-6" X 12'-4"
BOOK SHELVES
GUEST ROOM / STUDY 12'-0" X 13'-0"
PORCH 9'-4" X 4'-8"
© 2000 NELSON DESIGN GROUP, LLC.
ARCHED ENTRY

Upper Floor

HOME THEATER / GAME ROOM 27'-6" X 25'-0"
9' WALL
DN
READING / TV NOOK 11'-8" X 18'-10"
COMPUTER CENTER
BEDROOM 2 10'-0" X 13'-2"
STOR.
OPEN TO BELOW 23'-2" X 20'-5"
BATH
M.C.
BATH
LIN.
DN
BEDROOM 3 11'-10" X 12'-4"
OPEN TO BELOW 9'-4" X 9'-0"
BEDROOM 4 13'-2" X 12'-0"
ARCHED ENTRY

Designed For:

JBL

RESIDENTIAL SYSTEMS
COMPLETE HOME ENTERTAINMENT NETWORKS & DISTRIBUTED AUDIO

JBL
Home Theater

Designed For:

Pioneer
sound.vision.soul
Pioneer Sound System

632 Cherry Street

Width: 85' 0"
Depth: 90' 6"
Main Floor: 2,958 sq. ft.
Upper Floor: 1,376 sq. ft.
Total Living: 4,334 sq. ft.*
*Optional Bonus: 723 sq. ft.

Price Tier: G

Main Ceiling: 10 ft.
Upper Ceiling: 9 ft.
Bedrooms: 4
Baths: 4
Foundation: Crawl, Slab, Optional Basement, Optional Daylight Basement
Plan Options: page 282

BUILDING SYSTEM
NGI Next Generation Industries
COMPATABLE

To Order Call 1.800.590.2423   Similar plans can be viewed and ordered at www.nelsondesigngroup.com   261

Upper Floor

ATTIC STORAGE

MEDIA CENTER

GAME ROOM/
HOME THEATER
20'-4" X 20'-8"

BATH

BEDROOM 4
12'-0" X 14'-0"

DN

FRENCH DOORS

WET BAR
REF

OPEN TO BELOW

BEDROOM 2
14'-0" X 16'-0"

BEDROOM 3
11'-0" X 13'-8"

LIN

BATH
10'-8" X 5'-4"

LIN

671 Dogwood Avenue

Width: 74' 4"
Depth: 74' 8"
Main Floor: 2,836 sq. ft.
Upper Floor: 1,524 sq. ft.
Total Living: 4,360 sq. ft.

Price Tier: G

Main Ceiling: 10 ft.
Upper Ceiling: 9 ft.
Bedrooms: 4
Baths: 3, 2-1/2
Foundation: Crawl, Slab,
Optional Basement,
Optional Daylight Basement
Plan Options: page 282

BUILDING SYSTEM
NGI
Next Generation Industries
COMPATABLE

Designed For:

JBL
RESIDENTIAL SYSTEMS
COMPLETE HOME
ENTERTAINMENT NETWORKS
& DISTRIBUTED AUDIO
JBL
Home Theater

Designed For:

Pioneer
sound.vision.soul
Pioneer Sound System

Main Floor

SHOWER
SEAT
K.S.
LB.

M. BATH
15'-10" X 23'-8"

WHP TUB

SITTING AREA
10'-8" X 8'-10"

COVERED GRILLING PORCH
20'-4" X 10'-0"

KEEPING ROOM
11'-0" X 15'-8"

MASTER SUITE
15'-6" X 15'-0"

GREAT RM.
20'-4" X 20'-2"

BREAKFAST ROOM
10'-10" X 13'-6"

KITCHEN
18'-0" X 11'-6"
ISLAND

UP

REF.

DW

C.T.

OUT OF SEASON CLOSET

BUILT-INS

PANTRY

MW
OVEN

LAU.
9'-4" X 6'-1"

STRG
5'-8" X 6'-0"

LINEN

GALLERY
20'-4" X 5'-6"

BENCH W/ HANGING

D.
W.

KID'S NOOK

10" COLUMNS

LINEN

1/2 BATH
5'-0" X 7'-0"

FOYER
9'-10" X 12'-2"

OPEN ABOVE

DINING ROOM
13'-6" X 14'-10"

STUDY
13'-10" X 12'-0"

ENTRY PORCH
9'-10" X 5'-0"

UP

3-CAR GARAGE
21'-10" X 35'-4"

© 2003 NELSON DESIGN GROUP, LLC.

262 Olive Street

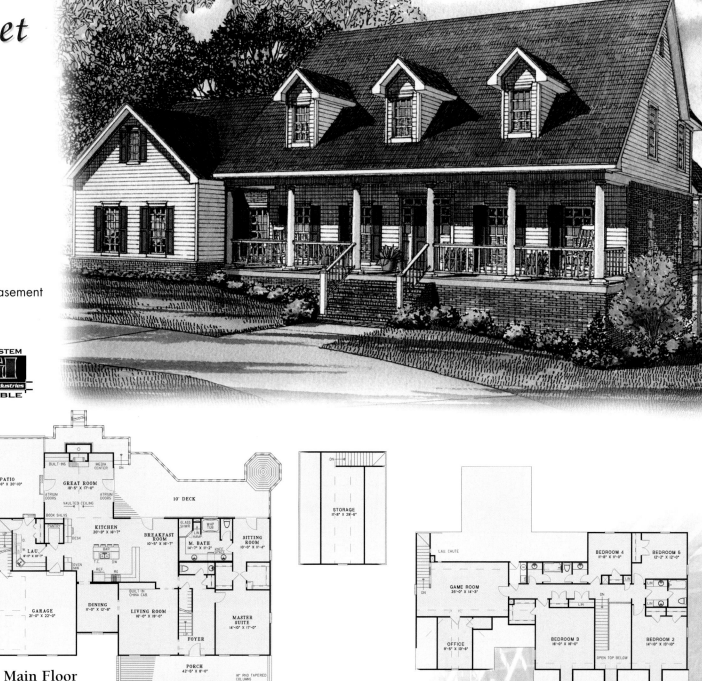

Width: 106' 5"
Depth: 65' 10"
Main Floor: 2,500 sq. ft.
Upper Floor: 1,882 sq. ft.
Total Living: 4,382 sq. ft.
Main Ceiling: 9 ft.
Upper Ceiling: 8 ft.
Bedrooms: 5
Baths: 3 1/2
Foundation: Crawl, Slab,
Optional Basement,
Optional Daylight Basement
Plan Options: page 282

Price Tier: G

BUILDING SYSTEM
NGi
Next Generation Industries
COMPATABLE

Designed For:

RESIDENTIAL SYSTEMS
COMPLETE HOME
ENTERTAINMENT NETWORKS
& DISTRIBUTED AUDIO

JBL
Home Theater

Main Floor

Upper Floor

Designed For:

sound.vision.soul
Pioneer Sound System

584 Hickory Place

Width: 79' 10"
Depth: 60' 6"
Main Floor: 2,861 sq. ft.
Upper Floor: 1,600 sq. ft.
Total Living: 4,461 sq. ft.*
*Optional Bonus: 250 sq. ft.
Main Ceiling: 10 ft.
Upper Ceiling: 9 ft.
Bedrooms: 5
Baths: 4 1/2
Foundation: Crawl, Slab,
Optional Basement,
Optional Daylight Basement
Plan Options: page 282

Price Tier: G

BUILDING SYSTEM
NGI Next Generation Industries
COMPATABLE

Main Floor

Upper Floor

© 1993 NELSON DESIGN GROUP, LLC.

Designed For:

JBL
RESIDENTIAL SYSTEMS
COMPLETE HOME
ENTERTAINMENT NETWORKS
& DISTRIBUTED AUDIO

JBL
Home Theater

Designed For:

Pioneer
sound.vision.soul
Pioneer Sound System

To Order Call 1.800.590.2423   Similar plans can be viewed and ordered at www.nelsondesigngroup.com

647 Dogwood Avenue

Width: 87' 8"

Depth: 60' 4"

Main Floor: 2,954 sq. ft.

Upper Floor: 1,534 sq. ft.

Total Living: 4,488 sq. ft.*

*Optional Bonus: 601 sq. ft.

Main Ceiling: 10 ft.

Upper Ceiling: 9 ft.

Bedrooms: 4

Baths: 3, 2-1/2

Foundation: Crawl, Slab,
Optional Basement,
Optional Daylight Basement

Plan Options: page 282

Price Tier: G

BUILDING SYSTEM
NGI
Next Generation Industries
COMPATABLE

Designed For:

JBL

RESIDENTIAL SYSTEMS
COMPLETE HOME
ENTERTAINMENT NETWORKS
& DISTRIBUTED AUDIO

JBL
Home Theater

Designed For:

Pioneer
sound.vision.soul
Pioneer Sound System

Best Seller
Designers Choice
NELSON DESIGN GROUP

Main Floor

Upper Floor

273 Dogwood Avenue

Width: 96' 10"
Depth: 76' 6"
Main Floor: 3,526 sq. ft.
Upper Floor: 1,347 sq. ft.
Total Living: 4,873 sq. ft.
Main Ceiling: 9 ft.
Upper Ceiling: 8 ft.
Bedrooms: 4
Baths: 4 1/2
Foundation: Crawl, Slab, Basement, Daylight Basement
Plan Options: page 282

Price Tier: **G**

BUILDING SYSTEM
NGI
Next Generation Industries
COMPATABLE

Main Floor

HEARTH ROOM / MEDIA ROOM 20'-4" X 29'-6"
10" BOXED CEILING
WET BAR
REF
BREAKFAST ROOM 13'-0" X 9'-5"
FRENCH DOORS
LANAI 33'-0" X 12'-0"
FRENCH DOORS
SITTING AREA
EXER. AREA 10'-2" X 12'-0"
GAS FIREPLACE
FRENCH DOORS
SEAT
KITCHEN 18'-4" X 16'-6"
DW
REF
GREAT ROOM 21'-0" X 19'-4"
BUILT-INS
MASTER SUITE 16'-4" X 26'-0"
LIN
SEAT
D-OVEN
OVEN WARMER BELOW
OPEN TO UPPER FLOOR CEILING
MAKE-UP CENTER
UP
PANTRY
OPT. DESK
BUILT-INS
FRENCH DOORS
WHP TUB
GLASS BLOCKS
STORAGE
LAU. CHUTE
GALLERY
BATH
M. BATH 10'-2" X 31'-6"
FRZR
LAU. 9'-10" X 12'-6"
8' COLUMNS
DINING ROOM 12'-6" X 15'-10"
OPEN TO ABOVE
GRAND FOYER 13'-0" X 13'-0"
UP
STUDY / GUEST RM. 12'-0" X 15'-6"
SHELVES
GARAGE 23'-6" X 34'-2"
© 1998 NELSON DESIGN GROUP, LLC.
VAULTED CEILING
COVERED PORCH

Upper Floor

© 1998 NELSON DESIGN GROUP, LLC.
BEDROOM 2 16'-4" X 16'-0"
BEDROOM 3 16'-4" X 14'-0"
OPEN TO BELOW
BATH
LIN
BATH
LAU. CHUTE
FUTURE ATTIC SPACE
8' LINE
ATTIC STORAGE
DN
BEDROOM 4 13'-0" X 13'-2"
OPEN TO BELOW

Designed For:

JBL
RESIDENTIAL SYSTEMS
COMPLETE HOME ENTERTAINMENT NETWORKS & DISTRIBUTED AUDIO

JBL Home Theater

Designed For:

Pioneer
sound.vision.soul
Pioneer Sound System

To Order Call 1.800.590.2423   Similar plans can be viewed and ordered at www.nelsondesigngroup.com

Upper Floor

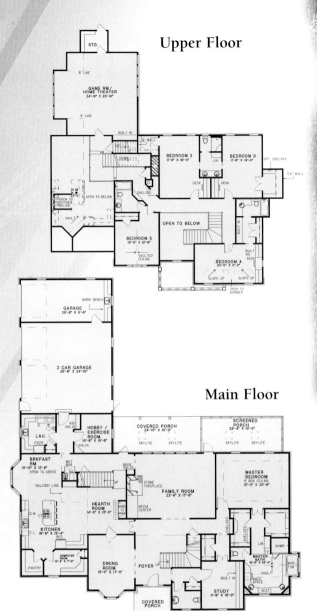

STO.

8' LINE

GAME RM /
HOME THEATER
24'-10" X 25'-10"

8' LINE

BUILT IN

BEDROOM 2
11'-8" X 18'-0"

BEDROOM 3
11'-8" X 18'-0"

LIN

OPT SHELVES

5/8" WALL

DESK   DESK

SHELVES

OPEN TO BELOW

OPEN TO BELOW

BEDROOM 5
13'-0" X 12'-8"

VAULTED
CEILING

BUILT
INS DESK

BEDROOM 4
20'-0" X 17'-2"

SLOPE UP   SLOPE UP

OPEN TO
DORMER

WORK BENCH

GARAGE
25'-6" X 11'-6"

2 CAR GARAGE
25'-8" X 24'-10"

Main Floor

KID SHLVS

L.AU.
FRZR

HOBBY /
EXERCISE
ROOM
10'-8" X 10'-8"

SHLVS

COVERED PORCH
24'-10" X 10'-0"

SKYLITE   SKYLITE

SCREENED
PORCH
22'-4" X 10'-0"

SKYLITE   SKYLITE

BRKFAST
RM
13'-10" X 12'-8"

OPEN TO ABOVE

WET
BAR

BOOK
SHLVS

BALCONY LINE

UP

STONE
FIREPLACE

FAMILY ROOM
22'-6" X 17'-6"

MASTER
BEDROOM
9' BOX CEILING
15'-0" X 20'-6"

HEARTH
ROOM
14'-0" X 13'-0"

MEDIA
CENTER

KITCHEN
18'-8" X 13'-4"
T.C.   REF

SHELVES

LIN

SHWR

D.W. CT.

COMPUTER
ROOM
12'-0" X 7'-4"

PANTRY

DINING
ROOM
13'-0" X 17'-0"

FOYER UP

MASTER
BATH
16'-8" X 20'-4"

WHP
TUB

VAULT

BUILT IN

STUDY
11'-8" X 13'-0"

KNEE
SPACE

SEAT

COVERED
PORCH

Designed For:

Pioneer
sound.vision.soul
Pioneer Sound System

Designed For:

JBL

RESIDENTIAL SYSTEMS
COMPLETE HOME
ENTERTAINMENT NETWORKS
& DISTRIBUTED AUDIO

JBL
Home Theater

138 Cherry Street

Width: 81' 6"	Main Ceiling: 9 ft.
Depth: 93' 2"	Upper Ceiling: 9 ft.
Main Floor: 3,276 sq. ft.	Bedrooms: 5
Upper Floor: 2,272 sq. ft.	Baths: 4 1/2
Total Living: 5,548 sq. ft.	Foundation: Crawl, Slab, Optional Basement, Optional Daylight Basement
Price Tier: G	Plan Options: page 282

BUILDING SYSTEM
NGI
Next Generation Industries
COMPATABLE

341 Dogwood Avenue

Width: 106' 0"
Depth: 87' 0"
Main Floor: 3,810 sq. ft.
Lower Floor: 1,914 sq. ft.
Total Living: 5,724 sq. ft.*
*Optional Bonus: 913 sq. ft.
Main Ceiling: 9 ft.
Lower Ceiling: 8 ft.
Bedrooms: 5
Baths: 4 1/2
Foundation: Daylight Basement
Plan Options: page 282

Price Tier: G

BUILDING SYSTEM
NGI
Next Generation Industries
COMPATABLE

Main Floor

Upper Floor

Lower Floor

Designed For:

JBL
RESIDENTIAL SYSTEMS
COMPLETE HOME
ENTERTAINMENT NETWORKS
& DISTRIBUTED AUDIO

JBL
Home Theater

Designed For:

Pioneer
sound.vision.soul
Pioneer Sound System

To Order Call 1.800.590.2423   Similar plans can be viewed and ordered at www.nelsondesigngroup.com

621 Birchwood Lane

Width: 117' 8"

Depth: 84' 8"

Main Floor: 5,338 sq. ft.

Upper Floor: 1,050 sq. ft.

Total Living: 6,388 sq. ft.*

*Optional Bonus: 1,460 sq. ft.

Main Ceiling: 10 ft.

Upper Ceiling: 9 ft.

Bedrooms: 4

Baths: 4, 2-1/2

Foundation: Crawl, Slab,
Optional Basement,
Optional Daylight Basement

Plan Options: page 282

Price Tier: G

BUILDING SYSTEM
NGi
Next Generation Industries
COMPATABLE

Designed For:

RESIDENTIAL SYSTEMS
COMPLETE HOME
ENTERTAINMENT NETWORKS
& DISTRIBUTED AUDIO

JBL
Home Theater

Designed For:

sound.vision.soul
Pioneer Sound System

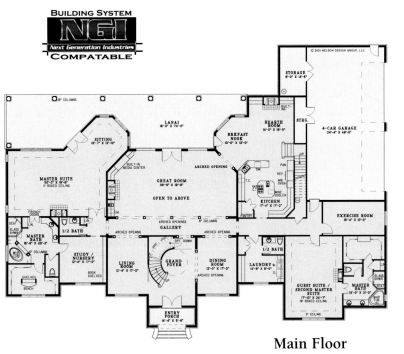

Main Floor

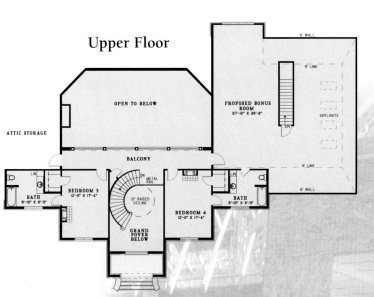

Upper Floor

... more plans

Address http://www.nelsondesigngroup.com/

Nelson Design Group LLC

RESIDENTIAL & COMMERCIAL PLANNERS - DESIGNERS
Home Plan Books

Nelson Design Group wants to ensure that our customers, whether consumers or builders, have the most helpful designs available. At NDG, we are constantly developing new plan publications in addition to our permanent collection. These books are valuable tools in selecting the home of your dreams, providing easy-to-read floor plans and specs, and detailed artistic renderings in full color. Each book showcases new plan collections, with minimal duplication, for optimum variety.

Builder Edition - Volume I ....(Black/White – 80 pages).......$10
Builder Edition - Volume II ....(Black/White – 80 pages).......$10
"New Beginnings" ....(Full Color – 156 pages).......$15
Builder's Special Edition I ....(Full Color – 288 pages).......$20
Builder's Special Edition II ....(Full Color – 288 pages).......$20
All 5 Plan Books $50

(shipping and handling not included)

Big Image On A Small Budget?

Feature Sheets
8.5" x 11" customized color rendering with floor plan, your color logo and customized bullet points. ..... 100 sheets/pack - 20% discount with 2 packs or more.... **$50**

Framed Prints
Professionally framed and matted 20" x 24" color renderings customized with your logo, floor plan and bullet points.
Black Metal **$89**
Wooden...**$89**
Gold **$150**

Outdoor Signage
24" x 36", similar to above but in vertical format laminated and weatherproofed, customized and ready for display in front of your construction site.
Color Laminated **$195**
Free blueprint of yard sign holder with sign purchase

Interior Signage
24" x 36", customized and ready for mounting on foamcore backing. Perfect for displaying on easels at Open Houses, Grand Openings, Sales Offices, Model Homes, etc.
Full Color **$150**

Brochures
Have your own customized brochure introducing and promoting your company or development as well as your benefits with photos and logo display ....**Call**

Logo and Artwork
Nelson Design Group's graphics and marketing team will develop a professional logo or other art design for your company, development, etc............From **$250**

Dura-trans
Special backlit 'Dura-tran' color images ready for display. Available in a variety of custom sizes.....................................**$125** to **$195**

Specialty Printing
Nelson Design Group can handle most every requirement: business cards, letterhead, envelopes, presentation folders, thank-you cards - and more ....**Call**

Video Presentations
We can produce a video presentation for you to play on VHS videotape and/or CD. Ask for the NDG video as an example! ....**Call**

3-D Virtual Reality Tours
Nelson Design Group provides this cutting edge service allowing you to view the home interior through 3-D visualization ....**Call**

Promotion, Ad Placement, Public Relations And More!
Nelson Design Group has experienced professionals to assist you in every phase of your marketing program ....**Call**

Home Plan Marketing Ideas

A. Home Plan Books
B. Collection Portfolios
C. Identity Packages
D. Feature Sheets
E. Computer Products

F. Framed Prints
G. Indoor/Outdoor Posters
H. Blueprints
I. Gold Framed Prints
J. Multi-media Products

Marketing

Nelson Design Group offers a wide variety of marketing tools that will assist you in selling your homes. Because we cater daily to a diverse marketplace with a broad mix of consumers, real estate professionals and home builders, we know what buyers want, how builders build, and how to design and market homes that sell quickly.

NDG offers a complete product line of marketing materials including full color feature sheets, framed and matted color renderings, street scapes and outdoor promotional signage allowing the builder/developer to have cost effective marketing materials on their homes and for their business.

Our in-house marketing and design staff provides you with everything you need to develop a turn-key marketing program and they can answer any questions you or your staff may have. We provide valued expertise throughout all phases of development from site selection and layout to final marketing strategies.

Dear Nelson Design Group Staff,

Thank you for helping me by providing me with concise and unique plans.. One of the major factors in my success has been attributed to your beautiful home plans and Tru-Cost Estimating program. Capital Development Group is pleased to be associated with a quality company such as Nelson Design Group and looks forward to a long and prosperous relationship.

Sincerely,
Robert A. Tyus, Sr.
Capital Development Group, LLC

My Work History...
Served as a Water Treatment Manager and General Manager for two local utilities for over 25 years. My duties included all capital improvement projects such as new buildings, treatment systems, tanks, and pipelines. My desire has always been to pursue residential development and home building.

Company History... Our company was established six years ago, and currently has approximately 500 acres under development and 9 homes ranging from $135,000.00 - $500,000.00 under construction. Six of these plans were purchased from Nelson Design Group.

Our Future Projects....Blackwell Oaks Subdivision will utilize some 8-10 different Nelson Design Group plans ranging from 1,250-1,800 square feet. This project is located in West Mobile directly in front of a new elementary school., and we believe the target market will be young families and first time homebuyers. Construction on the model home for the neighborhood will begin immediately.

My Family...I've been married for 31 years to my lovely wife Nedra. We have two children Jennifer and Robert Jr., and two grandchildren Tucker and Conner.

Capital Development Group, LLC
500 Blvd. Park East
Mobile, AL 36609 Phone: 251-344-8447
ratyus@capital-dev.com www.capital-dev.com

TYUS HOMES

That Works

Selling Your Home Faster

Feature Sheets

These 8 1/2" x 11" feature sheets include specifications, highlights and sales features describing each home plan as well as your company information. Customized logo work is available for an additional price.

Price: $50.00

per 100 quantity

Outdoor Posters

These 24" x 36" full color laminated posters are perfect for displaying at the Open House, Grand Opening, Sales Office or the Model Home. Metal Sign Holders & Brochure Box are available...

Price: Laminated Poster......$199.00

Metal Sign Holder:......$75.00   Brochure Box:......$45.00

Individuals shopping for a new home tend to drive by after work hours when no one is on the job site. These outdoor posters and feature sheets give the potential buyer much needed plan specs and your contact information to help you sell your home faster.

Framed Prints

Greet clients with an attractive display perfect for hanging in your office lobby or in a show home. Each finished 20" x 24" framed and matted print includes design highlights and your company's information.

Price: Gold Frame......$150.00   Black Frame......$89.00   Wooden Frame......$89.00

Big Image On A Small Budget

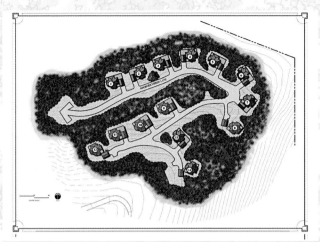

Land Use Planning & Design

Nelson Design Group works with builders and developers during the conceptualization phase of land use planning. We provide valuable expertise from site selection to proper land use. We can recommend the appropriate lot sizes to maximize the best use for the land and assist in creating effective neighborhoods. Our services during these early development stages help builders avoid costly revisions in design and engineering.

Identity Packages

Nelson Design Group's in-house design department can develop a professional image for your firm including company logos and brochures.

Professional Services

Utilizing Nelson Design Group's advertising services, you will save money and time in developing your marketing strategies. Nelson Design Group has a staff of experienced specialists to assist you in every phase of your project. We provide the following services: News Releases, Ad Design, Grand Opening Coordination and Home Development Consultation.

Development and Collection Portfolios

Builders will find individual designs and also several different groups of plans such as our new Wellington and Renaissance Collections. Our designs have complimentary themes that work together to build a single home, a neighborhood or a full-scale development.

Multi-Media Support

Nelson Design Group's website provides a builder with the opportunity to promote their firm's website and also link to our home plan search page. Nelson Design Group can also assist in the marketing of your firm and developments.

275

COMMERCIAL

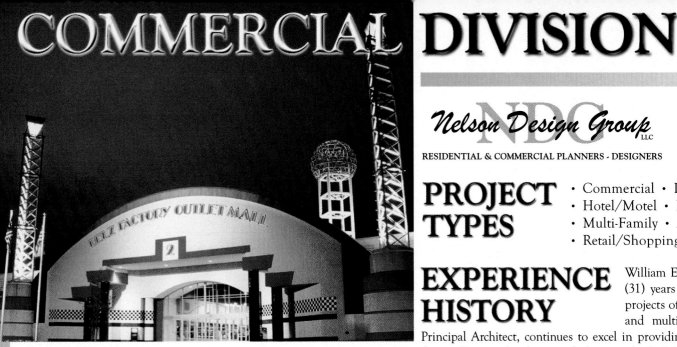

DIVISION

Nelson Design Group LLC
RESIDENTIAL & COMMERCIAL PLANNERS - DESIGNERS

Nelson Design Group, LLC., has the fresh eyes, new ideas and an objective evaluation of the performance of the construction industry.

PROJECT TYPES

- Commercial • Industrial • Religious
- Hotel/Motel • Hospital/Health Care
- Multi-Family • Assisted Living • Educational
- Retail/Shopping Centers • Historical

EXPERIENCE HISTORY

William E. Pace, AIA, utilizes experience of over thirty-one (31) years in the architectural industry. He has produced projects of a wide range of design types such as, commercial and multi-family. Of these design services, William, as Principal Architect, continues to excel in providing projects in architecture, planning and interior design. Projects for clients include not only the Mid-South Region, but National Area, also.

Those design types include religious, commercial, industrial, retail, residential and space planning projects. As the Principal Architect, he has designed over a billion square feet of building spaces. Refer to his individual resume for further details.

SERVICES

Nelson Design Group designers provide complete architectural services for commercial projects with many other services including strategic concepts, designs, renovation and/or retrofit, master planning and interior design including:

- Program Development Analysis
- Master Planning
- Existing Facilities Survey/Site Investigation
- Permit Coordination/Code Research
- Conceptual Designs/Sketches/Presentation Drawings
- Corporate Theme Design Development
- Space Planning • Fixture, Furnishings and Equipment Selections
- Prototype Site Adaptation
- Construction Documents and Specifications
- Food Service Layouts and Rough-Ins • Value Engineering
- Contract Negotiation and Construction Cost Evaluation
- Construction Administration • Tenant Related Services

We ensure our clients open communications, quality and consistency in producing design documents with a reduced completion time-frame.

AIA - Member of the American Institute of Architects
ICC - Member of International Code Council
NCARB - Member of the National Council of Architectural Registration Board

PROFESSIONAL REGISTRATION

State of Tennessee Architectural
 Registration #16524 and Interior Design #616

State of Arkansas Architectural
 Registration #1638

State of Mississippi Architectural
 Registration #2005

State of Georgia Architectural
 Registration #7395

State of Alabama Architectural
 Registration #3054

State of Texas Architectural
 Registration #11774

State of Missouri Architectural
 Registration #AR5367

State of Florida Architectural
 Registration #11496

State of Kentucky Architectural
 Registration - Applied For

State of Indiana Architectural
 Registration - #AR10300151

State of New Jersey Architectural
 Registration - #16130

State of North Carolina Architectural
 Registration - #9512

State of South Carolina Architectural
 Registration - Applied For

Materials List

Tru-Cost Estimating is a valuable tool for use in the planning and construction of your new home. Tru-Cost is available for each of NDG's plans.

We provide a complete estimate, similar to a bid, that will act as a checklist for all items you will need to select or coordinate during your building process. Tru-Cost will provide you a direct comparison to track your cost and help you stay within budget.

Tru-Cost has options that allow you to customize your estimate, to include labor rates and material prices for your area and can be imported into Tru-Cost software. The key to a successful project is to have a realistic budget, Tru-Cost is the solution.

Tru-Cost 111-1 - NDG111 W/ Slab

Item No Description

		Takeoff	Unit Price
373	2860 Vinyl Windows	11 EACH	$113.78
405	4040 Fixed Vinyl Windows	1 LS	
460	3660 Vinyl w/ Half Rnd	2 EACH	$306.70
471	4010 Vinyl Transom	1 EACH	$172.00
700	Shutters	8 PAIR	$50.00

$613.40
$172.00
$400.00

Division Total: $7,539.40

Division: 9 - Finishes

101	1/2 " Gypsum Drywall (4x12)	347 EACH	$11.13
102	Drywall Hang & Finish	16656 SQFT	$0.65
103	Drywall Nails	54 LBS	$0.85
104	Interior Painting Labor	2696 SQFT	$0.65
106	Exterior Painting Labor	2045 SQFT	$0.60
107	Interior Wall Primer	37 GAL	$9.91
108	Interior Wall Paint		$9.89
109	Wood Trim Paint	10 LS	$20.00
111	Carpet w/ Pad ($20 Per SqYd)	1854 SQFT	
112	Ceramic Floor Tile ($6 Per SqFt)	844 SQFT	

$3,862.
$10,82

Division To

2 EACH
4 EACH
3 EACH
88 SQFT
1 EACH
1 EAC
1 EA

Division: 10 - Specialties

	Shower Door
	Towel Bars
	Toilet Paper Holders
	Mirrors Installed
	Fireplace Allowance

Do You Know Your Homes Tru-Cost?

Tru-Cost
ESTIMATING

Tru-Cost is adaptable to a variety of estimating techniques and methods. By utilizing a ledger entry format, creating a bid is as simple as selecting items from the Master Database.

Tru-Cost Estimating provides a simplified method for calculating costs for equipment, labor, material and subcontractors, thus creating more accurate bids and easier cost tracking. Tru-Cost has multiple reports that assist a variety of tasks, from ordering materials to negotiating price with clients. Tru-Cost can automatically update pricing on previous bids to meet current prices within the Master Database.

Ledger Entry Form

Item Setup	No	Description	Total	Unit	Sub	Unit Price	Total	Del
	101	Wood Framing Labor	3733.00	SqFt		$3.00	$11,199.00	X
	102	Standard Trim Labor	2,698.00	SqFt		$1.25	$3,372.50	X
	104	Kitchen & Bath Cabinet Allowance	1.00	LS		$9,000.00	$9,000.00	X
	105	2 1/4 " Paint Grade Casing	968.00	LnFt		$0.33	$319.44	X
	106	Brick Mold Trim	350.00	LnFt		$0.60	$210.00	X
	108	2x4x9' Studs	872.00	Each		$2.85	$2,485.20	X
	110	1/2" Ornted Strand Board	108.00	Each		$8.39	$906.12	X
	111	1/2 " CDX Plywood	148.00	Each		$15.00	$2,220.00	X
	112	16D CC Sinker Nails	119.00	Lbs		$0.70	$83.30	X
	113	8D CC Sinker Nails	50.00	Lbs		$0.70	$35.00	X
	114	6D Finish Nails	12.00	Lbs		$0.70	$8.40	X
	120	9' x195' House Wrap	1.00	Each		$92.35	$92.35	X

Items   Division 6 - Wood & Plastics [111-1 - NDG111 w/ Slab]

Add New Item: Master Database | Division: ◄ 6 ► | Bid Calc | Div Summary | **Divison Total $47,923.21** | Close

Itemized Listing

Item Setup

Item No	Item Description		Take Off Unit	Take Off Method
101	Perimeter Footings		CuFt	V

	Formula	Buy Quantity	Unit Price	Extended Price
Equipment	1	752.00	$0.25	$188.00
Labor	1	752.00	$1.25	$940.00
Material	1	752.00	$2.50	$1,880.00
Other	1	752.00	$0.00	$0.00
Sub	1	752.00	$0.00	$0.00
Memo		Unit Price Total	$4.00	
			Item Total	**$3,008.00**

☐ MD Sync   MD Reset   Close

Advantages

– Quick startup

– Save time with material databases

– Import estimates from NDG

– Create a variety of reports

– Export reports to Excel or Palm Pilot

– Technical Support

– 16 Standard Construction Divisions

Bid Overview

Bid Calculations

	Base Cost	Adjust %	Adjustment	Adjusted Cost
Equipment	$13,188.00	10.00%	$1,318.80	$14,506.80
Labor	$28,342.00	10.00%	$2,834.20	$31,176.20
Materials	$62,292.22	10.00%	$6,229.22	$68,521.44
Other	$4,309.65	10.00%	$430.97	$4,740.62
Sub Bid	$71,537.17	10.00%	$7,153.72	$78,690.88
Total	**$179,669.04**		**$17,966.90**	**$197,635.94**
Overhead & Profit		10.00%		$19,763.59
			Bid Price	**$217,399.53**

Recalc   Report   Close

Features

– Organize subcontractor bids

– Itemize materials per category

– Easy to adjust material takeoff quantities

– Adjust overhead and profit margins

– Mark up individual categories, equipment, labor, materials, etc.

– Step-by-step instructional and interactive tutorial

279

WHAT'S INCLUDED IN YOUR NELSON DESIGN GROUP BLUEPRINTS

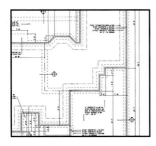

FOUNDATION PLANS

(1/4" or 1/2" = 1')
Most plans are available with a slab or crawl space foundation. Optional walkout style basement (three walls masonry with a wood framed side or rear wall) or full basement available if plan allows, at an additional cost. Please call for details.

FLOOR PLANS

(1/4" = 1')
Each home plan includes the floor plan showing the dimensioned locations of walls, doors and windows as well as a schematic electrical layout.

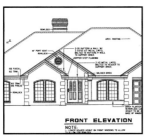

ELEVATION SETS

(1/4" = 1')
All plans include the exterior elevations (front, rear, right and left) that show and describe the finished material of the house.

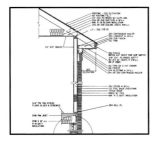

DETAIL SECTION(S)

(1/4" or 1/2" = 1')
The building sections are vertical cuts through the house showing floor, ceiling and roof height information.

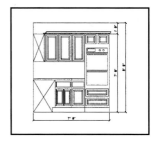

KITCHEN AND BATH ELEVATIONS

(1/2" = 1')
The kitchen and bath elevations show the arrangement and size of each cabinet and other fixtures in the room. These drawings give basic information that can be used to create customized layouts with a cabinet manufacturer.

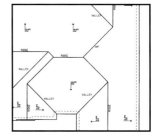

ROOF OVERVIEW PLAN

(1/4" = 1')
This is a "bird's eye" view showing the roof slopes, ridges, valleys and any saddles.

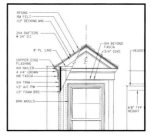

MISCELLANEOUS DETAILS

(3/4" = 1')
These are included for many interior and exterior conditions that require more specific information for their construction.

Nelson Design Group, LLC Home Plans can carry an architect stamp for an additional fee. CA is an exception.

Code Compliance: Our plans are drawn to meet the International Residential Code. Many states and counties amend the codes to adapt to their area. Consult your local building officials to determine the plan, code and site requirements.

Heated and Cooled Square Footage calculations are made from outside the exterior frame wall and do not include decks, porches, garages, basements, attics, fireplaces, etc. We include two story and vaulted areas only once in the calculations of the first floor. Stairs are counted once. Balconies and open walkways in two-story and vaulted areas are included in square footage of the second floor.

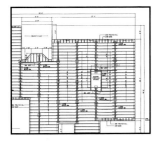

FLOOR FRAMING PLANS

(1/4" = 1'-0")
Each floor framing plan shows each floor joist indicating the size, spacing and length. All beams are labeled and sized.

$100.00 (includes one floor. Additional floors $50.00 each)

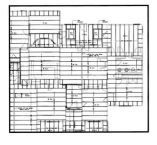

CEILING JOIST FRAMING PLAN

(1/4" = 1'-0")
The ceiling joist framing plan shows each ceiling joist indicating the size, spacing and length. All beams are labeled and sized.

$100.00

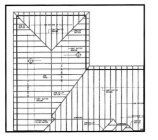

ROOF FRAMING PLAN

(1/4" = 1'-0")
The roof framing plan shows each rafter, valley, hip and ridge indicating the size, spacing and length. All beams are labeled and sized.

$100.00

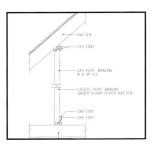

MISCELLANEOUS FRAMING DETAILS

Each framing plan sheet includes any framing details that are needed (boxed ceiling details, connection details, etc.) All of the framing is designed using conventional framing materials. Open web trusses are used in most one-and-a-half story and two-story plans.

RIGHT-READABLE REVERSED PLANS

Right-readable reversed plans are available should you wish to build your home reverse of the one shown in our book. The lettering and dimensions appear right reading. From the total number of sets ordered, all plans will be reversed. Check the appropriate area on the order form or let us know when placing your order.

TRU-COST ESTIMATING

Nelson Design Group has developed the Tru-Cost Estimating system to be a valuable tool for builders to use in the planning and construction of new homes. We have combined a thorough database of items required for construction. We offer three different options for our customers by providing estimates for all of our Stock Plans, as well as Modified and Custom Plans. Our Custom Estimate is not only available for our plans, it's also offered for our customer's plans. The Custom Estimate service allows the customer to modify or change any of the pricing or materials they may wish to use.

Base NDG Plan Estimate	**$125.00**
Revised Estimate for NDG Stock Plan	**$250.00**
Custom Estimate starting at	**$500.00**
Estimating Software	**$299.00**

REPRODUCIBLES

With the purchase of a reproducible set (vellums), a license and copyright release are also provided. Similarly, the purchase of reproducible home plans carries the same copyright protection as mentioned in this book. It is generally allowed to make up to a maximum of 10 copies for the construction of a single dwelling only. To use any plans more than once, and to avoid any copyright licenses infringement, it is necessary to contact Nelson Design Group, LLC to receive a release and a license for any extended usage. Nelson Design Group, LLC will make special provisions for plan usage within developments when previous arrangements have been made directly with Nelson Design Group, LLC.

CAD DISKS

CAD Disks are available on all NDG plans, with the exception of our Jim Barna Log System Collection. Standard formats are DWG and DXF. See order form for pricing.

MODIFY YOUR
NELSON DESIGN GROUP
STOCK PLAN

Not only do we have numerous designs created for various sized homes, we encourage the modification of our stock plans to meet personal specifications. Nelson Design Group will help you fulfill your dreams with a customized computer area, media center, hearth room, privacy nooks or whatever your needs entail.

Architectural in-house sealed prints are available for an additional fee with the exception of CA.

Modification work has a per plan set up charge and hourly fee or, is priced per total square footage under roof depending on the changes required or the complexity. To receive an estimated fee and completion time for modifications please call **1-800-590-2423** or fax us a copy of the floor plan, the changes you wish to make along with your daytime phone number.

A fee of the reproducible cost and the set up fee are required before revisions can be made, and the remaining fees are to be paid prior to shipping.

Any modifications made to the vellums by parties other than Nelson Design Group, LLC voids any warranties express or implied including the warranties of fitness for a particular purpose and merchantability. We recommend that an engineer in your area review your plans before actual construction begins due to local codes.

Foundation Alterations
Optional Basement Foundation - $250.00
Optional Daylight Basement Foundation - $250.00
Monolithic Slab - $250.00

Wall Options
2 x 6 cross-section for all plans included, upon request, at no additional charge.
2 x 4 to 2 x 6 Complete Wall Conversion - $250.00
2 x 4 to Concrete Block (up to 2,499 sq. ft.) - $450.00
            (2,500 sq. ft. and up) - $650.00

Exterior Alterations
Siding to Brick - $250.00   Brick to Siding - $250.00

Garage Alterations
Side Load to Front Entry - $250.00   Front Entry to Side Load - $250.00
Two Car to Three Car - $375.00   Three Car to Two Car - $375.00

Ceiling Alterations
8 ft. to 9 ft. - $250.00
9 ft. to 8 ft. - $250.00

For Architectural Stamps and additional modifications not listed, please call
1-800-590-2423.

COPYRIGHT LAWS OF
NELSON DESIGN GROUP

Reproduction of the illustration and working drawings of these home plans, either in whole or in part, including any form and/or preparation of derivative works thereof, for any reason without prior written permission is strictly prohibited. The purchase of a set of home plans in no way transfers any copyright or other ownership interest in it to the buyer except for a limited license to use that set of home plans for the construction of one, and only one, dwelling unit. The purchase of an additional set (s) of that home plan at a reduced price from the original set or as part of a multiple set package does not convey to the buyer a license to construct more than one dwelling. This is also the case with reproducible vellum, CAD disks or any multimedia.

Similarly, the purchase of reproducible vellum carries the same copyright protection as mentioned above. It is generally allowed to make up to a maximum of 10 copies for the construction of a single dwelling only. To use any plans more than once, and to avoid any copyright licenses infringement, it is necessary to contact the plan designer to receive a release and a license for any extended usage. Nelson Design Group, LLC will make special provisions for plan usage within developments when previous arrangements have been made directly with Nelson Design Group, LLC.

Whereas a purchaser of reproducibles is granted license to make copies, it should be noted that as copyright material, making photocopies from blueprints is illegal.

Copyright and licensing of home plans for construction exist to protect all parties. It respects and supports the intellectual property of the original architect or designer. Copyright law has been reinforced over the past few years. Willful infringement could cause settlements for statutory damages up to $100,000.00 plus attorney fees, damages and loss of profits.

CUSTOMER INFORMATION

Name: _____

Company Name: _____

Address: _____

City: _____ State: _____ Zip: _____

Phone: _____ Fax: _____

E-mail Address: _____

Credit Card #: _____ Exp. Date: _____

☐ VISA ☐ MasterCard ☐ AmEx ☐ Discover

☐ Check/Money Order Enclosed (U.S. Funds)

BLUEPRINT PRICING

Price Tier	Square Feet	One Set	Four Sets	Eight Sets	Twelve Sets	Repro Sets	CAD Disk
A	0-1499	$400	$435	$475	$520	$585	$1,060
B	1500-1999	$440	$475	$515	$560	$630	$1,105
C	2000-2499	$480	$515	$555	$605	$670	$1,145
D	2500-2999	$550	$585	$635	$675	$755	$1,430
E	3000-3499	$610	$645	$685	$730	$805	$1,480
F	3500-3999	$650	$685	$730	$780	$855	$1,530
G	4000 and up	$700	$735	$775	$820	$900	$1,575

NUMBER OF SETS

☐ **ONE SET** (stamped "not for construction")
Recommended for preview study

☐ **FOUR SETS**
Recommended for bidding

☐ **EIGHT SETS**
Recommended for construction

☐ **TWELVE SETS**
Recommended for multiple bids

☐ **REPRODUCIBLE SETS**
Recommended for construction/modifications

☐ **CAD Disks***
DXF/DWG Files

*Prices are subject to change. Special or grouped plans may vary in price.   *No CAD for Log Home Plans.*

SHIPPING AND HANDLING

	1-3 Sets	4-7 Sets	8 or more Sets	Repro Sets	CAD Disk
U.S. Regular (5-6 business days)	$17.50	$20.00	$25.00	$17.50	$15.00
U.S. Express (2-3 business days)	$35.00	$40.00	$45.00	$35.00	$30.00
Canada Regular (5-7 business days)	$40.00	$45.00	$50.00	$40.00	$35.00
Canada Express (2-4 business days)	$55.00	$60.00	$65.00	$55.00	$50.00
Overseas/Airmail (7-10 business days)	$70.00	$80.00	$90.00	$70.00	$60.00

Prices are subject to change.

Source Code: **BSEIII**

	Plan #	Plan #	Plan #
Price Tier			
Number of Sets			
Blueprint Cost			
Additional Sets @ $40 each			
Right Readable-Reversed Sets @ $50			
Tru-Cost Estimating @ $125			
CAD Disk			
Reproducible Sets			
☐ Crawl			
☐ Slab			
☐ Basement			
☐ Basement (Opt.) @ $250.00			
☐ Daylight Basement			
☐ Daylight Basement (Opt.) @ $250.00			
Tru-Cost Software @ $299.00			
☐ Other			
Sub-Total			
Shipping & Handling			
TOTAL			

Additional Sets - Additional individual sets of plan ordered at point of sale are **$40** each.

Right Readable-Reversed Plans - A **$50** surcharge. From the total number of sets you order above, all plans will be reversed. You pay only **$50**. Note: All plans are produced using computers, and all text is reversed as well.

All Nelson Design Group, LLC sales are non-credit purchases. The total amount is due when your order is placed. Orders may not be returned or exchanged. All orders are final.

MAIL TO: **Nelson Design Group, LLC**
2200 Fowler Ave. • Suite D, Jonesboro, AR 72401
Phone: 870-931-5777 • Fax: 870-931-5792
www.nelsondesigngroup.com

For Ordering and Technical Assistance call:
800-590-2423

283

NELSON DESIGN GROUP PLAN INDEX

Welcome to our
neighborhood...

84 LUMBER
Build on what we know.™

WHO WE ARE
84 Lumber Company is the largest privately held supplier of building materials in the United States. Founded in 1956 by Joe Hardy in the town of Eighty Four, Pennsylvania, 20 miles south of Pittsburgh, 84 Lumber is still growing. In 2002, we opened 20 new stores, raising the company's store count to 437 locations in 34 states coast-to-coast. In two of the past three years, 84 Lumber sold more building materials to professional contractors and remodelers than any other supplier, with 2002 sales exceeding $2 billion.

OUR MISSION
84 Lumber Company is dedicated to being the low cost provider of lumber and building materials to professional builders, remodelers and dedicated do-it-yourselfers, while adding value to our quality products through a trained, knowledgeable and motivated team of professional sales associates.

WHAT WE OFFER
- Competitive Prices
- Top Quality Products
- Knowledgeable Associates
- Special Order Program
- Convenient Hours
- Professional Delivery

INVENTORY & VOLUME BUYING POWER
With over 400 stores and a centralized buying system, customers can take advantage of our national purchasing power to save money and add more to their bottom line. Through our established relationships with national suppliers and bulk buying power, you can rely on 84 to have the products and quantities you need.

- Lumber
- Plywood
- Insulation
- Trim
- Mouldings
- Flooring
- Siding
- Drywall
- Decks
- Trusses
- Roofing
- Skylights
- Engineered Lumber
- Hardware
- Doors and Windows
- Kitchens and Baths
- Storage Buildings
- 84 Home Packages

MEETING THE NEEDS OF PROFESSIONAL BUILDERS
To meet the special needs of the professional builder, 84 Lumber has assembled a well-trained contractor sales force of more than 1,200 associates nationwide, with each of the company's stores having two to four contractor sales representatives (CSR's) on staff. Each new CSR goes through an extensive training and development program, and attends on-going courses throughout their career to stay current on the latest building trends and new services available. Our CSR's truly understand that every contractor has their own unique set of needs relating to service, product selection, delivery, and financing, just to name a few. Our CSR's strive to learn the operation of each contractor's business so that 84 Lumber may serve you as efficiently as possible.

FINANCING OPTIONS
84 Lumber provides many fast, builder-friendly financing options with our same down-to-earth value and convenience.

SPECIAL ORDER PROGRAM & BUILDING COMPONENTS
While our stores are well stocked with many basic building materials, we also have an outstanding special order program which allows virtually any custom product to be ordered through any 84 Lumber store associate or CSR. We will cater to a wide range of tastes by ordering those hard-to-find products, to be delivered when you need them, in most cases, directly to a job site if requested. 84 Lumber also operates building component manufacturing facilities in major markets, producing roof and floor trusses, as well as wall panels to help builders become more efficient and profitable.

COMPUTERIZED BIDS AND PRICING
Give us your materials list, blueprints, sketches or ideas and we will process your estimate within 24 hours and your blueprint take-off within 48 hours. If you're not ready to start your next project now, 84 offers a 30-day price guarantee. Pay for the materials now to lock in current prices, and you'll have up to 30 days to pick up your materials without any change in cost to you!

FAST AND RELIABLE DELIVERY
We know your time is important, and we won't waste it. Careful scheduling assures that materials are delivered to the job site when you need them. If you prefer, our convenient "drive up and load" sheds with express loading allow you to spend more time on your project and less time pulling carts through those crowded "superstores".

For the 84 Lumber location nearest you call:
1-800-359-8484

WHEN YOU FOLLOW A RECIPE, CAN YOUR KITCHEN KEEP UP?

Merillat cabinetry takes the extra steps out of creating a meal.
With Organomics® solutions that put items right at your fingertips.
So things are where you need them, when you need them.
Visit www.merillat.com

Merillat

Make perfect sense.

For Information on completing your homes' new kitchen, call: 1.800.575.8761

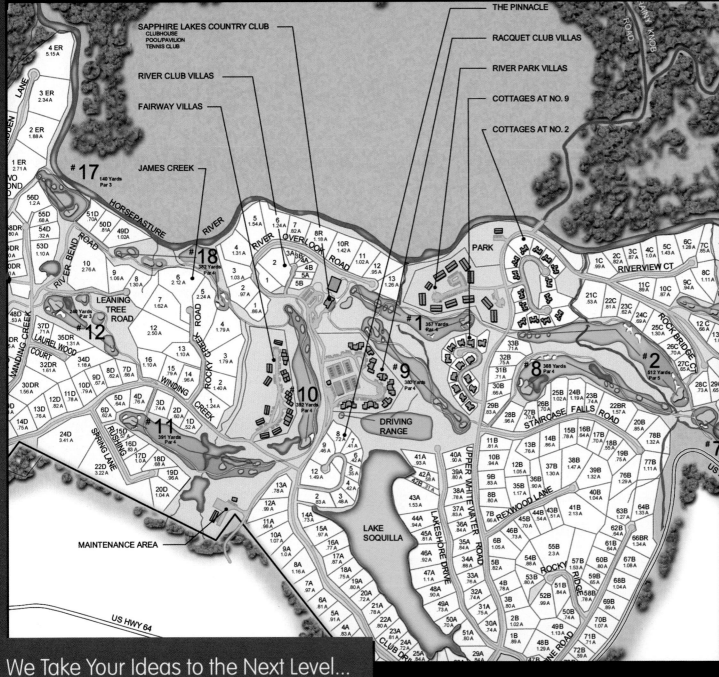

SAPPHIRE LAKES COUNTRY CLUB
CLUBHOUSE
POOL/PAVILION
TENNIS CLUB

THE PINNACLE

RACQUET CLUB VILLAS

RIVER CLUB VILLAS

RIVER PARK VILLAS

FAIRWAY VILLAS

COTTAGES AT NO. 9

COTTAGES AT NO. 2

JAMES CREEK

MAINTENANCE AREA

We Take Your Ideas to the Next Level...

Featured project development by Sapphire Lakes,

land planning by Luther E. Smith & Associates, PA

CANDLER COURT

www.bhmdesign.com
866.684.3820
Asheville, North Carolina

BHMdesign

BUILD YOUR DREAM HOME AND THE HOME THEATER OF YOUR DREAMS... TOGETHER

Are you aware that many lenders will allow you to include your home theater system in with your financing? Now you can enjoy a spectacular home theater experience the moment you walk through the door. By installing your Pioneer® recommended home theater while your dream house is being built, our authorized Pioneer installation professional will flawlessly integrate your system in with your living space. This way you'll benefit from a custom solution, seamlessly crafted to satisfy your exact requirements.

Pioneer products feature the most advanced technology to deliver the ultimate home theater experience.

• True High Definition Large Screen Displays

   - 43" and 50" Plasma Monitors Only 4" Deep

   - High Definition Ready Projection TVs From 53" to 64"

• High Performance Multi Channel Audio and Video Components

   - AV Surround Sound Receivers and Amplifiers for Every Size Room and Every Application

   - Award-Winning DVD Recording and Playback Components, PureCinema Progressive Scan, DVD Audio and Super Audio CD Capability

For more information, call 1-800-926-4329

Why an L.J. Smith Stair System is the best choice...

It's important to us that your stairway is not only functional and beautiful, but that it safely carries you and your loved ones from one floor to another for decades to come. L.J. Smith's stairway components are uniquely designed so they provide the strongest, most durable and attractive stairway, when installed properly. You will have peace of mind knowing you made the right choice with the stair components manufacturer who is recognized as the leader and innovator in the industry for over one hundred years...L.J. Smith.

Custom pre-built straight, circular and spiral stairways are also available from Woodsmiths Design and Manufacturing, a division of L.J. Smith. Woodsmiths uses only genuine L.J. Smith stair parts in their wood stairs, however, their abilities also include carved wood turnings, glass, metals and even molded plastics.

For more information on L.J. Smith products, visit www.ljsmith.net, contact your local lumber dealer or call us at (740) 269-2221.
For more information on Woodsmiths Design & Manufacturing capabilities, visit www.woodsmiths.net or call us at (800) 874-2876.

Today's homebuyer is looking at closets in a different way...

Are you?

The closet upgrade has come of age. Consumers are asking for more than a shelf and pole. ClosetMaid® MasterSuite laminate storage systems provide an attention-getting upgrade for closets, pantry and garage—at a surprisingly affordable cost. ClosetMaid also has a wide array of wire storage systems that can add profitable value to your homes.

Get ahead of your prospects—and the competition.
Contact your ClosetMaid dealer or call 1-800-221-0641.

CLOSETMAID®   www.closetmaid.com

EMERSON
Storage Solutions

Thickest Foam for Maximum Strength

Fast & Trouble-Free Installation

Contractor Training Available

Regional Technical and
Marketing Support

Reliable Local Service

Stringent
Quality
Control

Also Available
1/2 Height
(8") Forms

Logix™ walls are now available on many Nelson Design Group Home designs.

If walls could speak.

Bright Ideas for Better Living.

There's nothing that accents a room quite like real glass block from Pittsburgh Corning. Glass block adds beauty, light and class to any home, whether it's used in a wall, window or shower. Plus, our durable, scratch-resistant, 100% real glass block comes in a variety of patterns and shapes. Select from our pre-designed Shower Systems, pre-assembled LightWise® Windows, or draw on the expertise of our network of distributors/installers to take your ideas from concept to completion. For more information on creating a unique statement with glass block or to locate a distributor/dealer near you, visit www.pcglassblock.com or call 1-800-624-2120, ext. 800.

PITTSBURGH CORNING
GLASS BLOCK®

Feel the Intensity™

Wrap yourself in the warm, passionate embrace of Intensity – the world's most realistic gas fireplace. Once you've experienced Intensity, you'll want it in every room. Fortunately, with Heat-N-Glo's patented Direct Vent Technology, you can have Intensity in spots other fireplaces only fantasize about. And with the distinction of its furnace rating and ducting capabilities, you'll feel Intensity even when you're in the next room. If you've never experienced Intensity, you really should.

INTENSITY™

For FREE information, call 1-888-427-3973, visit www.heatnglo.com or www.fireplaces.com

HEAT-N-GLO®

No one builds a better fire

Promised myself
I'd improve my roll cast

Confirmed JELD-WEN
window and door delivery

Products arrived complete
in every detail

Promise kept

NO NEW
MESSAGES

Reliable JELD-WEN® windows and doors help ensure your job doesn't interfere with real life—the life of fishing lines, not phone lines. We're dedicated to providing orders on-time and complete, even if they include plenty of optional features. In addition, our products are backed by industry-leading warranties. To find a dealer near you or learn more about JELD-WEN products visit **www.jeld-wen.com or call 1-800-877-9482 ext. NDG**. We keep our promises, so you can keep yours.

RELIABILITY *for* real life™ |

"MY BUILDER HELPED TRANSFORM MY GARAGE FROM AN EMPTY SPACE INTO A ROOM THAT WORKS FOR ME USING GLADIATOR™ GARAGEWORKS."

GLADIATOR
GARAGEWORKS
by Whirlpool Corporation

IT'S TIME TO RETHINK THE GARAGE.™
IT'S EASY WITH GLADIATOR™ GARAGEWORKS.

Just as a great kitchen design can help sell a home to women, now there's something to attract the men – Gladiator™ GarageWorks. The Gladiator™ system is a complete line of quality products built to transform, organize and enhance the

garage. Men will love the industrial tread plate design, mobility and how all the components work together, or stand alone. So while women are attracted to your kitchens, men will be visualizing how they can store their gear with Gladiator™ GarageWorks. It's just one more way your homes can turn homebuyers' dreams into reality and turn more profit for you.

Make the garage the highlight of your homes with Gladiator™ GarageWorks. See it all at www.GladiatorGarageWorks.com. Only from Whirlpool Corporation. The Inside Advantage.™ Call Whirlpool Corporation at 800-253-3977.

Whirlpool
CORPORATION

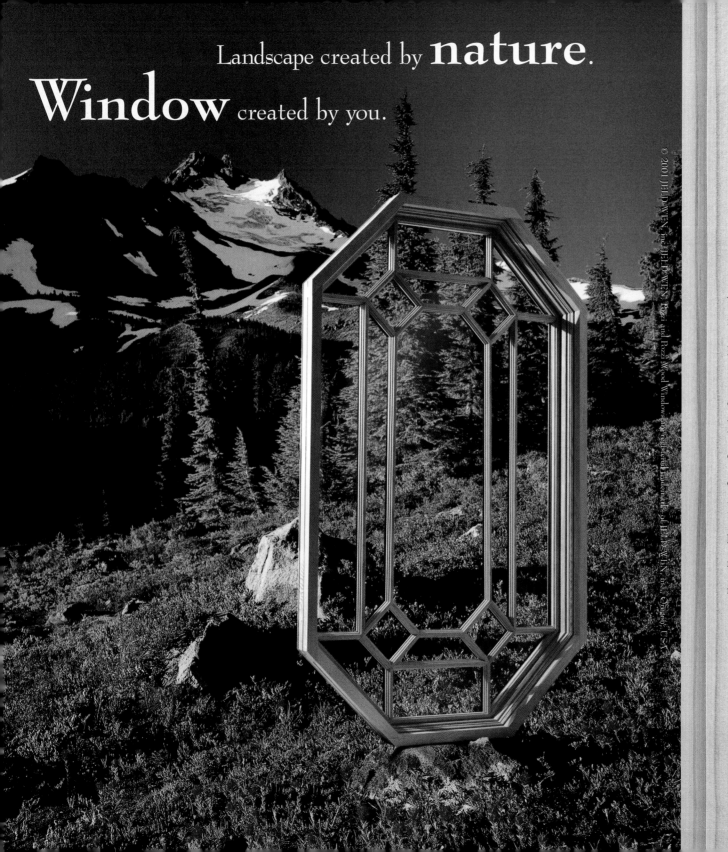

Landscape created by **nature**.

Window created by you.

© 2001 JELD-WEN, inc. JELD-WEN, Pozzi and Pozzi Wood Windows are registered trademarks of JELD-WEN, inc., Oregon, USA.

Eddie Markham,
Frame Builder

At Pozzi, some of Eddie Markham's best work is yours. Our Specials Builders, like Eddie, produce practically any design you dream up. In fact, 40 percent of Pozzi® wood windows and patio doors are custom designs. These can be personalized with color finishes on metal clad products. Pozzi offers 31 clad colors and copper. Our cladding feature a 70 percent Kynar 500® resin system and offers extra protection from nature. So even years from now, your window will be just as you first imagined it.

POZZI
WOOD WINDOWS®
Part of the JELD-WEN® family

"Handcrafted in Bend, Oregon"
Free Catalog:
1-800-257-9663 ext. P14
www.pozzi.com

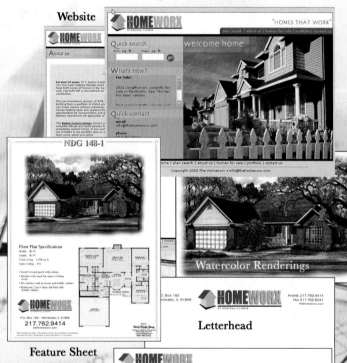